PSYCHOLOGICAL NARRATIVE ANALYSIS

PSYCHOLOGICAL NARRATIVE ANALYSIS

A Professional Method to Detect Deception in Written and Oral Communications

By

JOHN R. SCHAFER, Ph.D.

FBI Special Agent (Ret.)
National Security Division
Behavioral Analysis Program

CHARLES C THOMAS • PUBLISHER, LTD.
Springfield • Illinois • U.S.A.

Published and Distributed Throughout the World by

CHARLES C THOMAS • PUBLISHER, LTD.
2600 South First Street
Springfield, Illinois 62704

©2010 by CHARLES C THOMAS • PUBLISHER, LTD.

ISBN 978-0-398-07927-7 (hard)
ISBN 978-0-398-07928-4 (paper)

Library of Congress Catalog Card Number: 2009051484

Printed in the United States of America
CR-R-3

Library of Congress Cataloging-in-Publication Data

Schafer, John R., 1954-
  Psychological narrative analysis : a professional method to detect
deception in written and oral communications / by John R. Schafer.
    p. cm.
  Includes index.
  ISBN 978-0-398-07927-7 (hard) -- ISBN 978-0-398-07928-4 (pbk.)
  1. Deception. 2. Truthfulness and falsehood. 3. Content analysis
(Communication) I. Title.

BF637.D42.S33 2010
153.6--dc22
                                                      2009051484

PREFACE

Imagine you suspect your spouse is having an affair. Imagine your child comes home late and you suspect shenanigans. Imagine your clients or employees mislead you. If you're like most people, you ask yourself two questions: "How do I know the person talking to me is telling the truth?" and "What do I do if I think he's lying?" I ask myself these two questions every day when I speak with friends, colleagues, supervisors, used car salesmen, and the clerk in the grocery store who tells me that spaghetti is in aisle three. The list is long and continues to grow. When our three children became teenagers, they, too, were added to the list.

Most people lie to gain an advantage or to protect themselves from embarrassment, social reprimands, or even prison. During my 25 years as a police officer and Special Agent for the Federal Bureau of Investigation (FBI), I witnessed countless lies told for a variety of reasons in every imaginable circumstance from petty criminals to sophisticated international spies, each with differing levels of ability to lie convincingly.

Early in my law enforcement career, I catalogued how people told lies. Over time, patterns emerged. I found that liars typically use two methods to deceive: obfuscation and omission. Obfuscation creates verbal confusion to disguise the truth. With omission, liars tell the truth up to the point where they want to conceal information, skip over the information they want to conceal, and continue telling the truth. Generally speaking, liars prefer omission to obfuscation because it is easier to keep track of withheld information than to remember partially or entirely fabricated details.

I found that even though some people seem to be better liars than others, there were still significant similarities in the way in which they lied. As Yogi Berra once said, "You can observe a lot by watching." I tried to watch everything–closely. The more I watched, the more rigor I attached to the process. This led directly to my doctoral studies at Fielding Graduate University in Santa Barbara, California, where I studied psychology.

My studies at Fielding culminated with my dissertation, which examined the grammatical differences between truthful and deceptive narratives. This book contains much of that ground-breaking research. I organized the words and grammar patterns into a system that is easy to remember and easy to use. Since most of the material in this book is not found in other commercially available sources, I decided to label this system Psychological Narrative Analysis (PNA). PNA is a robust system that tests truthfulness in both written and oral communications and provides clues to the communication styles and behavioral characteristics of others. PNA techniques allow people to peer into the hearts and minds of others to discover what they are thinking and evaluate the veracity of what they say.

J.R.S.

INTRODUCTION

FIVE LESSONS IN BEHAVIORAL ANALYSIS

I was 14 years old, too old to ride a bicycle and too young to drive. The Chicago Transit Authority (CTA) extended my reach to every point in the city, but at a price. In 1968, a quarter for bus fare was hard to come by, especially for someone who was too young to work. Each school day, I rode three buses to and from Mount Carmel High School. I caught the bus at 115th Street and Vincennes Avenue, transferred at 87th Street, transferred at Stony Island, got off at 63rd Street and walked three blocks to Mount Carmel.

One day on my way to school, I looked at the transfer I was holding and noticed that the date and month were printed on the transfer but not the year. The driver hand-punched a clock printed at one end of the transfer. Transfers cost an extra quarter and could be used to ride buses on connecting routes within one-hour of the time punched by the driver. Without the year being stamped on the transfer, it meant that I could use the transfer on the same date and time the following year. I found a vulnerability in the system. As long as I got on the bus at a corner where two bus routes intersected, I could use a transfer and ride the bus for free, saving my money for more important things like nickel candy bars and 12 cent comic books.

The downside to my plan was I did not have a steady source of used transfers and even if I could secure used transfers, I could not start riding the bus for free until the same date and time the following year. I watched how bus drivers handled transfers. The first thing I noticed was that the drivers were too busy minding traffic, keeping schedules, and collecting cash fares to look at the printed date on the transfer, much less the hand-punched time stamp. They simply took the transfer, crumpled it, and put it into a canvas bag hanging from the fare box. This was my *first lesson* in behavioral analysis. *People prioritize their activities and pay more attention to the activities that they consider most important.* For bus drivers, checking the date and time stamp on transfers had low priority.

One afternoon, I got off the bus at 115th Street, the turn-around point, and noticed that the driver emptied the contents of the canvas bag into a nearby trash barrel. That trash barrel represented the pot of gold at the end of the rainbow. I watched the trash barrel for several days and noticed that only a few drivers emptied the canvas bags into the trash barrel. I later learned that drivers were supposed to take the used transfers back to the main depot to be shredded. I learned my *second lesson* in behavioral analysis. *Some people think that rules do not apply to them.*

Day after day, I collected transfers from that trash barrel. I ironed the transfers to eliminate wrinkles and indexed them according to bus route, date, and time in a wooden index box my grandfather had given me. I saved those transfers for use on the corresponding date and time one year hence.

Two weeks passed. I could not wait until next year. I wanted my freedom now. I needed an immediate solution. I took action. I began passing outdated transfers taking a chance I would not get caught. I handed the bus driver the outdated transfer with the same confidence I would a valid transfer. The probability of getting caught was low because I knew the driver was attending to more important tasks. On several occasions, when the driver questioned the validity of my transfers, I quickly pushed a quarter into the fare box and sat down. I learned my *third lesson* in behavioral analysis. *People tend to believe others if they act and speak with confidence.*

The first few times I passed outdated transfers, I felt as though the bus driver knew I was handing him a bogus transfer when, in fact, he was oblivious. I later labeled this feeling the Spotlight Effect. I learned my *fourth lesson* in behavioral analysis. *People think others readily recognize lies when, in reality, this is not the case.* As a law enforcement officer, I used the Spotlight Effect to my advantage by telling suspects that their lies were so transparent, it was like having a neon light on their forehead blinking "Liar" every time they opened their mouth.

During that first year, I also learned that distracting the driver with a friendly greeting further increased the probability of successfully passing outdated transfers. Since I took the same bus routes at the same time each day, I saw the same drivers. I made a point of developing a personal relationship with the drivers. I learned that the bus driver on the Vincennes Route was an avid Chicago White Sox fan. When I handed him my transfer, I made a slightly negative or slightly positive comment about the White Sox. In either case, the driver felt obligated to agree or disagree with the comment, which kept his attention away from the outdated transfer I handed him. The bus driver on the 87th Street Route was a proud grandmother. When I handed her my transfer, I asked her about her grandchildren. The Stony Island route rotated drivers, so I commented about general topics when I gave them the outdated transfer. I learned my *fifth lesson* in behavioral analysis. *The more people talk about themselves, the less time they have to observe the behavior of others.*

I rode the bus for free until I bought my first car two days after my 18th birthday. Free transportation was possible because I observed and catalogued human behavior. Thus began my life-long quest to understand human behavior. In retrospect, I realize that what I did was wrong, but I learned very valuable lessons from the experience.

I joined the Hinsdale, Illinois Police Department in 1980. For five years, I observed and catalogued human behaviors. In many instances, I instinctively knew what to say and do when I interviewed suspects, but I did not have a specific name for the techniques I used. In 1985, I became an FBI Special Agent. As an FBI Special Agent, I continued to hone my interviewing skills.

My interest in human behavior increased in 1998 when I was selected to be a behavioral analyst for the FBI's National Security Behavioral Analysis Program (BAP). The BAP differs from the more familiar Behavioral Sciences Unit (BSU). BSU investigators analyze crime scenes and, based on the artifacts at the crime scenes, develop hypotheses as to who may have committed the crime. The focus of the BAP is on national security investigations such as espionage, counterintelligence, and preventing the transfer of cutting edge technology to foreign governments. Unlike the BSU, the BAP typically has a known target. BAP team members assess the target's behavioral weaknesses and use those weaknesses to prevent the target from further damaging national security.

When I joined the BAP team, I decided to formalize my education in behavioral analysis. In 2000, I enrolled in a Ph.D. program at Fielding Graduate University. For my dissertation, I chose to examine the grammatical differences between truthful and deceptive narratives.

I chose to examine the grammatical differences between truthful and deceptive narratives because research has shown that nonverbal cues to detect deception are not consistently reliable. Researchers theorized that physiological changes occur when people lie because they fear getting caught. These changes, however, are not consistent from one person to the next, making lie detection difficult. A liar who does not fear getting caught or controls his reaction to fear will appear truthful. Conversely, a truthful person who is nervous often experiences the same physiological changes as does a liar and consequently displays the same nonverbal cues as a deceptive person.

Based on my research, I developed Psychological Narrative Analysis (PNA). PNA is the study of word choices and grammar structures people choose when they speak or write. PNA techniques identify specific words, speech patterns, and grammar structures that reveal a person's truthfulness and provide clues to a person's personality and behavioral characteristics.

Words represent thoughts and grammar formats those thoughts. Both truthful and deceptive people use the same grammar rules to construct sentences. When people obfuscate or omit the truth, they must use accepted grammar structures or their sentences would make no sense. The only difference between truthful statements and deceptive statements is the omission or obfuscation of the truth. PNA techniques identify and exploit those differences.

Although words can represent several meanings depending on context, writers and speakers intend one meaning when they write or speak with the exceptions of double entendre, puns, and sarcasm. For example, the word *hot* describes temperature, spiciness, or passion depending on the context of the sentence. In the sentence "The weather is hot," temperature is the intended meaning for the word *hot*. PNA analyzes words within the context of the writer or speaker's intended meaning. If the meaning of a word remains unclear within the context of one sentence, then the ambiguous word should be analyzed within the global context of the communication. With few exceptions, word definitions remain consistent throughout a single communication.

The first part of this book presents a full range of PNA techniques in concise, everyday language. Examples accompany each technique where applicable. The second part of this book offers examples of PNA using oral and written communications. Where possible, the examples I used were taken from actual cases or from real-life situations I experienced. The last part of this book contains examples of oral and written communications that have been analyzed using PNA techniques.

The words *interviewer* and *interviewee* are used throughout this book for convenience and do not exclusively refer to the police investigator-suspect relationship. The interviewer-interviewee paradigm also includes relationships such as parent (interviewer) and child (interviewee); lawyer (interviewer) and client (interviewee); superior (interviewer) and subordinate (interviewee); friend (interviewer) and friend (interviewee); and wife (interviewer) and husband (interviewee). Similarly, the pronoun "he" will be used to avoid the awkward use of the combined pronouns he/she.

CONTENTS

PSYCHOLOGICAL NARRATIVE
ANALYSIS

Chapter 1

WORD CLUES

In 1997, I fell off my horse and suffered a severe brain injury. I lost parts of my memory. I could not remember words, but I knew the meanings of words. I often gave my wife and children a definition and asked them to tell me the word that associated with the definition. Once I reconnected the definition with the correct word, I retained the word and its meaning. Over the next year, I did crossword puzzles to recover my vocabulary. I spent endless hours hunting for words that matched the clues in crossword puzzles. After an extensive rehabilitation, I resumed my career as a FBI Special Agent.

My rehabilitation taught me a valuable lesson. Words have meaning. They don't just plop out of a person's mouth. Once a thought is created, it moves to the part of the brain that contains the meanings of the words. The thought and the corresponding meaning then go to the part of the brain that stores vocabulary. Therein the meaning is associated with the correct word. The combined signal then goes to yet another part of the brain that directs our tongues, larynx, and lips how to move to formulate the word. When we write words, our brains go through a similar process. Speaking and writing words are deliberate processes, albeit complex. My injury severed the pathways between the part of my brain that contains the meanings of words and the part of my brain that contains my vocabulary. Doing crossword puzzles established new pathways between the two parts of my brain.

Words represent thoughts. The closest one person can get to understanding another person's thoughts is to listen to the words that he speaks or writes. Certain words reflect the behavioral characteristics of the person who spoke or wrote the words. I labeled these words, Word Clues. Word Clues increase the probability of predicting the behavioral characteristics of people by analyzing the words they choose when they speak or write. Word Clues alone cannot determine a person's personality traits, but they do provide insights into a person's thought process and behavioral characteristics. Interviewers can develop hypotheses based on Word Clues and test those hypotheses with subsequent information elicited from interviewees and third-party corroboration.

The human brain is incredibly efficient. When we think, we use only verbs and nouns. Adjectives, adverbs, and other parts of speech are added during the transformation of thoughts into spoken or written language. The words we add reflect who we are and what we are thinking.

The basic sentence consists of a subject and a verb. For example, the simple sentence "I walked" consists of the pronoun "I," which is the subject and the word "walked," which is the verb. Any words added to this basic sentence modify the meaning of the noun or verb. These deliberate modifications provide clues to the personality and behavioral characteristics of the speaker or writer.

Word Clues allow interviewers to develop hypotheses or make educated guesses regarding the behavioral characteristics of interviewees. For example, in the sentence "I quickly walked," the Word Clue "quickly" infused a sense of urgency, but it did not provide the reason for the urgency. A person might "quickly walk" because he is late for an appointment or anticipates being late for an appointment. Conscientious people see themselves as reliable and do not want to be late for appointments. People who want to be on time tend to respect social norms and want to live up to the expectations of others. People with this behavioral characteristic make good employees because they do not want to disappoint their employers. People "quickly walk" when they encounter general threats. A general threat might occur while walking through a bad neighborhood. Approaching bad weather could also present a threat. Walking quickly to avoid a thunderstorm reduces the threat of a lightning strike or getting wet. People might add the word "quickly" for a variety of reasons, but there is a specific reason for their choice.

The following examples demonstrate how Word Clues provide interviewers with simple insights into the behavioral characteristics of interviewees.

INTERVIEWEE: I won another award.

The interviewee used the Word Clue "another" for a reason. The word "another" conveys the notion that the interviewee won one or more previous awards. The interviewee wanted to ensure that other people knew that he won at least one other award, thus bolstering his self-image. The interviewee may need the adulation of others to reinforce his self-esteem. The interviewer could exploit this vulnerability by using flattery and other ego-enhancing comments.

INTERVIEWEE: I worked hard to achieve my goal.

The interviewee selected the Word Clue "hard" for a reason. Perhaps the interviewee values goals that are difficult to achieve. Perhaps the goal the interviewee achieved is more difficult than the goals that he usually attempts. The Word Clue "hard" also suggests that the interviewee can defer gratification or holds the belief that hard work and dedication produce good results. A job applicant with these characteristics would likely make a good employee because he would likely accept challenges and have the determination to complete those tasks.

INTERVIEWEE: I patiently sat through the lecture.

The interviewee added the Word Clue "patiently" for a reason. Perhaps the interviewee was bored with the lecture. Perhaps the interviewee had to return an important telephone call. Perhaps the interviewee had to use the restroom. Regardless of the reason, the interviewee was preoccupied with something other than the content of the lecture. A person who waits patiently for a break before he leaves the room is probably a person who adheres to social norms and etiquette. A person who receives a telephone call, immediately gets up, and leaves the lecture is a person who probably does not have rigid social boundaries. People with social boundaries make good employees because they follow the rules and respect authority. Conversely, a person who does not follow social conventions would probably be suited for a job that requires novel thinking. A person with the predisposition to act outside social norms would make a better spy than a person who is predisposed to follow social conventions because spies are routinely asked to violate social norms.

INTERVIEWEE: I decided to buy that model.

The interviewee chose the Word Clue "decided" for a reason. The word "decided" indicates that the interviewee weighed various options prior to the purchase. Perhaps the interviewee struggled to some degree before making the decision to purchase. This behavior trait suggests that the interviewee thinks things through, especially if the purchase was a minor one. The word "decided" also indicates that the interviewee is not likely to be impulsive. An impulsive person would likely say or write, "I just bought that model." The Word Clue "just" suggests that the interviewee bought the item without giving the purchase much thought.

Based on the Word Clue "decided," the reader can develop a hypothesis that the speaker or writer is an introvert. Introverts think before they act. They carefully weigh each option before rendering a decision. Extroverts tend to be more impulsive. The use of the verb "decided" does not positively identify the interviewee as an introvert, but it does provide an indication that the interviewee might be an introvert. A definitive personality assessment requires a more comprehensive psychological assessment; nonetheless, an interviewer can exploit a person if he knows that person tends toward extroversion or introversion.

Extroverts get their energy from being with other people and seek stimulation from their environments. Extroverts often speak spontaneously without thinking and confidently use the trial and error method. Conversely, introverts expend energy when they engage socially and seek alone time to recharge their batteries. Introverts seek stimulation from within and seldom speak without thinking. Introverts carefully weigh options before making decisions. Prior to entering into any type of business negotiations, knowing whether your opponent tends toward extroversion or introversion can provide a strategic advantage. Sales persons should allow their introverted customers time to think about sales proposals. Introverts take in the information, mull it over, and then come to a decision. Pressing introverts for impulsive decisions may force them to say "No" because they are not comfortable making immediate decisions. Extroverts, on the other hand, can be pressured to some degree to make immediate decisions because they are more comfortable making impulsive decisions. Rarely do people exhibit entirely extroverted or entirely introverted characteristics. Personality traits slide along a continuum. Many people exhibit both extroverted and introverted characteristics. Additionally, introverts who are comfortable with their surroundings often display behaviors associated with extroversion. Likewise, extroverts can display introverted characteristics.

INTERVIEWEE: I did the right thing.

The Word Clue "right" suggests that the interviewee struggled with a legal, moral, or ethical dilemma and overcame some level of internal or external opposition to make a fair and just decision. This behavioral trait indicates that the interviewee has sufficient strength of character to make the right decision even when confronted with opposing views.

On October 17, 1994, Susan Smith, mother of two young children and secretary at Conso Products located in Union, South Carolina received a letter from Tom Findlay, the son of the owner of Conso Products. In the letter, Findlay told Smith that he was breaking off their love affair. The letter read in part, "You will, without a doubt, make some lucky man a great wife. But unfortunately, it won't be me." Findlay further wrote, "Susan, I could really fall for you. You have some endearing qualities about you, and I think that you are a terrific person. But like I have told you before, there are some things about you that aren't suited for me, and yes, I am speaking about your children." Smith was devastated. Her chance at happiness was dashed because of her children. To make matters even more complicated, Smith was still married but in the process of getting a divorce.

During the night of October 25, 1994, eight days after receiving Findlay's letter, Smith strapped her two sleeping children, Michael age three, and Alex age 14 months, in the back seat of her 1990 burgundy Mazda Protégé and drove to John D. Long Lake. She drove her car onto the boat ramp, got out, and watched as the car drove off the boat ramp and into the lake. The car filled with water and sunk to the bottom of the lake drowning her two children.

To cover the murders, Smith made up a story that she was carjacked by an African-American male as she waited for the light to turn green at an intersection. The carjacker forced Susan out of her car and drove off with her children still in the back seat. This story was later discredited and Smith eventually admitted that she murdered her children. The following is an excerpt from the first portion of the written statement she provided to police investigators shortly after she reported that she was carjacked.

(1) I arrived home around 6:00 p.m. on Tuesday, October 25, 1994. (2) It had been an upsetting day for me. (3) When I walked in the door, my phone was ringing but before I could answer it, they hung up. (4) I have call return on my phone so I dialed back and it was my mom. (5) I asked her if she was going to be home because I might come over. (6) (When I am upset, I have to go somewhere or do something). (7) She told me that she was going to Nick's ball game at 7:00 and it would probably only last an hour so she would be back home some time after 8:00. (8) She asked me if she wanted me to just let her come by my house and I told her no I would rather come see her. (9) (She didn't know that I was upset). (10) We ended the conversation with me planning on coming to her house. (11) I hung up the phone and went into the living room w/Michael & Alex. (12) If I recall correctly, he put a movie in the VCR. (13) I went into the kitchen and (strikeout) tried to find them something to eat. (14) I decided to fix them (strike out) a pizza. (15) They played in the meantime and I played with them. (16) Because of my conversation with Tom earlier, I was concerned about him and knew that he was at Hickory Nuts with Susan Brown. (17) So called Hickory Nuts with Susan Brown. (18) So I called Hickory Nuts to talk to Susan to see how Tom was. (strikeout) (19) I could tell by talking to her that she couldn't say much about Tom because Tom was sitting beside her. (20) She told me she would call me later and talk to me. (21) I said o.k. (22) I really don't remember what else I did after that.

Smith provided several Word Clues revealing her state of mind. In Sentence 2, the Word Clue "upsetting" indicates that something occurred that day that caused her anxiety; however, she did not provide the cause for her anxiety. Exploring what caused her anxiety on the day of the murders may have provided insight into her motives and intent. In Sentence 6, the Word Clue "upset" supports the hypothesis that something happened that day to cause her anxiety and that this anxiety was so great that she had to go somewhere or do something to relieve the anxiety. The Word Clue "upset" in Sentence 9 indicates that, for unknown reasons, Smith did not want to tell her mother the reason or reasons for her anxiety. If Smith was upset to the extent she wrote in her statement and she was able to hide her emotions from her mother indicates that she can effectively mask her true emotions. Knowing this, puts investigators on notice that Smith may be able to lie more convincingly because she can control her emotional responses.

In Sentence 14, the Word Clue "decided" indicates that she thought about preparing foods other than pizza. Smith probably told the truth about this activity because she describes the mental process of choosing one item over another. Liars typically do not include mental processing in their lies.

The Word Clue "concerned" in Sentence 16 indicates that Smith experienced anxiety because of her earlier conversation with Findlay. In fact, Smith was so concerned about Findlay that she called Susan Brown to see how he was. The anxiety Smith expressed at the beginning of her statement, could have stemmed from her conversation with Findlay. In Sentence 19, Smith wrote, "I could tell by talking to her that she couldn't say much about Tom because Tom was sitting beside her." This sentence serves as a Word Clue. Smith's relationship with Findlay was strained to the point where she did not feel comfortable talking directly to him. Smith initiated the telephone call, which suggests that she wanted to continue the relationship, but he did not want to. One hypothesis suggests that Smith and Findlay had a major falling out and this may have been the cause of the anxiety she expressed in the beginning of her statement. A corollary to this hypothesis suggests that Smith's relationship with Findlay may have taken precedence over her relationship with her children. Smith wrote this statement after she was supposedly carjacked and her children kidnapped. The focus of the first part of Smith's statement is on her, her anxiety, and her concern for Findlay. Smith's concern should have been on her children whose fate was supposedly yet unknown. This is not appropriate behavior for a mother who was carjacked and her children kidnapped. Word Clues provide insight into what Smith was thinking. Smith was thinking only of herself and she should have been thinking about her missing children. This unusual behavior suggests deception.

Smith subsequently confessed to killing her children and is serving a life sentence in prison at South Carolina's Leath Correctional Institution. She will be eligible for parole in 2025, when she is 53 years old.

Chapter 2

HUMAN COMMUNICATION
AND DECEPTION

I protested vehemently, but, in the end, I had no choice but to accept my new assignment as a training agent. The last thing I needed was a new agent following me around with a clip board asking a bunch of stupid questions. I told the new agent to just watch and listen as I worked and he might learn a thing or two. The new agent watched me, a bit too close. He asked a lot of questions and few of the questions were stupid ones. He was like a two-year old always asking "Why did you do this?" and "Why did you do that?" As it turned out, I didn't know why I did what I did. I just did it. Having no answer, I told the new agent that after 18 years of experience he, too, would know how to do what I did. He did not accept this answer. He wanted to know what I knew, now. He could not wait 18 years.

I agreed to conduct a postmortem with him after each interview. He put everything I said or did under a microscope and took detailed notes, always asking the question, "Why?" Specifically, he wanted to know how to detect deception. His persistent inquiries forced me to organize my thoughts and actions, which, in part, formed the foundation for this book.

Deception involves at least two people, the deceiver and the deceived. Formulating false messages requires deceivers to fabricate lies to emulate the truth. People who communicate false information under the assumption that the information is true are not liars. Likewise, mentally ill people who cannot form the intent to deceive are not liars. Acting and magic tricks do not meet the definition of deception because audiences voluntarily suspend reality in exchange for entertainment. Deceptive communication also excludes social pleasantries. No one expects an honest answer to the greeting, "How are you?" Social pleasantries do not communicate substantive information but, rather, acknowledge the presence of other people. Social pleasantries are harmless and, in fact, necessary to maintain personal and business relationship. Dads who feign delight at receiving ugly ties on Father's Day to avoid hurting the feelings of their children are not liars. Guests who tell their hosts that they had a splendid time at a boring dinner party are not liars. The targets of social pleasantries understand that the comments serve to acknowledge their efforts and not to communicate information. Deception does not include satire and sarcasm because the writer's tone of voice and mannerisms ensure that the recipients understand the intended meaning of the message. Deception does include unsuccessful attempts to tell the truth. A cheating husband who playfully tells his suspicious wife that he was late getting home because a siren lured him to her lair constitutes a lie because the context within which the husband couched the truth appeared unbelievable, even though his words were accurate.

Actions can deceive. Faking illness to avoid attending an unpleasant social gathering constitutes deception. Temporal distortions constitute deception. For example, a teenager who went to the library for five minutes on his way to a party deceived his parents when he reported that he was at the library the entire previous evening. Withholding information to cause the recipients of communications to believe that something is true when it is not constitutes a lie. True statements juxtaposed can form a lie. For example, a person attempting to cash a forged check at a supermarket might say, "I'd like to cash this check. The manager said it was okay." to mislead the cashier into thinking that the manager authorized the transaction. The forger did speak to the manager about the availability a certain grocery item, not about cashing a check, and the forger did want to cash the check. These two statements are true in and of themselves, but form a lie when presented in sequence. For the purpose of this book, deception represents any intentional act, successful or unsuccessful, that creates in another person a belief that the writer knows to be untrue.

The ability to lie goes beyond speaking or writing words. The target of the lie must also believe that the words are true. Several psychological principles give liars an advantage by predisposing their targets to believe something is true when it is not. These psychological principles include the Truth Bias, Miller's Law, Primacy Effect, and the Land of Is.

TRUTH BIAS

People tend to believe others. This phenomenon, referred to as the Truth Bias, allows society and commerce to run efficiently. Absent the Truth Bias, people would spend an inordinate amount of time checking data collected from others. The tendency to believe others serves as the social default. Relationships with friends and business colleagues would become strained if their veracity were constantly questioned. Consequently, people typically believe others until evidence to the contrary surfaces.

The Truth Bias provides liars with an advantage because people want to believe what they hear, see, or read. If a story is basically true, the Truth Bias causes people to excuse away the loose ends that do not fit into the otherwise comprehensive narrative by saying, "He really didn't mean to say that?" or "He must have made a mistake," or "What she really meant was . . ." The Truth Bias favors liars when they lie by omission because the story they tell is true without the inclusion of the omitted information. The Truth Bias diminishes when people become aware of the possibility of deception. Judicious skepticism acts as a defense against the Truth Bias.

MILLER'S LAW

George Miller, a Princeton professor and respected psychologist, formulated the golden rule of communication. Miller's Law states, "To understand what another person is saying, you must first assume what the person said is true and then try to imagine what it could be true of." Practiced liars routinely use Miller's Law to tell the truth, but the truth about what?

My oldest son demonstrated that even seven-year olds can instinctively use Miller's Law to deceive. As punishment for some misdeed, I sent my son to his room after dinner without dessert. Earlier that afternoon, we made his favorite dessert, chocolate chip cookies. At about 7 o'clock that evening, I heard pajama clad feet heading toward the kitchen. The pantry door opened. The clink of the cookie jar lid was unmistakable. I knew my son was taking a cookie. I crept to the kitchen and opened the door. There he sat. I did not catch him in the act, but there were cookie crumbs on his face and hands and the cookie jar was tightly positioned between his crossed legs. The conversation went something like this:

> **ME:** Did you take a cookie?
> **MY SON:** No, I didn't take a cookie.
> **ME:** Don't lie, Son, there are cookie crumbs on your hands and face.
> **MY SON:** I didn't take a cookie, Dad.
> **ME:** How can you lie with the evidence all over your hands and face?
> **MY SON:** I didn't take a cookie.

My reputation was at stake. If I could get heinous criminals to confess, I could get my son to confess. I put him in a chair and interviewed him. A few minutes later, he admitted his guilt. I then focused on his lack of candor.

ME: Why did you lie to me, Son?

MY SON: I didn't lie to you, Dad. You asked me if I took a cookie. I didn't take a cookie; I took two cookies.

According to Miller's Law, my son did not lie to me. He told the truth, but the truth about what? He restricted his definition of "a cookie" to mean one cookie. The first cookie he took fits the definition of "a cookie." My son instinctively used Miller's Law to restrict the definition of the words "two cookies" to exclude the lesser-included first cookie.

Sixteen years later, my wife, my son, and I were sitting at the breakfast table. I was reading the newspaper and my wife was talking to my son. My wife asked my son if he used alcohol at college. I thought to myself, "Some questions are best left unasked." Nonetheless, I waited to see how my son would answer this question without lying to his mother. He responded, "I am not using alcohol, Mom." My wife answered, "You're a good kid. I'm so proud of you."

According to Miller's Law, my son told the truth, but the truth about what? He answered in the present tense, which rendered his answer true because he was not consuming alcohol at the moment my wife asked him the question. My son may have consumed adult beverages before talking with his mother and will certainly tip a few after talking with his mother, but he was telling the truth when he answered in the present tense. I thought for a brief moment to challenge my son's answer, for I knew he consumed alcohol on more than one occasion. I chose family harmony over the truth. Had I wanted the truth, I would have asked my son, "When was the last time you consumed alcohol?" This question would have challenged his present tense assertion and uncovered the truth, but perhaps destroyed his mother's faith in him. I remained silent, chuckling to myself, but silent.

Lawyers often encounter witnesses and defendants who maintain that they are telling the truth despite evidence to the contrary. The following excerpt is from the murder trials of Ritch Bryant, Randy Rojas, and Jessica Colwell. They were tried for the murder of Milton Walter, an African-American transient living in a vacant lot in Lancaster, California. Bryant, Rojas, and Colwell, along with Michael Thornton were members of a white supremacist gang called Nazi Low Riders. Gang members had to earn the right to wear certain tattoos, which gave them status in the gang. One of the most coveted tattoos was a set of two lightning bolts. Lightning bolts were the symbols used by the Nazi SS troops in WWII. The Nazi Low Riders adapted this symbol to represent their belief that the white race was superior to all other races. In order for gang members to earn the right to wear lightning bolt tattoos, referred to as bolts, they had to murder an African-American.

On November 25, 1995, Bryant, Rojas, and Thornton decided to earn their bolts. They happened upon Milton Walker in the vacant lot where he slept. Thornton ran up to Walker, hit him and kicked him several times. As Walker tried to make his escape, Rojas hit him in the face with a 2 x 4. Walker fell to the ground motionless. Rojas hit him in the face 12 more times as he lay motionless on the blood soaked ground. The attackers then casually walked to a nearby fast food restaurant to wash the blood off their hands, clothes, and shoes. Shortly thereafter, they met Colwell and told her that they just earned their bolts. Colwell became excited and wanted to see the dead body. Bryant took Colwell back to the vacant lot to view the body. Rojas did not accompany them because he read in a crime magazine that criminals should never go back to the scene of the crime. Thornton did not go because he had a 10 o'clock curfew and he did not want to make his mother angry.

At the crime scene, Bryant checked Walker for a pulse. He found one. Colwell picked up a metal pipe that was lying nearby and poked it in Walker's eye. Bryant picked up the bloody 2 x 4 Rojas used earlier and struck Walker in the face two times. He stopped breathing. Bryant and Colwell were so excited about earning their bolts that they walked to the home of a tattoo artist, woke him up, and asked him to tattoo them on the spot. The tattoo artist told them to come to his shop the next day and he would apply the tattoos.

The trial took place in Judge Lance Ito's courtroom. As you may recall Judge Ito gained notoriety in the O. J. Simpson murder trial. Rojas, Bryant, and Colwell demanded separate trials. Judge Ito ordered that the three trials take place simultaneously in the same courtroom with three separate juries. The evidence was color coded and the juries were ushered in and out of the courtroom depending on what evidence a particular jury was allowed to see.

The defense attorney for Colwell contended that Walker was already dead when his client arrived and she merely hit a corpse, a misdemeanor in California. Contradicting extant evidence, the forensic pathologist hired by the defense testified that Walker was dead at the time Colwell struck him. A closer examination of the forensic pathologist's testimony revealed that he did tell the truth, but the truth about what? After 20 minutes of verbal sparring, the prosecutor discovered the value of Miller's Law when she asked this final series of questions.

> **PROSECUTOR:** In terms of determining cause of death, you're familiar with the term brain dead?
> **PATHOLOGIST:** Yes, Ma'am.
> **PROSECUTOR:** Can someone be brain dead but still have heart and lung activity?
> **PATHOLOGIST:** Yes, Ma'am.

PROSECUTOR: When you say Mr. Walker was dead are you talking about brain dead or are you talking about no heart or lung activity?

PATHOLOGIST: I'm talking about what I consider a clinical brain death.

PROSECUTOR: So, when you say Mr. Walker was dead for an hour or so, you're talking about brain dead is that correct?

PATHOLOGIST: Yes, Ma'am.

PROSECUTOR: Mr. Walker still could have had a heartbeat and be dead by your definition?

PATHOLOGIST: Yes.

PROSECUTOR: Could you determine if Mr. Walker had any brain activity at the time the defendant struck him?

PATHOLOGIST: No, but based on the extent of his injuries at the time the defendant struck Mr. Walker, I concluded that Mr. Walker's brain ceased to function.

PROSECUTOR: Without medical equipment, can you know for sure if Mr. Walker had no brain activity at the time the defendant struck him?

PATHOLOGIST: No, Ma'am.

The prosecutor defined the word "death" as no heart and lung activity. The pathologist defined death as a person with no brain activity regardless of their heart and lung activity. The pathologist told the truth, but the truth about what?

THE PRIMACY EFFECT

The Primacy Effect does not change reality but, rather, manipulates the way in which people perceive reality. First impressions illustrate the Primacy Effect. People form first impressions when they meet someone for the first time. A single word can make the difference between liking a person and disliking that person. If a friend describes the person you are about to meet for the first time as untrustworthy, then you will be predisposed to view that person as untrustworthy. The word "untrustworthy" creates a filter that predisposes you to view the person you are about to meet as untrustworthy. Thereafter, you will tend to view everything that the person says or does as untrustworthy. Overcoming negative Primacy Effect is difficult but not impossible. The more times you meet the "untrustworthy" person and do not experience instances of untrustworthiness, the more likely you are to view the "untrustworthy" person as trustworthy, thus overriding the negative primacy filter. The inherent problem with a negative primacy filter is that you are less likely to meet an untrustworthy person a second time because you perceive that person as untrustworthy. Conversely, if before meeting a person for the first time, a friend tells you that the person you are about to meet is friendly, then you will likely view that person as friendly. However, if you meet the "friendly" person several times and do not experience friendliness, then you will tend to excuse the unfriendly behavior. Such excuses may include "He must be having a bad day," "I must have caught her at a bad time," or "Everybody has a bad day once in awhile." An unfriendly person initially described as friendly gains an advantage from a positive primacy filter because the people they meet will tend to allow the unfriendly person multiple opportunities to demonstrate friendliness despite numerous instances of unfriendly behavior.

Lawyers can benefit from the Primacy Effect. The prosecutor delivers the first opening statement in a criminal trial. The first opening statement is important because the prosecutor has the opportunity to establish the Primacy Effect. The prosecutor creates a filter through which the jurors will view the defendant and the evidence presented. After the prosecutor delivers the opening statement, the defense attorney presents the second opening statement. The jurors will tend to interpret the defense attorney's opening statement through the filter established by the prosecutor. The Primacy Effect gives the prosecution a distinct advantage at the onset of a trial. The Primacy Effect can also play an important part in determining how lawyers schedule witnesses to testify. The first witnesses called by defense attorneys should highlight the positive characteristics of the suspect, thus creating positive filters through which the jurors will view the suspect when he testifies. A witness who presents strong evidence should testify before witnesses who present weaker evidence. After the presentation of stronger evidence, jurors may create a primacy filter that the suspect is either guilty or innocent. If primacy occurs, then jurors will tend to view the weaker witness through the primacy filter created by the stronger witnesses, thus making the weaker evidence appear stronger.

The Primacy Effect can significantly affect learning. High achieving students labeled as poor performers typically perform poorly. Poor performing students labeled as high achievers tend to perform as high achievers. Students told by their teachers that a lesson is difficult tend to experience difficulty learning the lesson. Conversely, students who are told that a lesson is easy tend to experience less difficulty learning the lesson.

My younger brother let me in on one of his dating secrets. He used the Primacy Effect in a novel way to get women to call him and ask him out on dates. He lived in a small apartment in Los Angeles along with three other college students. One evening, they decided to go to a club. Clubbing cost money, so they went to an ATM machine. While his friends were using the ATM, he saw several ATM receipts lying on the ground and picked them up. One of the receipts listed a balance of $107,568. He quickly formulated a plan and pocketed the receipt. At the club later that evening, he met a girl who was clearly above his station. He offered the girl his phone number. She was reluctant. He acted as though he was fumbling for a piece of paper to write on. He finally pulled out the ATM receipt, looked at it, shrugged his shoulders acting as if this was the only piece of paper he had, and said, "I guess I can use this." He wrote his telephone number on the receipt and gave it to her. The trap was set. He knew that the girl would, at least, glance at the ATM receipt. When she did, she would become curious and look at the balance. The large balance would create a Primacy Effect. The girl now saw my brother from a different perspective. He was no longer a poor college student. His economic status did not change but through the Primacy Effect the ATM receipt created, he was now a college student with means. Bingo! Pop star status. Several days later the girl called him and asked him out on a date. My brother did not change reality; he changed the way the girl perceived reality. This technique did not work all the time, but it worked often enough that my younger brother and his friends routinely went fishing for ATM receipts in trash containers in front of banks in Beverly Hills. On one occasion, he told a girl who called him for a date that he was previously engaged. In reality, he did not have enough money to buy gas to drive the distance to her house in Beverly Hills.

The downside to this technique is that the Primacy Effect diminishes with skepticism. When my brother picked the girl up in a junker car and took her to a bowling alley for dinner, she began to suspect that he was not the person she envisioned. However, the Truth Bias may have caused the girl to excuse away my brother's behavior as eccentric. Over time, though, she would eventually realize that he was a poor college student and stop dating him. The other alternative my brother had was to use the time the Primacy Effect bought him to build rapport. Healthy skepticism is a good defense against the Primacy Effect.

THIRD-PARTY INTRODUCTIONS

Adolescents experience a difficult time coming of age. I was no exception, especially when it came to meeting teenage girls. I was infatuated with Vickie. She was the prettiest girl I had seen since I crossed the threshold of puberty. I wanted to spend time with her, but she was not my social equal. Vickie was a cool kid. I was not a cool kid, but neither was I a nerd. I was stuck in social limbo. I devised a plan exploiting the Primacy Effect to meet her without subjecting myself to social humiliation. I later referred to this technique as the Third-Party Introduction. Nancy was Vickie's closest friend. I knew if I told Nancy that I thought Vickie was cute, had a good sense of humor, and that I wanted to take her out on a date, the message would be conveyed to Vickie in a matter of minutes. I knew Vickie would be faced with two options. If she liked me, she would have a favorable opinion of me because she would see me as a person who liked her. If she did not like me, then she would avoid me at all cost because she would know my intentions to ask her out on a date. The next day, I saw Vickie walking down the hallway. Our eyes met. I saw panic. She took a hard right turn into an empty classroom and shut the door. I had my answer without suffering an unbearable public rejection. I tried the same technique on Paula, who was also in social limbo, with great success. I learned another lesson in behavioral analysis. People like others who share common interests, values, and backgrounds. Paula shared more commonalities with me than Vickie did.

Criminal interviewers can take advantage of Third-Party Introductions. I routinely brought suspects into the interview room. As I am shutting the door, my partner is ostensibly called out to take an emergency telephone call. I casually talk to the suspect as if I were waiting for my partner to return. I tell the suspect he is lucky to have my partner investigating the case because he is a fair person, who listens to both sides of a story before making up his mind. I further comment that the reason I like working with him is that he possesses the uncanny ability to detect deception, even with the most practiced liars. A few minutes later, my partner returns. The primacy filter I established predisposes the suspect to view my partner as a fair person who listens to both sides of a story before making up his mind, but more importantly, the suspect will perceive him as a human lie detector. The Primacy Effect predisposes the suspect to believe that my partner is an expert lie catcher. The Spotlight Effect heightens this belief.

As I discussed earlier, the Spotlight Effect heightens a person's self-awareness of lying or doing something wrong or secretive. Liars tend to think that their targets readily detect their lies when, in fact, they do not. For example, the feeling I experienced the first several times I passed out-of-date transfers is a good example of the Spotlight Effect. I thought the bus drivers knew I was passing out-of-date transfers when, in reality, they did not. Another common example of the Spotlight Effect is when a person has a small spot on their shirt. The person automatically thinks that everybody sees the spot and tries to cover it up. The act of trying to cover the spot draws more attention to the spot thus increasing the intensity of the Spotlight Effect.

The Spotlight Effect also occurs when police officers conduct surveillance. They tend to think that the suspect identified them as law enforcement when, in fact, the suspect did not discover the surveillance. I tested the Spotlight Effect after a long surveillance. My colleague was absolutely convinced that the suspect identified him as law enforcement. After the suspect was arrested while robbing a bank, I asked him if he made surveillance. His answer stunned me back to reality. He said, "Of course not. If I knew I was being followed, do you think I would have robbed the bank?"

A cousin to the Third-Party Introduction is the Third-Party Compliment. If you directly compliment someone, they may or may not think that you are genuine in your praise. A better way to compliment someone is to sing their praises to their friends or close associates. Your message will be transmitted to your target within minutes. The next time your target sees you, he will be predisposed to like you because you like him. Third-Party Compliments take advantage of the Primacy Effect and are more effective than direct compliments.

Employees can combine the Third-Party Introduction and the Third-Party Compliment to their advantage. For example, George, Tom, and Bill work for a large company and are competing for resources to fund their respective projects. The president of the company will review each proposal and then decide which project will receive funding. Due to restricted resources, only one project will be funded. Several months before the deadline for the submission of the proposals, George, knowing the power of the Primacy Effect, seeks out Greg, who has daily access to the president. During their *chance* meeting, George casually mentions that he likes the management style of the president, thinks that the president makes good business decisions, and likes the president's ability to communicate with the employees. Shortly thereafter, Greg will likely tell the president what George said because people tend to gossip. The Primacy Effect creates a filter through which the president will view George and, by extension, his proposal. All things being equal, the probability increases that George's project will be funded. When the president sees George's name on his proposal, he will view George as a person who mutually shares the same management style. People like other people who share the same qualities they value. This phenomenon is called mirroring. Mirroring gestures, posture, language, and speech patterns quickly builds rapport.

The Primacy Effect can be very subtle. Simply referring to a person as a suspect predisposes listeners or readers to assume that the person interviewed is guilty to some degree. If the word "interviewee" were used instead of the word "suspect," readers or listeners would be less inclined to assume guilt. If the word "witness" were used instead of the word "suspect" or "interviewee," then readers would be even less likely to assume guilt.

If the word "interrogation" were used instead of the word "interview," the likelihood increases that readers would assume that the person being questioned was guilty. Interviewers view interrogations as adversarial and, at some point prior to interrogations, they either consciously or unconsciously form the opinion that the interviewee is guilty to some degree. If this were not the case, then the interviewers would be conducting interviews not interrogations. Taking this approach creates two negative primacy filters. The first negative primacy filter is that the interrogation will be confrontational. If interviewers go into the interrogation with the preconceived notion that the suspect will be confrontational, then the interrogation will likely become confrontational because the interviewers will tend to interpret anything the suspect says or does through the filter of confrontation. Interviewers begin interrogations with a heightened sensitivity to confrontation; therefore, the slightest provocation by the suspect triggers responses that are more aggressive because interviewers anticipate confrontations. The same actions that interviewers perceive as aggressive during interrogations would probably be judged as less aggressive or neutral during interviews because interviewers perceive interviews as nonconfrontational. The second negative filter is that interviewers will likely view the interviewees as guilty before the interrogations commence and perceive everything the interviewees say or do as support of their guilt and discount or excuse away any evidence that does not support their preconceived notion of guilt.

The media harnesses the power of the Primacy Effect. In today's busy world, people typically do not consult multiple news sources to get a balanced view of world events; therefore, people tend to perceive world events through the filter created by a single newspaper, television newscast, or radio report. Media has the power to influence the way in which people view world events. If a media outlet, especially a reputable one, introduces a bias into the news story, the readers or listeners will tend to view the event through the biased filter established by the media report. The filter created by the biased news report will remain in place until the readers are exposed to other more balanced news reports; however, this is unlikely to occur because people generally do not consult multiple news sources.

I was sitting in Dulles Airport just outside of Washington, D.C. when I got a cell phone call from a producer from Good Morning America. He asked me if I would be willing to analyze the video statement of John Mark Karr, the "self-confessed" murderer of JonBenét Ramsey. Good Morning America sent a limousine to the airport and drove me to their studio in Washington D.C. to conduct a PNA of the videotaped confession made by Karr and comment on my analysis during an interview. I was given the following summary when I arrived at the studio.

On August 16, 2006, Thai authorities arrested John Karr. While in custody, Karr confessed that he murdered JonBenét Ramsey, the six-year-old found in the basement of her family's home in Boulder, Colorado one day after Christmas in 1996. Over a period of four years after the murder, Karr exchanged e-mails with Michael Tracey, a journalism professor at the University of Colorado, in which Karr alluded to the fact that he killed Ramsey. Tracey notified authorities and the search for Karr began. After Thai authorities arrested Karr, Peter Maguire, a deputy district attorney in Boulder, Colorado made the following statement at a news conference.

> This guy confessed on numerous occasions in great detail. He confessed in e-mails. He confessed in telephone conversations. He admitted it to a police officer. Karr even confessed on international TV, telling the world that he was with JonBenét Ramsey when she died, a claim he had been making to University of Colorado journalism professor Michael Tracey for years.

The media saturated the public with Maguire's statement along with countless conjectures posited by subject matter experts which set up the Primacy Effect. Maguire and the media determined without having full command of the facts that Karr murdered Ramsey. Thereafter, the press interpreted everything that Karr said and did as proof of his guilt. This is a good example of how Karr used the combination of Miller's Law and the Primacy Effect to camouflage the truth.

Karr made the following confession to the international press correspondents covering his case in Thailand.

> **KARR:** I love JonBenét. And she died accidently.
> **REPORTER:** Are you an innocent man?
> **KARR:** No.
> **REPORTER:** What happened?
> **KARR:** Her death was an accident.
> **REPORTER:** So, you were in the basement?
> **KARR:** Yes.
> **REPORTER:** Can you tell us about your connection to the Ramsey family?
> **KARR:** No comment to that.

The Primacy Effect did not distort reality, only the media's perception of reality. Good Morning America asked me to analyze Karr's videotaped confession. I will go over the same sentence-by-sentence examination of Karr's confession as I did with the producers.

> **KARR:** I love JonBenét. And she died accidently.

First, Karr stated that he loved JonBenét. Karr often expressed his love for children. His expression of love for JonBenét, albeit fanciful, is a true statement. For that matter, every opinion we hold is truthful regardless of its merits. Second, Karr may believe that JonBenét died accidently. This statement is, again, Karr's opinion. His opinion does not have to be truthful. These two sentences taken separately are each truthful but no logical connection exists between Karr and JonBenét's murder. However, through the filter of the Primacy Effect, the press, law enforcement, and much of the country perceived Karr's statement as an admission of guilt.

> **REPORTER:** Are you an innocent man?
> **KARR:** No.

The Primacy Effect predisposed the media to interpret Karr's answer as an admission of guilt. Karr's reply to this question is truthful, for who amongst us is an innocent person? While the statemetent itself is true, no logical connection exists between Karr and JonBenét's murder, except in the minds of the people who perceived Karr as guilty.

> **REPORTER:** What happened?
> **KARR:** Her death was an accident.

Again, Karr expressed his opinion. He did not admit to killing JonBenét. People in the United States are free to express their opinions regardless of the truthfulness of those opinions. Karr told the truth, but the truth about what?

> **REPORTER:** So, you were in the basement?
> **KARR:** Yes.

The media made the false assumption that Karr was in the Ramsey's basement at the time of JonBenét's death. According to Miller's Law, if Karr was in any basement prior to uttering this sentence, he answered truthfully. The reporter failed to specify if Karr was in the Ramsey's basement.

> **REPORTER:** Can you tell us about your connection to the Ramsey family?
> **KARR:** No comment to that.

Karr simply stated that he had no comment to the reporter's question. The comment "No comment" forms a secondary Primacy Effect. In America, the words "no comment" have a negative connotation because only guilty people are reluctant to make full disclosures. This connotation is magnified by the overarching Primacy Effect established by the media that Karr killed JonBenét.

REPORTER: How did you get into the basement to play with her?
KARR: No comment to that.

The analysis is the same as in the previous exchange.

Karr told the truth, but the truth about what? Karr made several admissions; however, murdering JonBenét was not among them. He did not admit to killing her. Several weeks later, after a close examination of Karr's whereabouts at the time of Ramsey's death, law enforcement authorities determined that Karr did not murder Ramsey. The media fell victim to the Primacy Effect and, in turn, created the Primacy Effect for the American population at-large. Reality did not change; however, people's perception of reality did change. People saw what they wanted to see.

COMPETING HYPOTHESES

Developing Competing Hypotheses reduces the Primacy Effect. A hypothesis in nothing more than an educated guess. A Competing Hypothesis is an educated guess that supposes a different outcome based on the same or similar set of circumstances. Interviewers should initially begin interviews with Competing Hypotheses. The first hypothesis posits that the person is going to tell the truth. The Competing Hypothesis posits that the person is going to lie. The interviewer then gathers evidence to support one of the hypotheses or develops additional Competing Hypotheses. For example, when we speak to someone our initial hypothesis is that the person is telling the truth. This is due, in large part, to the Truth Bias. The Truth Bias induces the Primacy Effect. We want to believe that the person we are talking to is telling the truth; therefore, we perceive everything that person says or does as truthful. To offset the Truth Bias and the Primacy Effect we would develop the Competing Hypothesis that the person is lying. During the conversation, we should seek evidence to support the initial hypothesis or the Competing Hypothesis. Rarely does all the evidence support the initial hypothesis or the Competing Hypothesis because honest people often say and do things that make them look dishonest and, conversely, dishonest people often say and do things that make them look honest. In the end, however, the weight of the evidence should support one hypothesis over the other.

I once interviewed a suspect who I thought committed murder. The murder occurred in a neighborhood where drugs were routinely sold. The evidence suggested that the murder victim, a drug dealer, was killed as a result of a drug deal that went bad. The suspect was affluent and lived in an upper-middle class suburb. He was out of place. I assumed that he came to this neighborhood to buy drugs. The drug deal obviously went bad and he killed the drug dealer. He was picked-up in the vicinity where the murder took place. When I interviewed him, I saw the classic nonverbal signs of deception, so I pushed harder. The harder I pushed the more signs of deception I saw. I was sure he murdered the drug dealer. An hour later, he confessed, but not to murder. He went to the neighborhood to meet with a prostitute and witnessed the murder. He was reluctant to tell the truth, not because he committed murder, but because he did not want to be identified as a witness. If he told the truth, he thought he would be summoned to court to testify against the real murderer. In doing so, he would have to confess to his wife that he had visited a prostitute. His feared that his wife would end the marriage and he would be destitute after alimony and child support payments. I fell victim to the Primacy Effect. Everything the man said or did I construed as evidence of murder. The man lied, not because he murdered someone, but because he did not want to tell his wife he visited a prostitute. If I had developed a Competing Hypothesis, I would have been less likely to jump to the conclusion that the man was a murderer. Rather than seeing everything the man said or did through the filter of deception, I should have developed Competing Hypotheses, gathered the facts, and determined at the conclusion of the interview which Competing Hypothesis carried the most weight.

The Primacy Effect is a double-edged sword. The Primacy Effect can influence others to view events from the perspective you choose or you can become a victim of the Primacy Effect by allowing others to choose the filters through which you view events. The Primacy Effect is a powerful tool of influence. When listening to spoken words or reading narratives, establish the habit of creating Competing Hypotheses.

Competing Hypotheses add to the flexibility and power of PNA. If more than one investigator is assigned to an investigation, each investigator can develop his own hypothesis based on his perspective of the evidence. As more facts become available, Competing Hypotheses are eliminated because the facts no longer support the supposition of a particular hypothesis or hypotheses. At the conclusion of the investigation, the evidence typically supports one of the Competing Hypotheses. Investigators have the freedom to pursue their own Competing Hypothesis, which is counterbalanced against the Competing Hypotheses of the other investigators. Competing Hypotheses reduce the impact of the Primacy Effect and allows the truth to surface.

THE LAND OF IS

Yes or No questions deserve "Yes" or "No" answers. When interviewees elect not to answer "Yes" or "No," they go to the Land of Is. The Land of Is occupies the space between truth and deception. This murky area contains a labyrinth of half-truths, assumptions, and suppositions. The lack of clear "Yes" or "No" answers forces listeners or readers to form their own conclusions and interpret those conclusions as either "Yes" or "No" answers, which may or may not comport with the reality or the interviewee's intent.

President Clinton's grand jury testimony in the Monica Lewinsky investigation inspired the concept of the Land of Is. The following is an excerpt from Clinton's grand jury testimony:

> **PROSECUTOR:** Your statement is a completely false statement. Whether or not Mr. Bennett knew of your relationship with Ms. Lewinsky, the statement that there was no sex of any kind in any manner, shape or form with President Clinton was an utterly false statement. Is that correct?
>
> **CLINTON:** It depends upon what the meaning of the word is means. If is means is, and never has been, that's one thing, if it means, there is none, that was a completely true statement.

Clinton took the prosecutor to the Land of Is. The prosecutor asked Clinton a Yes or No question. Clinton chose not to answer "Yes" or "No," and, in fact never answered the question. An analysis of Clinton's statement suggests that Clinton was truthful. If "is" means never has been, then "is" equals nothing or "is" = 0. If *is* means there is none then 0 = "is." The proposition "is" = 0 and 0 = "is" is, indeed, a truthful statement. Clinton told the truth, but the truth about what?

The prosecutor did not listen to what Clinton said and missed an opportunity to gain full disclosure. The prosecutor should have pressured Clinton to answer the question posed by responding, "I didn't ask you the meaning of the word "is." I asked you if that statement was false. Was that a false statement, "Yes" or "No?"

As a behavioral analyst, I reviewed videotaped interviews conducted by police investigators to determine the behavioral characteristics and veracity of suspects. In one case, the suspect was a college student. He was the prime suspect in the rape and murder of a female student who attended the same college. The suspect met the victim at a party where she drank heavily. Witnesses at the party saw the suspect push the victim to the floor, hold her down, and attempt to forcibly kiss her. Later that evening, the victim passed out on a couch. At about 1:00 a.m., the suspect woke the victim and walked her to her dormitory. The suspect was the last known person to see the victim alive. Three weeks later, volunteer searchers found the victim's body in a wooded area not far from the campus. A forensic examination determined that the victim was raped and murdered. No DNA evidence was recovered. The following excerpt from the police interview of the suspect demonstrates how the suspect took the interviewer to the Land of Is.

> **INTERVIEWER:** Did you want to kiss her?
> **SUSPECT:** I . . . I . . . I didn't feel . . . I didn't remember feeling any attraction towards her, so . . .
> **INTERVIEWER:** Okay, Alright. Let's move on.

The interviewer asked a Yes or No question, "Did you want to kiss her?" The suspect did not give a "Yes" or "No" answer to that question, but instead answered, "I didn't remember feeling any attraction towards he, so. . . ." The question was, "Did you want to *kiss* her?" not "Did you feel any *attraction* toward her?" The suspect told the truth, but the truth about what? The interviewer failed to listen to what the suspect said and missed an opportunity to gain valuable information. The interviewer should have followed up with, "I didn't ask if you felt any attraction towards her. I asked if you wanted to kiss her. Did you want to kiss her, yes or no?" The interviewer could have prevented the suspect from going to the Land of Is by forcing him to answer the investigator's initial question.

Referring back to the murder trial of Milton Walker in Lancaster, California, Thornton agreed to testify against Bryant, Rojas, and Colwell. Thornton testified without any promises of immunity. Thornton answered each of the prosecutor's Yes or No questions with "Yes" or "No" answers. His narrative answers were short and direct. Thornton's testimony serves as a good illustration of how truthful people answer questions. He made no attempt to take the prosecutor to the Land of Is.

> **PROSECUTOR:** Mr. Thornton, at this time, I'd like to draw your attention to Saturday, November 25th, 1995 at approximately seven-thirty in the evening. Where did you go?
> **THORNTON:** We were going to McDonald's to . . .
> **PROSECUTOR:** When you say "we" are you referring to you, Randy, and Ritch?
> **THORNTON:** Yes.
> **PROSECUTOR:** Did you, Randy, and Ritch then go to McDonald's?
> **THORNTON:** Uh . . . we headed towards McDonald's, and—until we saw a woman walking down the sidewalk.

PROSECUTOR: Did this woman approach you?

THORNTON: No, she did not.

PROSECUTOR: What happened?

THORNTON: Ritch asked her, "What's up? How are you doing?"

PROSECUTOR: And what did the woman say?

THORNTON: She said, "Not too fucking good. Some black guy just kicked me in the back."

PROSECUTOR: Did the–uh–woman indicate the vicinity where the black guy was?

THORNTON: Yes, she did.

PROSECUTOR: Where did she indicate?

THORNTON: In the vacant lot behind McDonald's.

PROSECUTOR: What happened next?

THORNTON: I walked up to the black guy, and said, "Did you hit that woman back there?" And before he replied, I kicked him, and then I punched him.

PROSECUTOR: Let me stop you right there. When you were approaching him, was he facing you?

THORNTON: Yes.

PROSECUTOR: As you were facing him, did you see him armed with any type of weapon?

THORNTON: No.

PROSECUTOR: Before you actually hit him in the side, and hit him with your fist, did he ever try to assault or attack you?

THORNTON: No.

PROSECUTOR: After you hit him, what did the black man then do?

THORNTON: He took a couple of steps back, and then proceeding, walking away, kinda–kinda fast.

PROSECUTOR: After you hit him did he ever try to hit you?

THORNTON: No.

PROSECUTOR: When–when he started to walk away, was that away from you?

THORNTON: Yes.

PROSECUTOR: What then happened?

THORNTON: He got seven to ten feet away from me, and then Randy Rojas struck him in the side of the head with a two-by-four.

PROSECUTOR: Before Randy Rojas stuck the black man in the head with the two-by-four, did you ever see the black man try to attack or assault Randy Rojas?

THORNTON: No.

PROSECUTOR: After Randy struck the black man across the head, what happened next?

THORNTON: He fell flat on his back.
PROSECUTOR: Did he appear conscious?
THORNTON: No, he didn't move.
PROSECUTOR: Did he say anything?
THORNTON: No.
PROSECUTOR: Did he move his arms?
THORNTON: No.
PROSECUTOR: Did he move his legs?
THORNTON: No.
PROSECUTOR: Did he pose a threat at all to you, Randy or Ritch?
THORNTON: No.
PROSECUTOR: What happened then?
THORNTON: Randy took the two-by-four and hit him squarely in the face with it, grunting as he hit him.
PROSECUTOR: Approximately how many more hits did Randy deliver with the two-by-four to the victim's face, while the victim lay on the ground?
THORNTON: Two or three. The man never moved after Randy hit him for the first time.

Rojas and Bryant were found guilty of murder with special circumstances and are currently serving life in prison without the possibility of parole. Colwell was found guilty of voluntary manslaughter and was sentenced to serve nine years in prison.

Chapter 3

LYING BY OBFUSCATION

Truthful people answer direct questions with direct answers. Liars provide evasive answers, ambiguous responses, and use misdirection to avoid the truth. People go to the Land of Is to be polite or to avoid making a commitment to a specific ideology or cause. Politicians go to the Land of Is to pander to diverse constituencies. Managers go to the Land of Is to avoid making decisions. Direct questions threaten people who, for whatever reason, cannot provide direct answers. Recognizing the words and grammar structures people use to go to the Land of Is provides interviewers with a distinct advantage during interviews. This chapter identifies techniques people use to go to the Land of Is.

MISDIRECTION

Misdirection shifts answers away from threatening questions. The overuse of this technique tends to discredit interviewees, especially when interviewers recognize the technique and force interviewees to provide direct answers to the questions posed. The following exchange between a politician and a reporter illustrates misdirection. The politician shifted the focus from his views on abortion to healthcare.

REPORTER: Where do you stand on abortion?
POLITICIAN: Without a doubt, abortion is a controversial issue. It is a personal decision. I've come here today to talk about how my ideas give people the opportunity to choose better health care. It's appalling that 32 percent of the children in our community go without health care. As mayor, I will work hard to provide health care to all the people in our community.

The reporter could have prevented the politician from going deeper into the Land of Is with the response, "Thank you for sharing your views on health care. Where do you stand on abortion?" This response would have forced the politician to talk about his views on abortion. If he returned to the Land of Is, then the reporter could again ask the question, "Where do you stand on abortion?" At this point, however, it becomes very clear that the politician wants to avoid the question. The politician rapidly looses credibility if he continuously goes to the Land of Is using Misdirection to avoid answering the question.   The following excerpt is from President Clinton's grand jury testimony. He used Misdirection to shift the focus of his discussions with Lewinsky about what she meant to write in her affidavit to the fact that there was no employment, sexual harassment, or benefit in exchange with his relationship with Lewinsky.

> **PROSECUTOR:** Did you talk with Ms. Lewinsky about what she meant to write in her affidavit?
> **CLINTON:** I didn't talk to her about her definition. I did not know what was in this affidavit before it was filled out, specifically. I did not know what words was used–were used specifically before it was filled out or what meaning she gave to them. But I'm just telling you that it's certainly true what she says here, that we didn't have–there was no employment or benefit in exchange. There was nothing having anything to do with sexual harassment. And if she defined sexual relationship in the way I think most Americans do, meaning intercourse, then she told the truth.

The prosecutor could have prevented Clinton from going deeper into the Land of Is with the response, "I understand there was no quid pro quo in your relationship with Ms. Lewinsky, but did you talk with her about what she meant to write in her affidavit?" If Clinton returns to the Land of Is, then deception is likely.

FALSE PREMISE

False Premise is a form of Misdirection. A basic argument consists of a premise, an inference, and a conclusion. An argument is a collection of statements or propositions that attempt to support a premise. Inference is the process whereby new beliefs are formed based on established beliefs. The premise provides support or evidence for the inference. A liar establishes a False Premise to support an inference that is not true. For example, a liar states, "I am telling the truth because I am an honest person." In other words, the interviewee said, "I am an honest person (Premise). Honest people do not lie (Argument); therefore, I am telling the truth (Inference)." The truth is honest people lie. Being an honest person does not necessarily mean a person is telling the truth.

My daughter tried to use a False Premise to convince my wife and me to buy her a cell phone. She began her argument, "I need a cell phone because everyone else in school has one, besides, I will be able to contact you in emergencies." In other words, she said, "Everyone at school has a cell phone (Premise). I need a cell phone to communicate with my friends (Argument). I need a cell phone to communicate with my parents in emergencies (Argument); therefore you should buy me a cell phone (Inference)." My daughter established the False Premise that everyone at school has a cell phone. This premise is false because not every student at my daughter's school has a cell phone; she does not have one. Further, her friends could communicate with her face-to-face. The second argument can be neutralized by agreeing with the false premise. I counter argued, "If everyone at school has a cell phone, then you could easily use another student's cell phone to call your mom or me in emergencies." Identifying the premise of any argument is the quickest way to uncover a False Premise. We eventually bought my daughter a cell phone when she learned how to present a solid argument as to why she needed one.

Liars create a False Premise by ignoring the question presented, asking themselves another question or making a statement, and then answering their own question or responding to their own statement. A military officer was charged with plagiarizing his War College thesis. The school conducted a formal hearing. The lawyer showed the officer a copy of a thesis presented by a student several years earlier and then presented the officer with the thesis he submitted. The two papers were remarkably similar. The following exchange was excerpted from the hearing transcript.

> **LAWYER:** Why don't you take a look at this one? This is a different paper. Do you recognize that paper? Should be your signature on the second page.
> **OFFICER:** That's my signature.
> **LAWYER:** Okay.
> **OFFICER:** Do I recognize it as being my paper?
> **LAWYER:** Yes sir.
> **OFFICER:** I couldn't tell you that. It has my signature on the second page. Could I look at it and tell you that I wrote this? No, I couldn't do it. Not at this point. I just couldn't-couldn't do it.

The officer took the lawyer to the Land of Is by setting up a false premise. He ignored the lawyer's question, posed his own question, and answered his question instead of the lawyer's question. The lawyer asked the Yes or No question, "Do you recognize that paper?" The officer responded, "That's my signature." The officer did not answer the Yes or No question with a "Yes" or "No," which signals the possibility of deception. Instead, the officer posed his own question, "Do I recognize it as being my paper?" The officer answered his own question, "I couldn't tell you that." The officer admitted in his previous answer that the signature on the second page was his, but now he cannot recognize it as being his paper. The officer posed a second question, "Could I look at it and tell you that I wrote this?" to which he answered, "No, I couldn't do it. Not at this point. I just couldn't-couldn't do it." The Push-Pull Word "Not at this point" indicates the officer could tell the lawyer he wrote the thesis at some point in the future. The only conditions in which the officer could use the Push-Pull Word, "Not, at this point" is if the officer already knew a point in the future when he could admit that he wrote the paper. Push-Pull Words will be discussed later in this book. Additionally, answering a question with a question signals deception. Answering a question with a question will be discussed later in this book. The officer's responses support the hypothesis that the officer plagiarized his thesis.

From the officer's perspective, his answer, "No, I couldn't do it. Not at this point. I just couldn't-couldn't do it" makes perfect sense. If the officer admitted he plagiarized his thesis, he would face military discipline. At this point, the officer was not prepared to admit he plagiarized his thesis; however, at some point in the future he would be willing to admit plagiarism. The responsibility of the lawyer is to discern when in the future the officer would admit to plagiarism, and more importantly, under what conditions would he admit to plagiarism. An effective follow-up question would have been, "At what point could you tell me that it is your paper?"

REAFFIRMATION OF A FALSE PREMISE

When a False Premise is referred to a minimum of three times, people tend to believe that the False Premise is true. Liars establish a False Premise and refer to the False Premise as many times as possible with the hope that the False Premise will be believed. The following excerpt from President Clinton's grand jury testimony demonstrates Reaffirmation of a False Premise.

PROSECUTOR: Mr. President, I want to go into a new subject area, briefly go over something you were talking about with Mr. Bittman.

The statement of your attorney, Mr. Bennett, at the Paula Jones deposition–counsel is fully aware–it's page 54, line 5. Counsel is fully aware that Ms. Lewinsky is filing, has an affidavit, which they were in possession of, saying that there was absolutely no sex of any kind in any manner, shape or form with President Clinton. That statement was made by your attorney in front of Judge Susan Weber Wright.

CLINTON: I had told you, Mr. Wisenberg–I will tell you for a third time–I am not even sure that Mr. Bennett made that statement that I was concentrating on the exact words he used. Now, if someone had asked me on that day, are you having any kind of sexual relations with Ms. Lewinsky–that is asked me a question in the present tense–I would have said no. And it would have been completely true.

Clinton stated, "I had told you, Mr. Wisenberg–I will tell you for a third time. . . ." Clinton previously established a false premise and referred to the premise three times, which increases the likelihood that the people will believe the false premise. Additionally, this comment disparages the prosecutor by alluding to the fact that he did not understand what Clinton said two times before.

Politicians running for office are often the victims of half-truths, innuendo, and vicious rumors from the opposing candidates. As soon as a radio, television, or Internet ad targets candidates, they immediately respond with a like ad refuting the accusations and launch counteraccusations. This immediate response is necessary because if attack ads go unchallenged, people will tend to believe the attack ad after hearing it for a minimum of three times. John Kerry, the democratic presidential candidate opposing George W. Bush in the 2004 presidential election, learned this lesson when he failed to challenge the "swift boat" controversy challenging his actions in the Vietnam War. Bush went on to win the election. Likewise when you find yourself the target of a vicious rumor, you should respond immediately to prevent people from believing the rumor. If people hear false information enough times, they tend to believe the false information is true.

IF/THEN CONDITIONAL

The If/Then Conditional sets up a false premise by establishing specific parameters wherein the answer to a question is true. These parameters typically exclude the information sought by the interviewer. Conditional statements contain two parts. The first part establishes a hypothetical situation. The second part provides the consequences of the hypothetical situation, if it were to come to pass. If the liar's response meets the restricted conditions of the If/Then Conditional, then he would be telling the truth under the restricted hypothetical conditions.

The following excerpt was taken from a police interview of a murder suspect whose wife's skeletal remains were found in the suspect's car, which rested at the bottom of a lake for several decades after her mysterious disappearance.

> **DETECTIVE:** Was she drinking?
> **SUSPECT:** Had she been drinking that day? She'd drink every day.
> **DETECTIVE:** She drank right up until the time she went to bed?
> **SUSPECT:** Yeah, normally.
> **DETECTIVE:** Was she drinking that night at the time she went to bed?
> **SUSPECT:** If, ah, if, ah, it was a normal day, yes.

The detective asked the Yes or No question, "Was she drinking that night at the time she went to bed?" The suspect could not or chose not to answer "Yes" or "No." Instead, the suspect set up a False Premise using the If/Then Conditional. The hypothetical condition is "if it was a normal day." The implied consequence is that on the night she disappeared she drank up until the time she went to bed. By using the If/Then Conditional, the suspect referred to a normal day and not the day his wife disappeared. The detective could have prevented the suspect from going to the Land of Is by stating, "I understand that she drank every day, but did she drink on the night that she disappeared?" The suspect would be forced to answer "Yes" or "No" or return to the Land of Is. If the suspect returns to the Land of Is, the probability of deception significantly increases. If the suspect returns to the Land of Is, a more direct approach such as, "That was a Yes or No question. Is the answer "Yes" or "No?" would force the suspect to answer "Yes" or "No." In many instances, a person may answer "Yes" or "No" and then add reasons to mitigate his answer. Notwithstanding the interviewee's mitigation, he made an admission. The interviewer should focus on the admission and then address the motivations as to why the interviewee did what he did.

The following excerpt is from President Clinton's grand jury testimony. He established a false premise by using an If/Then Conditional.

> **PROSECUTOR:** Did you talk with Ms. Lewinsky about what she meant to write in her affidavit?
> **CLINTON:** I didn't talk to her about her definition. I did not know what was in this affidavit before it was filled out, specifically. I did not know what words was used—were used specifically before it was filled out or what meaning she gave to them. But I'm just telling you that it's

certainly true what she says here, that we didn't have--there was no employment or benefit in exchange. There was nothing having anything to do with sexual harassment. And if she defined sexual relationship in the way I think most Americans do, meaning intercourse, then she told the truth.

Clinton used the IF/Then Conditional ". . . if she defined sexual relationship in the way I think most Americans do, meaning intercourse" to support his answer that Monica Lewinsky told the truth. If Lewinsky defined sexual relationship in any other way, she would not be telling the truth. The hypothetical condition is if Lewinsky defined "sexual relationship" in the way Clinton thinks most Americans do. Clinton added the Word Qualifier "think," which indicates that he did not know with certainty how Lewinsky defined "sexual relationship" nor did he know with certainty how most Americans defined sexual relations. Word Qualifiers will be discussed later in this book. Clinton established such vague parameters that almost any response he would have made would have been truthful. Clinton told the truth, but the truth about what?

ELASTIC TRUTH

Each person constructs an internal dictionary of the words he uses. With few exceptions, people share the same or similar definitions for the words they use. The similarity of definitions allows people to communicate efficiently. When one person speaks, he automatically assumes that the definitions of the words he speaks approximate the definitions listeners apply to the words they hear. Fortunately, the overwhelming majority of people share similar word definitions. If this were not the case, then communication would be difficult. When a speaker holds up an object and says, "cup," the listener registers the same object as a cup. Communication problems occur when a speaker holds up an object, says "cup," and the listener registers an object other than the object the speaker is holding. When buyers make purchases, they rely on shared definitions. The words buyers use to describe the goods and services they want to purchase must approximate the definitions of the words the sellers use to describe the goods and services offered for sale. If this were not the case, then commerce would be extremely difficult.

Describing emotions and ideas becomes more difficult because these concepts are less tangible. Nonetheless, the definitions of the words people use to communicate their ideas and emotions correspond, with few exceptions, to the definitions listeners or readers use to decode communications. People who act in good faith effectively communicate with one another with little difficulty.

Liars, on the other hand, elongate or restrict their personal word definitions to introduce definitional relativity. Problems arise because liars typically do not notify listeners or readers of the change in their personal word definitions.

Liars can ostensibly tell the truth based on the elongated or restricted personal definitions of the words they use. The recipient of a deceptive communication ascribes the generally accepted word definitions, oblivious to the fact that the deceiver changed his internal word definitions. Elongating or restricting the personal definitions of the words people use becomes Elastic Truth. Consider the following illustration.

Jimmy put three drops of poison in a cup, gave it to his wife to drink, and she died. During the subsequent investigation, a detective asked Jimmy if he put three drops of poison in a cup and gave it to his wife. Jimmy responded, "I did not put poison in a cup." Jimmy's response is truthful because, unbeknownst to the detective, Jimmy changed his internal definition of the word "cup" to "a ceramic vessel that holds liquidy substances." Now, if the detective had asked Jimmy, "Did you put poison in a ceramic vessel that holds liquidy substances and give it to your wife," Jimmy could truthfully respond, "No" because unbeknownst to the detective, Jimmy again changed his internal definition of the word "cup" from "a ceramic vessel that holds liquidy substances" to "a temporary reservoir for drinkable fluids." Liars routinely use this technique to lie. Liars introduce definitional relativity by either elongating or restricting the definitions of words or concepts to include or exclude the questionable activity.

Effective liars do not notify their targets of the change in their personal word definitions. To do so would alert the targets to the deception. Without prior notification of definitional differences, interviewers tend to apply their own internal definitions to the liar's words. Parents often encounter this problem when questioning their children. For example, mom comes home and finds a broken lamp. She suspects that her son, against strict house rules, flew his radio controlled helicopter indoors. She made the following inquiry.

MOM: Did you break the lamp?
SON: No.
MOM: Did you knock it off the table?
SON: No.
MOM: Did you have anything to do with the lamp breaking?
SON: No.
MOM: Were you flying your helicopter in this room.
SON: Yes.

MOM: Did your helicopter break the lamp?

SON: It was an accident, Mom. It just flew off on its own and hit the lamp, honest!

Mom used the trial and error method to uncover the truth. Her son changed his definition of the word "break" and, more specifically, what caused the lamp to break. Her son did not break the lamp. The helicopter did. The helicopter did not knock the lamp off the table. It flew into it. Even though her son was at the controls, the helicopter somehow flew off on its own and hit the lamp. Her son told the truth because he kept changing his internal definitions for the words his mother used. He only told the truth when his mother used the exact words as those words were defined by her son in his internal dictionary. Her son told the truth, but the truth about what?

Clinton, in his grand jury testimony, used elastic truth to obfuscate his relationship with Monica Lewinsky. The unique feature about Clinton's testimony is that he notified the grand jurors that he changed his internal definition of the concept "present tense." By changing his internal definition of the concept "present tense," Clinton told the truth, but the truth about what? The following is an excerpt from Clinton's grand jury testimony.

PROSECUTOR: I just want to make sure I understand you correctly. Do you mean today that because you were not engaging in sexual activity with Ms. Lewinsky during the deposition that the statement Mr. Bennett made (OFF MIKE)?

The off-mike conversation was not recorded in the grand jury transcripts; however, Clinton provided the following answer.

CLINTON: No, sir. I mean that at the time of the deposition, we had been–that was well-beyond any point of improper contact between me and Ms. Lewinsky. So that anyone generally speaking in the present tense saying that was not an improper relationship would be telling the truth if that person said there was not, in the present tense–the present tense encompassing many months. That's what I meant by that–I wasn't trying to give you a cute answer to that.

In his answer, Clinton elongated his definition of the word "present." Most people would define the word "present" as here and now. Clinton not only changed his internal definition of the word "present," but he notified the prosecutor of this change. Good liars typically change their internal definitions of words, but do not notify their targets of the change for obvious reasons. Nonetheless, Clinton defined the word "present" as many months. Many months could mean one month or 100 months depending on each person's internal definition of the words "many months." If Clinton defined many months to include the entire time he spent with Monica Lewinsky, then any statement Clinton made using the present tense would be a truthful statement because his activities with Lewinsky, in his mind, occurred in the past not the present. Clinton elongated his definition of "present tense," which, of course, excludes any activity with Lewinsky that occurred in the past. The prosecutor should have asked Clinton to specifically define his meaning of the concept "present tense" and then ask follow-up questions using Clinton's definition of the concept "present tense." This line of questioning would have prevented Clinton from taking the prosecutor to the Land of Is.

A second prosecutor asked Clinton to clarify his previous answer regarding his sexual activities with Monica Lewinsky.

> **PROSECUTOR:** Mr. President, I want to go into a new subject area, briefly go over something you were talking about with Mr. Bittman. The statement of your attorney, Mr. Bennett, at the Paula Jones deposition–counsel is fully aware–it's page 54, line 5. Counsel is fully aware that Ms. Lewinsky is filing, has an affidavit, which they were in possession of, saying that there was absolutely no sex of any kind in any manner, shape or form with President Clinton. That statement was made by your attorney in front of Judge Susan Weber Wright.
>
> **CLINTON:** I had told you, Mr. Wisenberg–I will tell you for a third time–I am not even sure that Mr. Bennett made that statement that I was concentrating on the exact words he used. Now, someone had asked me on that day, are you having any kind of sexual relations with Ms. Lewinsky–that is asked me a question in the present tense–I would have said no. And it would have been completely true.

Like the first prosecutor, Clinton took the second prosecutor to the Land of Is. Clinton's personal definition of the concept "present tense" allowed him to tell the truth, but the truth about what? The second prosecutor attempted to find his way out of the Land of Is with the following line of questioning.

> **PROSECUTOR:** . . . Counsel is fully aware that Ms. Lewinsky has filed–has an affidavit, which they are in possession of, saying that there is absolutely no sex of any kind in any manner, shape or form with President Clinton.
>
> **CLINTON:** Where is that?

WISENBERG: That is on page 54, beginning at line 1. About midway through line 1.
CLINTON: Well, actually, in the present tense, that's an accurate statement. That was an actual—that was an accurate statement. If—I don't—I think what Mr. Bennett was concerned about, if I—maybe it would be helpful to you and to the grand jurors, quite apart from these comments, if I could tell you what his state of mind was and what my state of mind was and why I think he read it to him in the first place. If you don't want me to do it, I won't. But I think it will help to explain a lot of this.

This response is even more convoluted than Clinton's previous answers. Clinton used his personal definition of "present tense," to take Mr. Wisenberg deep into the Land of Is. Clinton also used Misdirection to shift the focus of his answer from his sexual relationship with Lewinsky to what his attorney thought and what might be helpful to the grand jurors. Once trapped in the Land of Is, finding a way out becomes a difficult task. The best interview strategy is to prevent interviewees from going to the Land of Is in the first place.

WORD QUALIFIERS

Most people are reluctant to lie outright, so they add Word Qualifiers to sentences to make the sentences appear truthful. In order to maintain the truth, people use words that are less assertive, reduce certainty, and weaken personal commitment. Word Qualifiers tend to make deceptive statements appear true under the restricted parameters established by the writer or speaker. Some common Word Qualifiers are probably, think, believe, kind of, like, maybe, perhaps, presumably, roughly, about, sort of, generally, and mostly. Word Qualifiers modify the meanings of nouns and verbs. As stated earlier, any words added to the subject-verb paradigm have meaning. Identifying Word Qualifiers reveals the thought process and veracity of interviewees. The following exchange, excerpted from the previously referenced police interview of a rape and murder suspect, demonstrates how the suspect used Word Qualifiers to take the interviewer to the Land of Is.

INTERVIEWER: Okay. I mean, if someone told us that—you had contact with her [the victim] at the party . . .
SUSPECT: No contact. I think she might have said "Hi" to me twice maybe.
INTERVIEWER: Do you remember runnin' into her in the hall?
SUSPECT: I don't remember at all talking to her in the hallway.

In the first exchange, the suspect used the Word Qualifier "No contact," but did not provide a definition for the word "contact." The suspect added that the suspect might have said "Hi." Based on this comment, the suspect does not define brief social exchanges as "contact." The suspect used the Word Qualifiers "think" and "might," which indicate that the suspect did not know for certain if the victim said "Hi" to him. The suspect then used the Word Qualifiers "twice" and "maybe," which indicate that the victim may have said "Hi" to him at least two times during the party. The suspect used Word Qualifiers to distance himself from the victim and, at the same time, provide an explanation as to why some people at the party said they saw the suspect interact with the victim.

In the second exchange, the suspect used the Word Qualifier "talking" to instead of the word "runnin'" which was in the question. If the suspect did not talk to the victim in the hallway, then his statement is true. The suspect avoided answering the interviewer's question by using the Word Qualifier "talking." The suspect could justify the substitution of the word "talking" for "runnin'" because the word "runnin'" could mean talking with someone. For example, the question "Do you remember runnin' into Joe the other day?" could be answered by the response, "Yes, I ran into Joe the other day and he told me. . . ." The suspect also used the Word Qualifier "hallway," which indicates that he may have talked to the victim somewhere other than the hallway.

In this same exchange, the suspect used the Word Qualifier "at all" to describe the act of talking to the victim. The suspect tried to convince the interviewer rather than merely convey information. Liars try to convince people that they are telling the truth rather than merely conveying information.

Later in the interview, the interviewer attempted to obtain detailed information about what the suspect did when he walked the victim home.

> **INTERVIERER:** Alright. You don't remember havin' any conversation with the victim–from the time you left the party 'til the time you dropped her off . . .
> **SUSPECT:** No, I don't remember any conversation at all.
> **INTERVIEWER:** Do you find that odd?
> **SUSPECT:** Well, it's possible we small talked but–not that I remember any other unless, you know, I don't remember having any conversations but–I'm like . . .
> **INTERVIEWER:** Do you remember talkin' to the victim?
> **SUSPECT:** No. I don't remember–I don't remember . . . any conversation, I guess, you know it's–it's like I was on the bus, you know, it's like I–I–I remember I talked to one guy but I don't remember how many kinds of people I talked to.

INTERVIEWER: I'm talking about the victim not a guy.
SUSPECT: Well, I was just thinkin' for like today is like say, I was on the bus. You know, I remember getting' on it, don't remember anything I was talking' about, don't remember how many people . . .
INTERVIEWER: Okay. Okay.

In the first exchange, the interviewer asked the suspect if he had a conversation with the victim. The Word Qualifier "at all" suggests that the suspect may have not had a conversation with the victim, but may have had words with the victim, chatted with the victim, spoken with the victim, exchanged word groups with the victim, etc. When the suspect used the Word Qualifier "at all," he restricted his internal definition of the word "conversation;" however, he did not reveal his definition of the word "conversation." The Interviewer should have asked the suspect how he defined the word "conversation."

In the second exchange, the suspect used the Word Qualifier "small talked." The suspect also used the Word Qualifier "possible," which suggests that the suspect may have small talked with the victim or he may have not small talked with the victim. According to the suspect, the exchange of words did not constitute a conversation but rather as small talk. The suspect then reemphasized this difference when he added, "I don't remember having any conversations…" The suspect's internal definition of the word "conversation" did not include "small talk." The use of the Word Qualifier "possible" leaves open the possibility that the suspect spoke to the victim while her walked with her. The interviewer could have responded, "So there is a possibility that you spoke with the victim. Let's talk about that. What did you possibly talk about?" or "Described what you and the victim small talked about."

In the third exchange, the interviewer asked the victim if he remembered "talkin" to the victim. The suspect answered that he did not remember having any conversation with the victim. The suspect used the Word Qualifier "conversation," which does not include the word "talkin." The suspect qualified the interviewer's question to exclude the word "talkin'" by using the Word Qualifier "conversation." The suspect told the truth, but the truth about what?

In the third and fourth exchanges, the suspect used Misdirection to shift the focus from his conversations with the victim to his experiences on the bus. The suspect's experiences on a bus have nothing to do with having a conversation, small talk, or talkin' to the victim on the way home from the party. The suspect took the interviewer deep into the Land of Is using Word Qualifiers, Miller's Law, and Misdirection.

The earlier referenced excerpt from President Clinton's grand jury testimony demonstrates how he used Word Qualifiers to take the prosecutor to the Land of Is.

> **PROSECUTOR:** Did you talk with Ms. Lewinsky about what she meant to write in her affidavit?
>
> **CLINTON:** I didn't talk to her about her definition. I did not know what was in this affidavit before it was filled out, specifically. I did not know what words was used—were used specifically before it was filled out or what meaning she gave to them. But I'm just telling you that it's certainly true what she says here, that we didn't have-there was no employment or benefit in exchange. There was nothing having anything to do with sexual harassment. And if she defined sexual relationship in the way I think most Americans do, meaning intercourse, then she told the truth.

Clinton restricted his answer to "definitions" and excluded the concept what she "meant to write." If Clinton talked about what Lewinsky "meant to write" but did not talk to her about the "definitions" of the words she wrote, then Clinton told the truth, but the truth about what? Clinton further answered, "I did not know what was in this affidavit before it was filled out, specifically." Clinton used the Word Qualifiers "specifically," which restricted his answer to the final draft of Lewinsky's affidavit. The word "specifically" also serves as a Push-Pull Word. The only condition in which Clinton could say "specifically" is if he "generally" knew what was in Lewinsky's affidavit. Push-Pull Words will be discussed latter in this book. Clinton may not have known specifically what was in the final draft of Lewinsky's affidavit, but he may have known what was generally going to be in the final draft of her affidavit. Clinton also used the Word Qualifier "before." Clinton restricted his answer to before the final draft of Lewinsky's affidavit was written. The Word Qualifier "before" excludes the review of any drafts before the final draft was written. The Word Qualifiers "this affidavit" "before" and "specifically" restrict the parameters of Clinton's answer to the final draft of Lewinsky's affidavit. Clinton excluded the review of any drafts of Lewinsky's affidavit except for the final draft. Clinton told the truth, but the truth about what?

Clinton also used Misdirection to take the prosecutor to the Land of Is. The prosecutor asked, "Did you talk with Ms. Lewinsky about what she meant to write in her affidavit?" Clinton answered, "I didn't talk to her about her 'definition'." Clinton changed the focus of the question from "Did you talk with Ms. Lewinsky about what she "meant to write" in her affidavit?" to "I didn't talk to her about her 'definition'." Clinton used Miller's Law and

Word Qualifiers to create the illusion of truth. Clinton told the truth, but the truth about what?

Clinton continued his answer, "I did not know what words was used–were used specifically before it was filled out or what meaning she gave to them." Clinton used the Word Qualifiers "words," "specifically," "before it was filled out," and "the meaning she gave to them" Clinton used these Word Qualifiers to restrict his answer to the following parameters: (1) Clinton did not know the specific words Lewinsky wrote in the final draft of her affidavit; (2) Clinton did not know the specific words Lewinsky wrote in the final draft of her affidavit before she wrote the final draft; (3) Clinton did not know the meaning of the words Lewinsky used in the final draft of her affidavit; and (4) Clinton limited his response to the final draft and excluded the review of any drafts of Lewinsky's affidavit except for the final draft. These parameters are very restricting. According to Miller's Law, Clinton told the truth, but the truth about what?

Clinton continued his answer, "But I'm just telling you that it's certainly true what she says here, that we didn't have–there was no employment or benefit in exchange. There was nothing having to do with sexual harassment." As discussed earlier, Clinton used Misdirection to change the focus of the question from, "Did you talk with Ms. Lewinsky about what she meant to write in her affidavit? to the fact, "There was no employment or benefit in exchange," which is a less anxiety provoking topic for him. Clinton used the Word Qualifier "just" to minimize the first part of his answer. Clinton then used the Word Qualifier "certainly" to emphasize that Lewinsky told the truth when she wrote, "there was no employment or benefit in exchange" or "sexual harassment." The Word Qualifier suggests the possibility that Lewinsky did not tell the truth elsewhere in her affidavit.

Clinton ended with the Word Qualifier "here," which restricted what Clinton thought was truthful in Lewinsky's affidavit to the fact that there was no employment or benefit in exchange or sexual harassment. The word "here" also serves as a Push-Pull Word. The word "here" pushes off the word "there." The only circumstances in which Clinton could say ". . . it's certainly true what she says here . . ." is to push off ". . . it's certainly not true what she says there. . . ." Push-Pull word will be discussed later in this book. This statement supports the hypothesis that Lewinsky's affidavit may not be entirely truthful.

As previously discussed, Clinton ended his response with the If/Then Conditional, "if she defined sexual relationship in the way I think most Americans, do meaning intercourse, then she told the truth." Clinton further restricted the If/Then Conditional with the Word Qualifiers "think," which indicates that he did not know with certainty how Lewinsky defined sexual relationship nor did he know with certainty how most Americans define sexual relationship. Clinton used the Word Qualifier "most Americans" to give the impression that the majority of Americans are on his side and would support him in how he thinks Lewinsky would define sexual relationship. This logic makes little sense. Clinton is conjecturing on a conjecture that he is not certain is true.

Clinton took the prosecutor deep into the Land of Is. The prosecutor asked the Yes or No question, "Did you talk with Ms. Lewinsky about what she meant to writ in her affidavit?" Clinton should have answered, "Yes" or "No." Clinton chose not answer "Yes" or "No" and took the prosecutor to the Land of Is. Investigators should stay focused on the question they asked. If the interviewee does not answer "Yes" or "No," the investigator should redirect the interviewee to answer the question either "Yes" or "No." If the interviewee answers "Yes" or "No" and still wants to go to the Land of Is to qualify his "Yes" or "No" answer, let him do so. A "Yes" or "No" answer is an admission. What follows is justification for the answer.

TAG QUALIFIERS

The simplest method to qualify an answer is to add a Tag Qualifier. Tag Qualifiers specifically identify actions that took place but were not included in the question. If a specific action was omitted from an otherwise true account, then the liar could honestly answer the question by adding a Tag Qualifier. Tag Qualifiers include, but are not limited to, this, that, these, those, and though. For example, Timmy's third-grade teacher telephoned Timmy's mother and told her that during recess, Timmy ran up to Vickie, a fellow classmate, and pulled her hair causing her to fall down and hurt her head. The following conversation took place:

> **TIMMY'S MOTHER:** Your teacher called and said that during recess you ran up to Vickie and pulled her hair causing her to fall down and hurt her head.
> **TIMMY:** She's lying. I didn't do that.

Timmy used the Tag Qualifier "that" to give the illusion of truth. Timmy did pull Vickie's hair causing her to fall down and hurt her head, but he did not run up to Vickie and pull her hair, he walked up to Vickie and pulled her hair. According to Miller's Law, Timmy told the truth, but the truth about what? The Tag Qualifier "that" also functions as a Push-Pull Word. It there is a "that," then there is a "this." Timmy cannot use the word "that" without considering at least one alternate action. The mother's follow-up question should be, "If you didn't do that, what did you do?" Push-Pull Words will be discussed later in the book.

In the earlier referenced excerpt from President Clinton's grand jury testimony, he used a Tag Qualifier to take the prosecutor to the Land of Is. Clinton told the truth, but the truth about what?

> **PROSECUTOR:** Did you talk with Ms. Lewinsky about what she meant to write in her affidavit?
>
> **CLINTON:** I didn't talk to her about her definition. I did not know what was in this affidavit before it was filled out, specifically. I did not know what words was used–were used specifically before it was filled out or what meaning she gave to them. But I'm just telling you that it's certainly true what she says here, that we didn't have–there was no employment or benefit in exchange. There was nothing having anything to do with sexual harassment. And if she defined sexual relationship in the way I think most Americans do, meaning intercourse, then she told the truth.

Clinton used the Tag Qualifier "this affidavit," which indicates that another affidavit existed. The word "this" also serves as a Push-Pull Word. "This affidavit" pushes off "that affidavit." The only conditions in which Clinton could have said "this affidavit" is if there was at least one other affidavit. Push-Pull Words will be discussed later in this book. Clinton restricted his answer to the final draft of Lewinsky's affidavit. If Clinton did not read the final draft of the affidavit but read previous drafts of the affidavit, he told the truth because he excluded the review of any copy of the affidavit except for the final draft. The Tag Qualifier "this affidavit" renders this statement truthful.

On December 24, 2002, Laci Peterson, who was eight months pregnant, disappeared from her Modesto, California neighborhood. Her husband, Scott Peterson, told interviewers he last saw her that morning as she left their house to walk their dog. Shortly thereafter, he went fishing at the Berkeley Marina. On April 13, 2003, a baby's body, with his umbilical cord still attached, washed up on a beach three miles north of the Berkeley Marina. Several days later, a woman's body came ashore near the same location. DNA tests identified the bodies as Laci Peterson and her baby. A jury subsequently found Peterson guilty of murdering Laci and her unborn baby boy.

On January 28, 2003, Diane Sawyer interviewed Peterson on Good Morning America. The following is an excerpt from that interview:

> **SAWYER:** Because again you know that people sitting at home have imagined that either you were in love with someone else, therefore you

decided to get rid of this entanglement, namely your wife and your child, or there was just an angry confrontation.

PETERSON: Neither of those was the case. It's–it's that simple.

Peterson used the Tag Qualifier "those," which indicates that he did not kill Laci to get rid of an entanglement or because of an angry confrontation. If Peterson did not kill Laci for those two reasons, then for what reason did he kill Laci?

Tag Qualifiers become less obvious in more complex interviews. The suspect in the rape and murder case referenced earlier in this book took the interviewer to the Land of Is using Tag Qualifiers. The interviewer asked the suspect several times about how he tried to kiss the victim at the party. Each time the suspect answered, he used Tag Qualifiers to take the interviewer to the Land of Is.

> **INTERVIEWER:** Well, let's go back to the party for a second. There's somebody at the party–not just somebody, maybe–how many? Four or five people? Four of five people told us that they saw you trying to kiss her–at the party. In fact, it was in the hallway at the party–and, uh, you were trying to kiss her. In fact, I think she fell down on the ground and you were, kind of laying down next to her. Trying to kiss her or something. What can you remember what happened with that?
>
> **SUSPECT:** I never even . . . I don't remember doing anything like that.
>
> **INTERVIEWER:** Okay. This is where some–just one person told us–several people saw this. So, we're–I was wondering what happened as far as you and the victim were concerned there. Was she kind of pulling you down on the ground or . . . ?
>
> **SUSPECT:** I don't even remember doing anything like that.
>
> **INTERVIEWER:** Nothin'?
>
> **SUSPECT:** Nuh uh.
>
> **INTERVIEWER:** Nothing like that happened?
>
> **SUSPECT:** Nothing.
>
> **INTERVIEWER:** Why do you think these four or five people would tell us that?
>
> **SUSPECT:** It's possible thought [sic] I was someone else.
>
> **INTERVIEWER:** Well, that's what we thought. That's why we showed your picture. And, uh, they picked you out of the picture. 'Cause we got–she was kissin' on a lot of guys that night. You know, there was other . . .
>
> **SUSPECT:** I never kissed her though.

In the first exchange, the suspect used the Tag Qualifier "that," which indicates that the incident did not happen exactly how the interviewer described it. The Tag Qualifier "that" rendered the response truthful.

In the same exchange, the interviewer used numerous Word Qualifiers to give the illusion that he knew what the suspect did at the party. An astute interviewee would have known that the interviewer was not truthful. The interviewer stated that "someone" and qualified "someone" as more than one person by stating, ". . . not just somebody." The interviewer then added the Word Qualifier "maybe," which suggests that the interviewer was not sure if there was more than one witness. The detective then asked the rhetorical question, "How many?" The interviewer answered his own question with the question, "Four or five people?" Answering a question with a question indicates deception. The interviewer shouted his message by using the Word Qualifier "In fact" two times. If the interviewer, in fact, talked to four or five witnesses, he would have simply reiterated what they said without qualification. The interviewer used the Word Qualifier "think" when he stated, "I think she fell down. The Word Qualifier "think" indicates that the interviewer did not know that the victim fell. The Word Qualifier "think" weakens the illusion that more than one witness described what happened at the party. The detective used the Word Qualifier "kind of," which indicates that he did not know for sure what the suspect did. The interviewer used the Word Qualifier "or something," which indicates that the interviewer did not know for certain what the suspect did. The interviewer's ambiguous description of the suspect's actions at the party made it easy for the suspect to use a Tag Qualifier to answer truthfully. A more effective question would have been, "Tell me what happened in the hallway." This open-ended question presupposes that something happened and puts the onus on the interviewee to provide details. Open-ended questions are more effective, especially if the interviewer does not know the facts.

In the second exchange, the Suspect used the Tag Qualifier "that," which indicates that the incident did not happen exactly how the interviewer described it. The Tag Qualifier "that" rendered the response truthful.

In the second exchange, the interviewer again used Word Qualifiers to give the illusion that he knew more than he actually did. The interviewer initially said that one person saw this, paused, and added that several people saw this. The interviewer initially used the pronoun "we," paused, and used the Personal Identifier "I," which suggests that only the interviewer possessed this knowledge not other interviewers. Pronouns use will be discussed later in this book. The interviewer used the Word Qualifier "kind of," which could represent many different actions making it easy for the suspect to use the Tag Qualifier to render his response truthful. A more effective question would have been, "What did the victim do?"

In the fourth exchange, the interviewer used the Tag Qualifier "that" to refer back to his description of the incident. The suspect answered truthfully because the incident did not happen exactly the way in which the interviewer described it the first time.

In the fifth exchange, the suspect used the Word Qualifier "possible" to dismiss the eyewitness accounts of the incident. The Word Qualifier "possible" indicates that the witnesses may have thought the suspect was someone else or the witnesses correctly identified the suspect. The suspect chose the option that discredited the witnesses. The interviewer should have countered with the statement, "Then, you would have to admit that it was also possible that the eyewitnesses correctly identified you, wouldn't you?"

In the sixth exchange, the interviewer used the Tag Qualifier "though," which suggests that he may have done the other actions the interviewer described but he did not kiss her. The Tag Qualifier "though" renders the suspect's response truthful. The suspect successfully took the interviewer to the Land of Is using Word Qualifiers and Tag Qualifiers.

CHANGE OF PERSPECTIVE

Word Qualifiers often signal a change in personal perspective. Two people can look at the same object and provide different descriptions of what they saw. Both descriptions are accurate because the observers viewed the same object from difference perspectives. Liars often change their perspective to give the illusion of truth. The following illustration demonstrates how a Change of Perspective can take the reader or listener to the Land of Is.

> **INTERVIEWER:** Did you ever have unauthorized contact with a foreign intelligence officer?
> **INTERVIEWEE:** I am not a spy.

The interviewee used the Word Qualifier "spy." The word "spy" has different connotations depending on perspective. The interviewer may define the concept "spy" as a person who betrays his country by providing secrets to a foreign government. The interviewee, on the other hand, may consider these same actions as acts of loyalty. If the interviewee switches his loyalty from Country A to Country B, then Country B becomes his homeland and Country A becomes a foreign government. Any contact with an intelligence officer from Country B is neither a foreign contact nor is it unauthorized because, from the interviewee's perspective, Country B is now his homeland

and these activities are authorized. From the interviewee's perspective, he can truthfully say that he never had unauthorized contact with a foreign intelligence officer.

CHANGE OF LANGUAGE

Change of Language is a form or Change of Perspective. When people have a Change of Perspective, they typically change the language they use to describe what they see, hear, feel, or do. Likewise, a Change of Language often indicates a Change of Perspective. In the rape and murder investigation referenced earlier in this book, the interviewer asked the interviewee about his sexual activity. The interviewee used a Change of Language, which indicates a Change of Perspective.

> **INTERVIEWER:** How many times have you had sexual intercourse?
> **SUSPECT:** Four times?
> **INTERVIEWER:** Four times? Okay. Well, who's this girl you had sex with?
> **SUSPECT:** I–I don't want to say anyone's name. So, it–it–it–it– it–it– it was someone I went to school with so…

The suspect first used the word "anyone," suggesting that he still considered the girl he had sex with as a person. In the next sentence, the suspect refers to the girl he had sex with as an "it." The suspect reduced the girl he had sex with to an inanimate object. This Change of Language is significant because it is easier for the suspect to talk about a violent act when the victim is dehumanized. The suspect also repeated the pronoun "I" twice and the word "it" seven times. Repeated Words signal anxiety, suggesting that the suspect was uncomfortable talking about his relationship with this girl. Repeated Words will be discussed later in this book. The fact that the suspect reduced the rape victim to an inanimate object and displayed anxiety about the rape indicates that the suspect may feel a degree of guilt.

The suspect also used the Word Qualifier "want," which indicates that he knew the name of the girl he had sex with but chose not to reveal her name. The interviewer should obtain the name of the girl the suspect had sex with because, as stated, the suspect is a controlling person, has poor social skills, only kisses girls when he is intoxicated and has only kissed several women. Another hypothesis posits that if the suspect raped the victim, she could be the girl he referenced in his statement and, for obvious reasons, did not "want" to reveal her identity. The fact that the victim attended the same school as the suspect supports this hypothesis. In further support of this hypothesis, the suspect used the Past Tense "went," which indicates that the girl the suspect had sex with no longer goes to the same school as the suspect. If the suspect raped and murdered the victim, he would naturally use the past tense to describe the victim. Obtaining the identity of the girl with whom the suspect had sex would eliminate this possibility.

WORD SCALES

Liars often minimize their actions using Word Scales. Word Scales allow liars to place words on a continuum. Word scales are replete in social situations. A common method to interrupt people who are otherwise engaged is to say, "I don't mean to interrupt but . . ." The Mean or Intent Scale is a continuum from 1 to 10, Low Intent being 1 and High Intent being 10. No matter where the person places "I don't mean to interrupt" on the Intent Word Scale, the person still intended to interrupt. If the person did not mean to interrupt, then why did he interrupt? Another common example of a Word Scale is, "I don't mean to pry." If the person did not mean to pry, then why did he? My favorite Word Scale is, "I don't mean to be devil's advocate." One time when I was an FBI special agent, I gave a case presentation to obtain funds for an undercover operation. Everything went well until near the end of my presentation. A high bureau official (HBO), and I use that term with great affection, said, "I don't mean to be devil's advocate. . ." I interrupted, "Sir, if you don't mean to be devil's advocate, either leave the room or sit down and be quiet." An eerie silence fell over the room. I thought to myself, "Perhaps I crossed the line, again." The HBO chuckled and said, "Well, I guess I do mean to be devil's advocate." Laughter broke the tension and with relief I continued my presentation. I later received the funds to run the undercover operation.

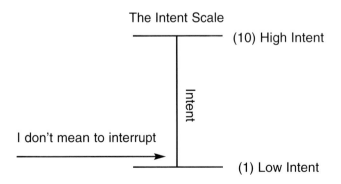

In another illustration, a person was caught doing a bad thing. The word "bad," in and of itself, has a negative connotation. Liars often soften the word "bad" by saying "It wasn't such a bad thing" The statement "It wasn't such a bad thing." reduces the perceived culpability of the interviewee. The interviewer should ask the interviewee to place the word "bad" on the Bad Word Scale. The Bad Word Scale is a continuum from 1 to 10, Low Bad being 1 and High Bad being 10. Most people would rank the statement "It wasn't such a bad thing," low on the Bad Word Scale. No matter how low interviewees place the statement, "It wasn't such a bad thing," the "thing" they did is still bad.

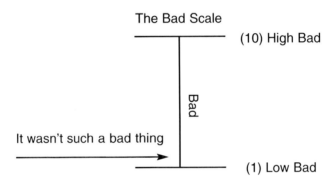

After the interviewee assigns a value on the Bad Word Scale, the interviewer should ask the interviewee where he or she would place the word "bad" on the Good/Bad Word Scale. The word "bad" is a Push-Pull Word. The interviewee could not utter the word "bad" without pushing off the word "good." Push-Pull Words will be discussed later in this book. Good is at one end of the Good/Bad Word Scale, Bad is at the other end of the Word Scale, and neutral occupies the midpoint. Logically, the interviewee must choose a point on the scale above neutral. The interviewer can now make the argument that in order for a person to judge something as bad, he must first judge the action on the Good/Bad Word Scale. Judging an action as either good or bad requires forethought. A person must weigh the attributes of the contemplated action in terms of being either good or bad and then conclude the activity is bad. Only after a person judges his actions as bad on the Good/Bad Word Scale can he create the Bad Word Scale. Therefore, the person made a conscious determination prior to conducting the contemplated action that the action was bad. The interviewer can now make the presumptive statement that the interviewee intentionally conducted the activity knowing that the activity was bad. Word Scales provide interviewers with a tool to logically examine the hedge words liars use to deceive.

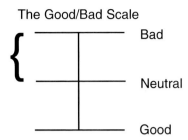

The Good/Bad Scale

Bad

Neutral

Good

In the interview referenced earlier in this book between the investigator and the rape and murder suspect illustrates the use of a Word Scale.

INTERVIEWER: Let me ask you this–I think I asked you once before– let's suppose–and I'm not saying that this happened. Let's just suppose that, you know, after–the victim kind of came on to you a little bit and you came onto her a little bit. You're a red-blooded American boy like any of us would be and, uh, you know, you got– played a little kissey face, a little touchy poo, this kind of stuff. You know, if–if you did that–would you tell us about it and not be afraid to tell us 'cause it's very important you tell us everything. 'Cause remember, we've talked to a whole lot of people. And they told us some things and we tried to fit all these pieces together. Now if–if something like that happened–it doesn't mean anything–but it's very important to this total picture that if–if you did do, you know, kissed her a little bit or touched her a little bit, which there's nothing wrong with it but if you did, it's really important that you tell us–so that we can fit all these pieces together based on what everybody's telling us–around here. And I could see somebody, you know, kissin' her or–or you know, especially when she comes onto him and then being afraid to say anything– 'cause now she's missin' and that person might think, 'Oh, God, I'm a suspect.' But, you know, we wouldn't think . . .

SUSPECT: Yeah.

INTERVIEWER: . . . but I–I need to have the whole . . .

SUSPECT: Yeah. No. It wouldn't . . .

INTERVIEWER: . . . picture.

SUSPECT: . . . it wouldn't really be a big deal, you know, me kiss on– because I've been partying and I've kissed someone before.

INTERVIEWER: Well, no. And this . . .

SUSPECT: So . . .

INTERVIEWER: . . . is no big deal at all.

SUSPECT: Yeah.

The words "it wouldn't really be a big deal" serve as a Word Scale. The investigator should have asked the suspect to place the words, "it wouldn't really be a big deal" on the Big Deal Word Scale, 1 being a Low Big Deal and 10 being a High Big Deal. The interviewee would probably have placed "it wouldn't really be a big deal" low on the Big Deal Word Scale. No matter where the interviewee places the words, "it wouldn't really be a big deal" on the Big Deal Word Scale, it was still a big deal for the suspect to kiss someone.

The suspect used the Word Clue "kiss on." The word "kiss" has several meanings depending on the context in which the word is used. The sentence, "I kissed her," implies a one-sided kiss. One person kissed a second person without that person kissing back. The sentence "He kissed me" implies a one-sided kiss. The man kissed another person without that person kissing back. The sentence "We kissed" implies a mutual kiss. Both people willingly engaged in the act of kissing. The words "kiss on" imply that one person kissed a second person without their consent.

A simple test to determine the appropriateness of the use of a word is to substitute the word in question into sentences that have accepted usage. For example, "I kissed on her," "He kissed on me," or "We kissed on each other" sound awkward and are rarely used in general conversation.

The Word Clue "kiss on" indicates that the suspect might be a controlling person. The Word Clue "because I've been partying" suggests that the suspect only kisses girls when he is partying or, in other words, when he is under the influence of alcohol or drugs. The suspect used the Word Clue "someone," which indicates that he has not kissed many girls in the past. The suspect answered, ". . . it wouldn't really be a big deal, you know, me kiss on– because I've been partying and I've kissed someone before." The suspect used the Word Scale "it wouldn't really be a big deal," which indicates that it was a big deal for the suspect to kiss a girl.

Based on Word Clues and a Word Scale, the hypothesis can be posited that the suspect is probably a controlling person with poor social skills and only kisses girls when he is intoxicated. Further, the suspect has not kissed many girls in the past and when he does kiss a girl, it is a big deal. The suspect may be socially isolated because he lacks the interpersonal skills to initiate and maintain extended personal relationships. These behavioral characteristics do not signify guilt, but they do provide investigators with possible motives as to why the suspect might have committed the crime. Of course, additional support for this hypothesis must be obtained before the investigator can make any conclusions as to the suspect's behavior characteristics or guilt.

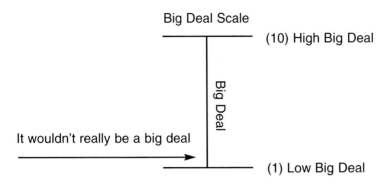

Big Deal Scale

(10) High Big Deal

Big Deal

It wouldn't really be a big deal

(1) Low Big Deal

Vickie, a promising actress living in Hollywood, received a letter from a stalker. In the first sentence of the letter, the stalker wrote, "Today I've decided to write instead of talking on the phone; maybe it'll be more effective and less upsetting for you." The writer used the Word Scale "less upsetting," which indicates that he intentionally wrote the letter knowing it would upset Vickie.

During a subsequent interview, the interviewer could ask the writer to rate "less upsetting" on the Upset Word Scale. No matter where the writer places "less upsetting" on the Upset Word Scale, the interviewer can then make the presumptive, "So, you intentionally wrote the letter to Vickie knowing that the letter would upset her." The writer would be forced to admit that he deliberately wrote the letter knowing the letter would upset Vickie. The interviewer can use this admission against the writer later in the interview when the writer tries to place the blame for his actions on anything or anybody other than himself. The interviewer could simply say, "You intentionally wrote the letter knowing that it would upset Vickie, so you can only blame yourself for the trouble that you caused."

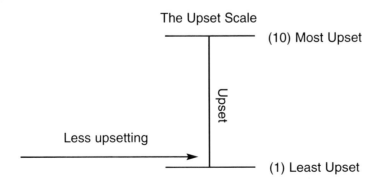

The Upset Scale

(10) Most Upset

Upset

Less upsetting

(1) Least Upset

The stalker also wrote, "I've never intended to be around too much or checking on you." The stalker used the Intent Word Scale. If the stalker "never intended to be around," then why did he intentionally place himself near Vickie? In one possible interview scenario, the interviewer could tell the stalker, "Since you were in Vickie's presence, you took some deliberate actions to get from where you were to where Vickie was. Maybe you didn't leave your house with the intent of seeing Vickie, but you knew in the back of your mind that you would eventually see her. On a scale of 1 to 10, 1 being Low Intent and 10 being High Intent, where would you rate your intentions?" No matter what number the stalker assigns on the Intent Word Scale, he still intended to see Vickie. The interviewer should ask the stalker to define the Word Qualifier "too much." The stalker must now quantify the concept "too much." Since the concept "too much" suggests a presence to some degree, the interviewer must provide a number above zero. Next, the interviewer could ask the stalker to provide a cutoff number that he deems "too much." The interviewer could now summarize the conversation by saying, "So, you intended to be near Vickie at least (insert the cutoff number) times knowing that your presence would upset her." The interviewer only used the words spoken by the stalker; therefore, he would be forced to admit to the interviewer's supposition, which is tantamount to a confession. Exploiting the stalker's Word Scales and Word Qualifiers could have revealed his true intent.

PUSH-PULL WORDS

Push-Pull Words require two or more words to complete their definitions. The word "upstairs" cannot be defined without the word "downstairs." The word "hot" cannot be defined without the word "cold." "Inside" cannot be defined with the word "outside." Some words need more than two words to complete their meanings. The word "medium" cannot be defined without the words "large" and "small." The word "warm" cannot be defined without the words "hot" and "cold." Push-Pull Words are like two poles positioned directly across from one another connected by a rope. One pole represents the word "hot" and the other pole represents the word "cold." The word "warm" represents a point somewhere between both poles. In some instances, one or both poles of a Push-Pull Word are partially buried or completely submerged rendering one or both poles partially visible or completely obscured. For example, the word "normal" pushes off the word "abnormal." A person cannot say the word "normal" without referencing the word "abnormal." The pole "abnormal" is often partially visible or completely obscured in normal conversions.

Interviewers can defend against Push-Pull Words by attacking the opposite meaning of the Push-Pull Word. For example, at the conclusion of one of my lectures on PNA, a student asked me for a copy of my slide presentation. I did not want to give the student a copy of my slide presentation because I was tired and did not want to go back to my office and photocopy my presentation. I could not say "No" because I would look like I was being insensitive to the needs of the student. I could not say "Yes" because I did not want to take the time to photocopy my slide presentation, so I took the student to the Land of Is. I answered, "I generally don't give out a copy of my slide presentation." The student recognized the Push-Pull Word "generally" and responded, "Sir, under what conditions do you hand out your slide presentation?" Instead of arguing with me about why I did not want to provide a copy of my slide presentation, the student attacked the opposite of the Push-Pull Word "generally." I could not utter the word "generally" without pushing off the word "specifically." If I do not generally give out my slide presentation, then I must specifically give my slide presentation. In other words, there are circumstances where I do give out my slide presentation. If the student could discover under what conditions I provide a copy of my slide presentation, then I would be forced to tender my slide presentation when those conditions are met. The student prevented me from going to the Land of Is by recognizing the Push-Pull Word "generally" and attacking the opposite meaning of the Push-Pull Word. I rewarded the student's cleverness by giving him a copy of my slide presentation.

The earlier referenced excerpt from President Clinton's grand jury testimony illustrates the use of Push-Pull Words.

> **PROSECUTOR:** Did you talk with Ms. Lewinsky about what she meant to write in her affidavit?
> **CLINTON:** I didn't talk to her about her definition. I did not know what was in this affidavit before it was filled out, specifically. I did not know what words was used–were used specifically before it was filled out or what meaning she gave to them. But I'm just telling you that it's certainly true what she says here, that we didn't have-there was no employment or benefit in exchange. There was nothing having anything to do with sexual harassment. And if she defined sexual relationship in the way I think most Americans do, meaning intercourse, then she told the truth.

Clinton stated, "I did not know what was in this affidavit before it was filled out, specifically." The Push-Pull Word "specifically" pushes off the word "generally." As previously stated, the Push-Pull Word "specifically" also functions as a Word Qualifier. Clinton may not have specifically known what was in Lewinsky's affidavit, but the possibility exists that he generally knew what was in her affidavit before the final draft was completed. Clinton further stated, "I did not know what words was used–were used specifically before it was filled out or what meaning she gave to them." The Push-Pull word "specifically" pushes off the word "generally." Clinton may have not specifically known what exact words or the meanings of the words Lewinsky intended to use in her affidavit prior to her writing it, but he may have generally known the words and the meanings of the words Lewinsky was going to write in her affidavit before she wrote the final draft of her affidavit.

In the excerpt referenced earlier in the book, a detective asked the suspect a series of questions regarding the death of his wife whose skeletal remains were found in the suspect's car, which rested at the bottom of a lake for several decades after her mysterious disappearance.

> **INTERVIEWER:** Was she drinking?
> **INTERVIEWEE:** Had she been drinking that day? She'd drink every day.
> **INTERVIEWER:** She drank right up until the time she went to bed?
> **INTERVIEWEE:** Yeah, normally.
> **INTERVIEWER:** Was she drinking that night at the time she went to bed?
> **INTERVIEWER:** If, ah, if, ah, it was a normal day, yes.

The detective asked the question, "Was she drinking that night at the time she went to bed?" The suspect answered, "If, ah, if, ah, it was a normal day, yes." The suspect used the Push-Pull Word "normal." The pole "normal" is readily visible; however, the pole "abnormal" is not readily visible. In order for the suspect to utter the word "normal" he had to push off the word "abnormal." The suspect telegraphed that something out of the ordinary happened that day. If it were truly a normal day, the suspect would have simply stated, "Yes, she was drinking" without adding the Push-Pull Word "normal." Additionally, the suspect added the If/Then Conditional "if it was a normal day." The suspect established parameters for his "Yes" answer. If it was a normal day, then she would have been drinking. The suspect took the interviewer to the Land of Is by establishing conditions for his "Yes" answer. The detective should have attacked the opposite meaning of the Push-Pull Word "normal" by asking, "What happened on that day that was out of the ordinary."

A Competing Hypothesis posits that the day an innocent man finds his wife dead is not a normal day. This is a viable argument but the detective stated, "Tell me what *you* did on the day your wife was murdered." A person without guilty knowledge simply relates the events of the day from his perspective. Conversely, a person with guilty knowledge knows that the day was not a normal day because he killed his wife. Based on this guilty knowledge, the suspect would spontaneously select the word "normal" because he referenced the killing of his wife, which was abnormal. In this instance, the detective could clarify matters by asking the suspect, "What was different about your activities before you came home and found your wife dead?" The suspect's answer may cause him to reveal additional clues regarding his activities prior to the discovery of the body of his dead wife.

The Push-Pull Word "I don't remember" pushes off "I do remember." A person cannot say that he does not remember something without having first remembered what it was he doesn't remember. When an interviewee says, "I don't know," the probability increases that the interviewee is telling the truth because the Push-Pull Word "I don't know" pushes off "I do know." A subtle difference differentiates the statement "I don't remember" from the statement "I can't remember." "I can't remember" suggests that the person put forth some effort to remember but had difficulty retrieving the information. When a person says, "I don't remember," he or she does not acknowledge any effort to remember what has been forgotten. Truthful people make an effort to scan their memories for the information that they have forgotten. Deceptive people do not have to scan their memories for the requested information because they know it is there. The probability increases that a person who says "I can't remember" is telling the truth compared to a person who says, "I don't remember." An effective technique to counter responses such as "I don't remember," I don't recall," or "I forgot" is to conduct a Full Sensory Interview.

FULL SENSORY INTERVIEW

Human memory is complex. Memories are not stored in just one place in the brain but rather in many areas of the brain. Each source of stimuli, eyes, ears, touch, emotions, and smell, is stored in a separate part of the brain. Accessing only one of these memory storage areas can limit the amount of information interviewees can retrieve. To increase memory retrieval, interviewers can conduct a Full Sensory Interview. A Full Sensory Interview takes longer than a conventional interview but can be more productive. A Full Sensory Interview begins with a narrative of the event or incident in question. After the interviewee finishes the general narrative of the incident or event, the interviewer instructs the interviewee to recount the incident or event by only describing the people and things the interviewee saw. After the visual rendition, the interviewee recounts everything he or she heard. After the audio rendition, the interviewee recounts everything he or she touched. After the tactile rendition, the interviewee recounts everything that he or she felt, and after the emotional rendition, the interviewee recounts what he or she smelled. In the event the interviewee is deceptive, the Full Sensory Interview allows the interviewer to capture six renditions of the incident or event that can be compared to test for inconsistencies and a PNA can be conducted. In the event that the interviewee is truthful, the interviewer significantly increases the amount of information obtained from the interviewee. Kip Kinkel, a 15-year-old student from Oregon, shot his parents and then went to his school cafeteria and shot 24 students killing two of them. After shooting his father in the head, he waited for his mother to return home from grocery shopping. Upon her arrival home, Kinkel helped her unload the groceries and then shot her to death. The following excerpt was taken from Kinkel's confession.

> **DETECTIVE:** What did you do to prepare yourself for you having to shoot your mom?
> **KINKEL:** I cried. I said I was so sorry. I had to though. I had to.
> **DETECTIVE:** You said you were waiting for her.
> **KINKEL:** Mm huh (yes).
> **DETECTIVE:** Where were you waiting for her at?
> **KINKEL:** In the living room so I could see when the car came up.
> **DETECTIVE:** And when she pulled in the garage and the garage door came down and she got out of her car, where were you?
> **KINKEL:** I don't know. I can't remember.
> **DETECTIVE:** Were you hiding somewhere in the garage so that she had to walk past you?
> **KINKEL:** No, I came down and helped her with her bags, bring them up.
> **DETECTIVE:** Where was the gun at this point?
> **KINKEL:** It was on my hip
> **DETECTIVE:** On your hip?
> **KINKEL:** Yeah.

The detective asked Kinkel where he was when his mother got out of the car. Kinkel responded, "I don't know. I can't remember." Kinkel probably told the truth. The Push-Pull Word "I don't know" pushes off "I do know," and the phrase "I can't remember" suggests that he made the effort to search his memory to retrieve the information but failed to retrieve it. In support of this hypothesis, Kinkel made a full voluntary confession and had no reason to lie about his location before she shot his mother. The detective asked Kinkel the follow-up question, "Were you hiding somewhere in the garage so that she had to walk past you?" Kinkel answered, "No, I came down and helped her with her bags, bring them up." The Push-Pull Word "I came down" pushes off "I came up," which indicates that Kinkel was upstairs when his mother got out of the car. Additionally, the push-pull phrase "bring them up" pushes off "bring them down" which supports the hypothesis that Kinkel was upstairs when his mother got out of the car. Exploiting the Push-Pull phrases Kinkel used, the detective could have asked the presumptive question, "Where upstairs were you when you heard the garage door open?" This question would have assisted Kinkel to search his memory more thoroughly, thus providing additional information that would have made his confession more complete.

STOPPED-ACTION WORDS

Stopped-Action Words signal that an action was begun but something interrupted the completion of the action. The most common Stopped-Action Words include started, began, continued, resumed, asked, tried, and continued. In the sentence, "I started to go to the store," the interviewee used the Stopped-Action Word "started" to give the impression that he went to the store, when, in fact, he did not. If the interviewer went to the store, he would have stated, "I went to the store." In the statement "I started to go to the store, but the phone rang," the interviewee provided the reason that prevented him from completing the action of going to the store. A Stopped-Action Word accompanied by a reason for the interruption indicates truthfulness. If interviewees do not provide a reason for the stopped action, then interviewers should identify the intervening action or actions that prevented the interviewees from completing their initial actions. The following exchange illustrates the use of Stopped-Action Words.

> **INTERVIEWER:** How did the accident occur?
> **DRIVER:** I saw an opening in traffic and I started to turn my turn signal on when the guy came out of nowhere and hits me. It wasn't my fault.
> **INTERVIEWER:** You stated that you started to turn your turn signal on. What prevented you from turning it on?
> **DRIVER:** The car hit me.
> **INTERVIEWER:** So, your turn signal was not on when you changed lanes.

The interviewee stated that he started to turn on his turn signal. He did not say that he actually turned it on. Liars use Stopped-Action Words to give the illusion that they completed the actions when, in fact, the actions may not have been completed. The interviewee used the Present Tense "hits," which indicates deception. Past Tense usage will be discussed later in this book. The interviewee also used the Spontaneous Negation "It wasn't my fault." Spontaneous Negations signal a high probability of deception. Spontaneous Negations will be discussed later in this book.

The following interview illustrates another example of Stopped-Action Words. In this case, the interviewee's actions allegedly caused the accident, although she was not involved in the accident. The interviewee denied that her actions were the cause of the accident. Witnesses reported that the interviewee was parked in the emergency lane on the expressway and when she drove back onto the highway, she caused the accident.

> **INVESTIGATOR:** Tell me what you did.
> **DRIVER:** I entered the freeway at Exit 23, continued driving, and exited at Exit 34. I didn't stop at all on the freeway. I periodically looked in the rearview mirror and didn't see anything out of the ordinary.

The driver used the Stopped-Action Word "continued," which indicates that she did something other than driving between Exit 23 and Exit 34 without stopping. If the driver entered the freeway at Exit 23 and exited the freeway at Exit 34 without stopping, she would have stated. "I got on the freeway at Exit 23 and exited the freeway at Exit 34." The driver also used the Push-Pull Word "ordinary." The driver could not utter the word "ordinary" unless she saw something out "of the ordinary." The Spontaneous Negation "I didn't stop at all on the freeway" indicates a high probability of deception. Spontaneous Negation will be discussed later in this book. The driver's use of a Stopped-Action Word, a Push-Pull Word, Word Qualifier and a Spontaneous Negation supports the hypothesis that the driver may have been aware that her actions caused the accident.

Referring back to the rape and murder cited earlier, the interviewer asked the suspect where he walked the victim. This was the last time the victim was seen alive and the suspect was the last known person who saw her alive. This was a critical part of the interview. The suspect took the interviewer to the Land of Is and the interviewer could not find his way out.

> **INTERVIEWER:** Okay. So, then you walked the victim up to where?
> **SUSPECT:** Up to, um . . . 'cause . . . well, it has the driveway. Must be over there and just like I remember–I–I walked with her to where the driveway was and then I went up to my dorm because the walkway goes that way towards my dorm and then she started walking that way.

The suspect used the Stopped-Action Word "started," which indicates that some action prevented the victim from "walking that way." The repeated word "I" indicates anxiety. Repeated Words will be discussed later in this chapter. The suspect used the Text Bridge "then" two times. The first text bridge created an information gap from the time the suspect walked the victim to where the driveway was to the time the suspect when went up to his dorm. The second Text Bridge creates an information gap from the time just before he went to his dorm to the time she walked "that way." Text Bridges will be discussed later in this book. The Stopped-Action Word "started" suggests some action prevented the victim from going to her dorm. The two Text Bridges signal missing information and the Repeated Word "I," suggests anxiety. Based on these PNA indicators, one hypothesis posits that the suspect may not be telling the truth. Since this is a critical area in the interview, the interviewer should have made more detailed inquiry of the suspect.

On January 29, 2003, Diane Sawyer interviewed Scott Peterson on Good Morning America. A jury found Peterson guilty of killing his wife Laci and her unborn child. The following is an excerpt from that interview:

> **SAWYER:** And the last time you saw her was?
> **PETERSON:** I believe it was about 9:30 that morning. Uh, the reason being we started to watch Martha Stewart Living while Laci was working in the kitchen and–uhm–I left sometime during that.

Peterson stated that he and Laci started to watch Martha Stewart Living, but he did not indicate what action prevented them from completing the viewing of that show. Peterson used the Personal Identifier "we," which suggests that he and Laci watched the show together, but he stated that Laci was working in the kitchen. Peterson's use of the Personal Identifier "we" does not comport with his descriptions of Laci's behaviors. Personal Identifiers will be discussed later in this book. These PNA indicators signal deception, especially since they occur during a critical portion of the interview.

The Communication Word "asked" also serves as a Stopped-Action Word. For example, a date rape suspect stated that the sex was consensual because "I asked her if she wanted to have sex;" but he failed to report the woman's response to the request. The suspect used the Stopped-Action Word "asked" to lead the interviewer to believe that the woman consented to his request, which was not the case.

On one occasion, I asked my supervisor if I could attend some local training at the FBI Field office in Los Angeles 70 miles away. He refused my request. I thought his refusal was unreasonable, so I went to the training anyway. At the registration desk, the clerk looked for my name but could not find it. She said, "I can't find your name on the registration list." I answered, "I asked my supervisor if I could attend." She replied, "Okay, I'll just pencil your name in at the bottom." I smiled obligingly and took a seat. I told the truth. I did ask my supervisor if I could attend the training. The clerk failed to ask what his response was. She automatically assumed that since I asked my supervisor if I could attend, the answer must have been "Yes" because I was at the training. Now, if the clerk would have asked me, "What did your supervisor say?", I would have responded, "He said, 'No'" and I would have walked away.

The Word Qualifier "tried" also serves as a Stopped-Action Word. A smoker who says, "I tried to quit smoking" is really saying, "My attempt to quit smoking failed because some action prevented me from quitting." An interviewee who says "I am trying to tell the truth" is really saying, "Something is preventing me from being completely truthful." An interviewee who says, "I'm trying to cooperate" is really saying, "Something is preventing me from fully cooperating." The use of the Word Qualifier "try" also suggests that the speaker or writer is not serious about the activity he is trying to complete because the Word Qualifier "try" has a built-in escape hatch. A smoker who tries to quit smoking and fails can always say, "I succeeded at trying but failed at quitting."

President Clinton used a Stopped-Action Word in his grand jury testimony:

> **CLINTON** . . . When they knew they couldn't win the lawsuit [Paula Jones], they thought, well, maybe we can pummel him. Maybe they thought I'd settle. Maybe they just thought they would get some political advantage out of it. But that's what's going on here. Now, I'm trying to be honest with you and it hurts me. And I'm trying to tell you the truth about what happened between Ms. Lewinsky and me.

Clinton used the Stopped-Action Word "try," which indicates that he was trying to be honest but did not succeed. Not only did he fail to be honest; he failed to tell the truth. In other words, Clinton said, "Something is preventing me from completing the act of being honest and truthful and it hurts to do so."

The following statement was written by a college student who alleged that she was date raped at a fraternity party by a person who she thought was her friend. Her use of Stopped-Action Words provides support for the hypothesis that she told the truth about being raped.

> (1) Gerry came over and started to massage my shoulders. (2) He then asked me if I wanted to see the house. (3) I said ok so we went inside. (4) We went through the kitchen and then down the hall to the foyer to a room that had a piano. (5) We stayed in that room for about 15 minutes. (6) We talked and I played the piano. (7) He said do you want to see the upstairs so I said alright.

(8) We went upstairs and then he took me to Stan's bedroom. (9) He then started kissing me. (10) While we were kissing we made our way to the bed and laid down. (11) We kissed for a couple of minutes and he started to unbutton my blouse. (12) Then he pulled my blouse off, undid my bra and took it off. (13) He then undid my pants. (14) I started feeling uncomfortable and tried to button them back up. (15) I said I would like to go back to the party, I started to sit up and he said no the party is here. (16) My heart was pounding and I kept trying to get up and he kept pushing me down. (17) I said no, no, I want to go. (18) He then started to finger me and I went limp. (19) He said so that's the way you're going to be now. (20) He got off me and I got up and got dressed. (21) I went to the door, opened it to leave and he shut the light off and then grabbed me around the neck and pulled me back on the bed. (22) I pulled away and screamed loud. (23) He pushed my head on the bed so I couldn't scream. (24) He twisted my neck. (25) He said, "I swear to God I'll kill you, drop you in a body bag in Philly and no one would ever know. (26) He pulled my pants off. (27) I was just crying and saying no, please don't hurt me. (28) He punched me about four times. (29) I told him I couldn't breathe. (30) Then he rolled me on my back and I felt him push his penis against me. (31) Then he put it in me and I started crying oh God, oh God.

In Sentence 1, the Stopped-Action Word "started" indicates that the act of massaging the victim's shoulders was interrupted. In Sentence 2, the victim provides the reason why the act of massaging was interrupted, "He then asked me if I wanted to see the house." The Stopped-Action Word accompanied with the reason why the initial action was interrupted supports the hypothesis that the victim is telling the truth.

In Sentence 15, the Stopped-Action Word "started" indicates that the act of sitting up was interrupted. In Sentence 15, the victim provides the reason why the act of sitting up was interrupted, "He . . . he said no the party is here." The Stopped-Action Word accompanied with the reason why the initial action was interrupted supports the hypothesis that the victim is telling the truth.

In Sentence 16, the Stopped-Action Word "trying to get up" indicates that the act of getting up was interrupted. In Sentence 16, the victim provides the reason why the act of getting up was interrupted, ". . . he kept pushing me down." The Stopped-Action Word accompanied with the reason why the initial action was interrupted supports the hypothesis that the victim is telling the truth.

In Sentence 18, the Stopped-Action Word "started" indicates that the act of fingering her was interrupted. In Sentences 18, 19, and 20, the victim provides the reason why the act of fingering her was interrupted, "I went limp. He said so that's the way you're going to be now. He got off me and I got up and got dressed." The Stopped-Action Word accompanied with the reason why the initial action was interrupted supports the hypothesis that the victim is telling the truth.

In Sentence 31, the Stopped-Action Word "started" indicates that the act of her crying was interrupted. The victim did not provide a reason why the act of her crying was interrupted. One hypothesis posits that she continued to cry for some time after the rape and the reason for her crying to be interrupted is outside the scope of her narrative.

Other PNA indicators and the outcome of the case will be discussed later in this book. The astute reader should already know the outcome of the case. I tried to keep my analysis of this event as neutral as possible so I would not create a Primacy Effect for the reader. I wanted readers to develop their own hypotheses as to the outcome of this case. However, when I edited this portion of the text, I realized that I inadvertently provided a Word Clue as to the outcome of this case. I decided not to change the Word Clues to demonstrate that our minds sometimes unconsciously reveal what we are thinking and it is difficult to defend against PNA, even if you are familiar with the techniques. The Word Clue will be revealed later in this book.

COMMUNICATION WORDS

Communication Words reveal the nature of a verbal exchange from the perspective of writer or speaker. Conversation Words must be analyzed within the context of a written statement or verbal narrative. Determining the meaning of a Communication Word in a written statement is more difficult because much of the meaning of a Communication Word is transmitted through verbal and nonverbal cues. For example, in the written sentence, "I had a chat with my friend" the Communication Word "chat" can be interpreted as a friendly exchange of information. However, the meaning of the Communication Word "chat" changes significantly in a verbal exchange between an angry supervisor who wants to have a "chat" with an errant subordinate. The supervisor's verbal and nonverbal cues alert the subordinate that the communication will be chiefly one-sided and not very friendly. The intended meaning of the Communication Word "chat" would be lost outside the context of the larger conversation. Word Qualifiers typically accompany Communication Words when the accepted meaning of the word changes. The meaning of a Communication Word is more easily understood in a written statement when a Word Qualifier accompanies it. For example, when a parent tells a teacher, "I had a little chat with my son last night. I can assure you that his classroom behavior will improve" the Word Clue "little" indicates that the father's conversation with his son was not cordial and was primarily a one-way exchange.

Communication Words divide into three categories; conversational, argumentative, and inquisitive. Conversational words include but are not limited to talk, discuss, tell, said, spoke, chat, and converse. Conversational words represent subtle nuances in conversations. The Communication Word "talk" suggests that the conversation is one-way and the speaker is dominating the conversation. The conversational word "discuss" connotes a two-way, give and take conversation. The conversational word "told" implies a one-way verbal exchange wherein the speaker dominates the conversation. The conversational words "spoke" and "chat" suggest casual exchanges, while the conversational word "converse" suggests a more formal communication.

Argumentative words indicate that the conversation is adversarial. Argumentative words include but are not limited to confront, argue, shout, and testify. The argumentative word "confront" indicates that one person challenges another person with a set of facts and expects an explanation. The argumentative word "argue" indicates a two-way, adversarial verbal exchange. The argumentative word "shout" indicates a one-way, hostile verbal exchange. The argumentative word "testify" indicates a more formal one-sided delivery of information.

Inquisitive words indicate that one person attempts to acquire information from another person. Inquisitive words include but are not limited to ask, inquire, query, request and muse. The inquisitive word "ask" indicates an informal attempt to gain information. The inquisitive words "inquire" and "request" indicate more formal attempts to gain information. The inquisitive word "muse" indicates a deep, questioning of a set of facts. The inquisitive word "query" indicates a request for information.

Communication Words can also serve as Word Clues because Communication Words can convey the emotional state of the speaker or writer. For example, in the sentence "I confronted my husband about his infidelity" the Word Clue "confronted" indicates that the speaker was emotionally upset when she confronted her husband. In another example, "I told you so, but you would not listen to me" the Communication Word "told" also serves as a Word Clue. The word "told" indicates a sense of superiority of the speaker over the person to whom he is speaking.

The following excerpt from the written statement of a rape victim demonstrates the use of communication words to evaluate the deteriorating relationship between a rape victim and her date. The victim's use of Personal Identifiers and Stopped-Action Words supports the hypothesis that the victim is truthful.

(1) So he picked me up and gave me a hug we left my house drove for about five mins and he told me that instead of going on the date that was planned he wanted to go back to his apartment. (2) On the way to his house he was kissing me, his friend came with him. (3) We then arrived at his house. (4) We

talked for a minute . . . and then went to his bedroom. (5) His friend stayed in the living room and watched T. . . . (6) So we sat down on his bed and talked. (7) He then starting kissing me and had me lay down. (8) He was all over me & forcing me to put my hands down his pants. (9) I told him I was not comfortable doing so, but he wouldn't stop. (10) I told him I didn't know him well enough to sleep with him. But he said "it's my birthday and you're going to give it to me like it or not."

In Sentence 1, the Communication Word "told" indicates that the victim's date made a unilateral decision to take the victim to his apartment. He did not discuss his plans with the victim. In Sentence 4, the victim wrote, "We talked," which indicates that this was a back and forth discussion between the victim and her date. In Sentence 6, the victim wrote, "So we sat down on his bed and talked," which indicates that the discussion is still give and take. In Sentence 9, the victim used the Communication Word "told," which indicates that this is a one-sided conversation and she is not consenting to the activities proposed by her date. In Sentence 10, the Communication Word "told" supports the hypothesis that this was a one-sided conversation. The use of Communication Words tracks the deterioration of the relationship between the victim and her date which is consistent with a truthful statement.

REPEATED WORDS

Repeated Words indicate that the writer or speaker is anxious or subjected to an increased cognitive load. Lying is not easy. Liars must keep track of their nonverbal behaviors to appear to be telling the truth. They must keep track of what they say to ensure that they do not contradict themselves. They must guard against slips of the tongue. They must keep track of their verbal cues, tone of voice, rises in voice pitch, and hesitations. If that were not enough, liars must also constantly monitor their target's nonverbal cues, verbal cues, and speech content to ensure that the target believes the liar. A liar's brain is operating at almost peak capacity and often needs time to process extra information. To gain extra time, liars will often repeat words.

In the rape and murder investigation referenced earlier in this book, the interviewer asked the interviewee, about his sexual activity. The following is an excerpt from the police interview:

> **INTERVIEWER:** How many times have you had sexual intercourse?
> **INTERVIEWEE:** Four times?
> **INTERVIEWER:** Four times? Okay. Well, who's this girl you had sex with?

INTERVIEWEE: I–I don't want to say anyone's name. So, it–it–it–it–it–it–it was someone I went to school with so . . .

The interviewee used the Repeated Word "it," which signals that he experienced anxiety with the topic. Additionally, the Word Qualifier "want," as described earlier, indicates that he knows the woman's name but is unwilling to reveal it to the investigator.

The following excerpt is from President Clinton's grand jury testimony:

PROSECUTOR: So you wanted to check her [Betty Currie's] memory for what she remembered, and that is...
CLINTON: That's correct.
PROSECUTOR: . . . . whether she remembered nothing, or whether she remembered an inappropriate, intimate relationship?
CLINTON: Oh, no, no, no, no. No, I didn't ask her about it that way. I asked her about what the–what I was trying to determine was whether my recollection was right because she was always in the office complex when Monica was there, and whether she thought she could hear any conversations we had or did she hear any.

Clinton used the Repeated Word "no," which indicates that he experienced anxiety about his conversations with Betty Currie. Clinton also used the Tag Qualifier "that way," which indicates that Clinton judged some part of the prosecutor's question as not true. The Tag Qualifier "that way" also serves as a Push-Pull Word. The Push-Pull Word "that way" pushes off "this way." The prosecutor's next question should have been, "In what way did you ask her?"

HANGING WORDS

Hanging Words indicate that the interviewee decided not to finish the thought. Liars often begin a sentence and then stop mid-sentence because the sentence is inappropriate or could expose the truth. Interviewers should pursue Hanging Words to determine why the interviewee decided not to complete the sentence. Hanging Words can provide additional information that the interviewee would have otherwise not provided.

The earlier referenced excerpt from President Clinton's grand jury testimony illustrates the use of a Hanging Word.

PROSECUTOR: Did you talk with Ms. Lewinsky about what she meant to write in her affidavit?

CLINTON: I didn't talk to her about her definition. I did not know what was in this affidavit before it was filled out, specifically. I did not know what words was used–were used specifically before it was filled out or what meaning she gave to them. But I'm just telling you that it's certainly true what she says here, that we didn't have–there was no employment or benefit in exchange. There was nothing having anything to do with sexual harassment. And if she defined sexual relationship in the way I think most Americans do, meaning intercourse, then she told the truth.

Clinton used the Hanging Word "But I'm just telling you that it's certainly true what she says here, that we didn't have. . . ." Have what? Clinton decided, for unknown reasons, not to finish his sentence. The prosecutor could have followed up with the question, "You said, ". . . we didn't have" and then stopped. What were you about to say? Please finish your thought." The following exchange between an accident examiner and a driver, the driver used a Hanging Word.

EXAMINER: My question was, was she traveling parallel along to your vehicle for some period of time?
DRIVER: I can't remember that. I just remember–and you got to realize you're going back to 2002. It's like.

The driver used the Hanging Word "I just remember," which indicates that the driver, for unknown reasons decided not tell the examiner what he remembered. The examiner could have asked the follow-up question, "You stated that you "just remember" and then stopped. What do you remember? Please tell me."

PERSONAL IDENTIFIERS

Personal Identifiers include I, me, we, us, ours, my, theirs, they, them, he, and she. The absence of the Personal Identifier "I" suggests that the speaker or writer is not committed to the statement. Liars often omit the Personal Identifier "I" because they are not committed to what they said or wrote. The effectiveness of the Personal Identifier "I" to detect deception may be changing because people who routinely use email or instant messaging often omit the Personal Identifier "I." This may be due to the shorthand associated with email and instant messages. Economy of words necessitates the omission of Personal Identifier "I" in favor of the implied "I." In light of this phenomenon, the absence of the Personal Identifier "I" person should be applied with caution.

Personal Identifiers can also provide insights into the relationship the speaker or writer has with the other people in their narratives. The Personal Identifier "I" suggests a singular activity. The Personal Identifier "we" indicates that the communicator feels a relational bond with other people described in the narrative. Consider the following examples:

INTERVIEWEE: We watched TV.

The use of the Personal Identifier "we" suggests that the speaker or writer felt as though she had a close kinship with the person or persons with whom she was watching TV.

INTERVIEWEE: I watched TV with Sue.

The use of the Personal Identifier "I "suggests that the writer or speaker, at the very least, does not share the same interest in the television show. The Personal Identifier "I" is at the beginning of the sentence and Sue is positioned at the end of the sentence suggesting there is a physical as well as a psychological distance between the writer and Sue. Distance in Communication in this book.

The following statement was written by Jane, a college student, who alleged that she was date raped at a fraternity party by a person whom she thought was her friend. Her use of Personal Identifier provides insight into the ebb and flow of her relationship with the person who raped her.

Gerry came over and started to massage my shoulders. He then asked me if I wanted to see the house. I said ok so we went inside. We went through the kitchen and then down the hall to the foyer to a room that had a piano. We stayed in that room for about 15 minutes. We talked and I played the piano. He said do you want to see the upstairs so I said alright. We went upstairs and then he took me to Stan's bedroom. He then started kissing me. While we were kissing we made our way to the bed and laid down. We kissed for a couple of minutes and he started to unbutton my blouse. Then he pulled my blouse off, undid my bra and took it off. He then undid my pants. I started feeling uncomfortable and tried to button them back up. I said I would like to go back to the party, I started to sit up and he said no the party is here. My heart was pounding and I kept trying to get up and he kept pushing me down. I said no, no, I want to go. He then started to finger me and I went limp. He said so that's the way you're going to be now. He got off me and I got up and got dressed. I went to the door, opened it to leave and he shut the light off and then grabbed me around the neck and pulled me back on the bed. I pulled away and screamed loud. He pushed my head on the bed so I couldn't scream. He twisted my neck. He said, "I swear to God I'll kill you, drop you in a body bag in Philly and no one would ever know. He pulled my pants off. I was just crying and saying no, please don't hurt me. He punched me about four times. I told him I couldn't breathe. Then he rolled me on my back and I felt him push is his penis against me. Then he put it in me and I started crying oh God, oh God.

At first, the victim felt comfortable with Gerry because she used the Personal Identifier "we" when she described her activities with him. The use of the Personal Identifier "we" suggests that the victim felt comfortable going into Stan's room and kissing Gerry. The Personal Identifier "we" suggests the victim was comfortable moving toward the bed, laying down, and continuing to kiss. The victim may even have been comfortable with Gerry taking off her bra because she did not express any discomfort until he undid her pants. After this point, there is a very clear distinction between the Personal Identifiers "I" and "he," which suggests that the victim did not engage in consensual sex.

The following statement was written by an employee who held a top secret clearance and worked on a highly classified Department of Defense project. A coworker observed the employee download classified information to a Palm Pilot memory chip and leave the building to go to a second facility. The coworker notified security. Security called the employee on his cell phone and instructed him to surrender his Palm Pilot to the gate guards upon arriving at the second facility. The employee surrendered his Palm Pilot but the memory chip was missing. The employee accused the guards of stealing the memory chip. A security investigator asked the employee to write a statement describing in detail his workday from the time he came to work until the time he arrived at the second facility. The employee provided the following written narrative.

> (1) I arrived to work at about 6:30 or so I really don't remember the exact time. (2) I needed to talk with Ken White regarding the verification of equipment at about 10:00 a.m. in that I needed concurrence on some documentation. (3) He started processing the paperwork and I broke out *my* Palm Pilot and started playing solitaire. (4) Although I used *my* Palm Pilot as a day planner and a means to store and quickly recall phone numbers, I use my Palm Pilot as entertainment on my weekly commutes to and from Dallas as well as other business trips. (5) I called for telephone messages and then Ms. Bell expressed her concern over it and asked that I turn it over to security, which I really didn't want to do. (6) I knew that I shouldn't have the system in the facility and that I could have my accesses revoked and job terminated. (7) With the pilot in my pocket, I exited the facility and placed the pilot in my trunk. (8) While I was dri-

ving, security paged me and requested that I surrender the Palm Pilot to the guard at the gate. (9) Within eye distance from the gate, I stopped my car and removed my brief case, my cassette music tapes, and the pilot from my trunk. (10) The guard asked to take *my* Pilot. (11) I gave him *my* Pilot and that was the last time I saw it. (12) I then called Ms Bell to let her know I was clean with security and that they confiscated *my* Pilot. (13) I also called my boss to let him know what happened.

In Sentences 3, 4, 10, 11, and 12, the writer used the Personal Identifier "my" to describe his Palm Pilot. The Personal Identifier "my" indicates that the writer took possession of his Palm Pilot. In Sentences 7, 8, and 9, the writer used the Article "the" to describe his Palm Pilot. The Article "the" indicates that the writer distanced himself from his Palm Pilot. Additionally, in Sentence 5, the writer used the pronoun "it" two times to describe his Palm Pilot. This Change of Language indicates a Change of Perspective, which supports the hypothesis that he wanted to distance himself from his Palm Pilot. The writer established a baseline in that he used the Personal Identifier "my" at the beginning of his statement and at the end of the statement. The use of the Article "the" in the middle of the statement, which indicates that something occurred to cause the writer to distance himself from his Palm Pilot. The change occurred from the time right after the writer talked with Ken White to the time he surrendered his Palm Pilot to the guard. During that time, Ms. Bell expressed her concern about the writer using his Palm Pilot in a secured area. One hypothesis posits that Ms. Bell saw the writer download the classified information to the memory chip and confronted him about the breach of security rules. The writer did not want to turn his Palm Pilot over to security as directed by Ms. Bell because he knew the memory chip contained classified information. The writer left the first facility and drove to the second facility. After receiving the telephone call from security, the writer removed the memory chip from his Palm Pilot and surrendered the Palm Pilot to the guard. Support for this hypothesis will be discussed later in this book.

In the earlier referenced interview between Diane Sawyer and Scott Peterson, he inappropriately used the Personal Identifier "we" which indicates the possibility of deception.

> **SAWYER:** And the last time you saw her was?
> **PETERSON:** I believe it was about 9:30 that morning. Uh, the reason being we started to watch Martha Stewart Living while Laci was working in the kitchen and–uhm–I left sometime during that.

The Personal Identifier "we" suggests that he and Laci watched Martha Stewart Living together but this may not have been the case. The Word

Qualifier "while Laci was working in the kitchen" suggests that Peterson may have been watching Martha Stewart Living, but Laci was doing something other than watching television. One hypothesis posits that Peterson wanted to give Sawyer and the television audience the illusion that all was well the last time he saw Laci. Peterson's inappropriate use of the Personal Identifier "we" does not comport with his description of Laci's behaviors and may indicate deception.

In another example, John Walker Linhd, also known as the American Taliban, was captured by American troops during the Battle of Qala-i-Jangi, a violent Taliban prison uprising where American CIA officer Mike Spann was killed. The revolt was eventually suppressed by the Northern Alliance and American air and ground support. During the battle, Lindh and 85 other Talaban fighters sought refuge in a basement. The Northern Alliance slowly flooded the basement with water. After several days, Lindh and his companions emerged and surrendered. Lindh is currently serving a 20-year prison sentence. Immediately after his capture, he made the following statement.

> **INTERVIEWER:** What made you leave the basement?
> **LINDH:** It was the last day. What happened was–yesterday–they had bombed us with airplanes, they had shot missiles, they had thrown grenades, they had shot us with all types of guns, they had poured gas on us and burned us, they had done everything you could imagine. So the last thing they did was they–they poured water down into the basement. They wanted to fill it up with water.

Lind used the Personal Identifier "they," which referred to the Northern Alliance and American troops. Within the context of Lindh's statement the Personal Identifier "they" is appropriate. Lindh and the Taliban are on one side and the Northern Alliance and American troops are on the other side.

> **INTERVIEWER:** Was it your goal to be shaheed–martyred?
> **LINDH:** It is the goal of every Muslim.

The interviewer asked Linhd a direct Yes or No question. Linhd chose not to give a "Yes" or "No" answer, but, instead, took the interviewer to the Land of Is.

> **INTERVIEWER:** Was it your goal though?
> **LINDH:** Huh?

The interviewer stopped Linhd from going to the Land of Is by repeating the question. Linhd answered the question with a question, which indicates deception.

INTERVIEWER: Was it your goal at that time?
LINDH: I'll tell you, to be honest, every single one of us, without any exaggeration, every single one of us was one hundred percent sure that we would all be shaheed. We'd all be martyrs.

Again, Linhd chose not to give a "Yes" or "No" answer and tried to take the interviewer to the Land of Is. Lindh never answered the question, which suggests that his goal was not to be martyred.

LINDH: What happened was, we spent the night under the basement then they led us out one by one. They would search each of us. Then they tied us up and they put us out on the lawn. So, as they were taking us one by one, somehow they started fighting with . . . . starting with a grenade, then one of them grabbed a Kalishnikov from one of the– Dostam–uh–army forces. And–uh–so the fighting began.

Lindh used the Personal Identifier "we," which indicates that he associated with the Talaban. Lindh used the Personal Identifier "they led," "They would," "they tied," "they put," and "they were" referred to the Northern Alliance and American troops. Lindh then used the Personal Identifier "they started" and "them" refering to the Taliban forces. Lindh considered himself as one of the Taliban fighters until the fighting started. When the fighting started, he distanced himself from the Taliban fighters. The contradictory use of Personal Identifiers indicates that Lindh was not dedicated to the Taliban forces. In support of this hypothesis, Lindh refused to commit to martyrdom after repeated questioning. Personal Identifiers revealed Lindh's true motivation.

DISTANCE IN COMMUNICATION

People tend to draw near to people and things that they like and tend to distance themselves from people and things that they don't like. This phenomenon occurs in both oral and written communications. The use of the article "the" instead of "my" or the use of the Personal Identifier "them" instead of "us" are signals that the writer or speaker wants to distance himself from the topic he is addressing. Word separations in sentences can also signal distancing. For example, in the sentence "I had lunch with Sue," the writer distanced himself from Sue, which suggests that he does not have a close relationship with Sue. In contrast, the sentence, "Sue and I had lunch" demonstrates less distancing. The sentence, "We had lunch" suggests that the writer and Sue had a close relationship.

Consider the following example: Vice President Dick Chaney issued a statement wherein he supposedly took full responsibility for shooting his friend Harry. A PNA analysis of the Vice President's statement suggests otherwise. The statement read:

"I'm the guy who pulled the trigger that fired the round that hit Harry."

The Personal Identifier "I" is the first word in the sentence and the name Harry is the last word in the sentence. The distance between Cheney and Harry could not be further. Cheney also blamed the trigger for firing the round that hit Harry. This suggests further distancing because the Cheney put the trigger between himself and the act of shooting Harry. The trigger is responsible for shooting Harry not Cheney; he just pulled the trigger. The Word Clue "hit" suggests distance because the word "hit" substitutes for the word "shot." If Cheney truly wanted to take full responsibility for shooting Harry, he would have said something to the effect, "I shot Harry" or "I accidentally shot Harry."

SIMPLE PAST TENSE

People who tell the truth retrieve information from their memories. Deceptive people either make up facts or modify facts from truthful events previously stored in their memories. When fabricating information or facts, liars mentally rehearse their stories in the present tense. When they are satisfied that the fabricated stories are plausible, they must then translate the present tense information or facts into the past tense to simulate a truthful narrative. Liars often fail to translate all the present tense verbs into the past tense and subconsciously speak or write narratives using both past tense and the present tense verbs. Information or facts spoken or written in the present tense suggest deception.

One exception to this rule is that people who retell personally traumatic events such as a rape or a near death experience often use the present tense because they are reliving the events in their minds as they relate the story. Another exception is that people sometimes use the past tense expressions when referring to the present tense. For example, When first meeting a person, people often say, "What did you say your name was?" instead of "What is your name?" When buying a airplane or train ticket, people often say, "I was looking for a ticket to Chicago" instead of "I am looking for a ticket to Chicago."

On January 28, 2003, Diane Sawyer interviewed Scott Peterson, who was later convicted of killing his wife, Laci and her unborn son, on Good Morning America. The following is an excerpt from that interview:

SAWYER: Tell me about the state of your marriage. What, what kind of marriage was it?

PETERSON: God, I mean the first word that comes to mind is–you know–glorious. I mean we took care of each other very well. Uhm–she was amazing – is amazing.

SAWYER: You haven't mentioned your son.

PETERSON: Hmm–that was–it's [it is] so hard.

Peterson used the past tense "was" to describe his relationship with Laci, quickly corrected himself, and used the appropriate tense. The quick change in tense suggests that Peterson realized that he made a mistake and corrected it because he wanted to portray himself as an innocent person. Peterson made the same mistake when he talked about his unborn son. The change and the immediate corrections support the hypothesis that he killed or, at least, had knowledge that his wife and unborn son were dead.

The following excerpt, written by a store clerk, demonstrates a change in tense from the simple past tense to the present tense, and then back to the past tense. This statement was written after the investigator's initial interview of the clerk, wherein she denied stealing the money.

> I closed the cash register at about 10 o'clock. I took my drawer to the back room and count the receipts. I see there are six $100 bills. I place the bills in the moneybag. I sealed the bag, dropped it in the drop box, and went home.

The clerk used the past tense verbs "closed," "took," and "count" before she counted the money. She used the present tense verbs "see," "are," and "place," while she was counting the money and used the past tense "sealed," "dropped," and "went" after she counted the money. The writer established a baseline because she used the past tense before and after she used the present tense. One hypothesis posits that the clerk stole the money in the back room when she counted the money. The investigator exploited the writer's change in tense in a creative way.

The investigator returned to the store and learned every motion the clerk went through on a typical day when she closed her register. Additionally, he memorized the physical surroundings in and around the cash register and in the back room. The investigator summoned the clerk for a second interview. He began the interview with the statement," Now, I know exactly what happened. You took the money in the back room." The clerk replied, "Yeah, tell me." Then investigator slowly and deliberately described in minute details what she did from the time she closed the cash register until the time she took the six $100 bills when she counted the money. The clerk began to cry and exclaimed, "I knew there was a security camera in the back room." The investigator lead the clerk to believe that there was a security camera in the back room. He accomplished this when he said, "Now, I know exactly what happened." The Push-Pull Word "now" indicates that he did not know what happened the first time he interviewed her but he now knows. The Word Qualifier "exactly" indicates that the investigator knows precisely what occurred. This introductory statement established the Primacy Effect for the clerk. She viewed everything the investigator said from the perspective that he, in fact, knew that she stole the money. The detective's detailed description of her actions enhanced the Primacy Effect causing the clerk to believe that there was a security camera in the back room. The Spotlight Effect magnified her belief that the investigator knew exactly what happened.

FIRST PERSON SIMPLE PAST TENSE

The formula First Person Simple Past Tense indicates truthfulness. Truthful people retrieve information from their memory and commit to that information by using the Personal Identifier "I." Liars, on the other hand, create information in the present tense and translate the action to the past tense to give the illusion that the information was retrieved from memory. Liars often cannot commit to the false information and omit the Personal Identifier "I" because they know the information is false. In many instances, liars will blend the truth with deception resulting in the mixed use of the Personal Identifier "I." Each sentence should be examined for the use of the First Person Simple Past Tense to determine if the speaker or writer is committed to the activities in that sentence. The lack of the First Person Simple Past Tense does not always signal deception but does identify areas in the spoken or written communication that require further inquiry, especially if the omission of the First Person Simple Past Tense deviates from the speaker or writer's baseline.

The following statement was written by a truck driver who mysteriously lost a pallet of three airplane tires off the back of his truck while he was driving from Los Angeles to Lancaster, California. The use of the Personal Identifier "I" deviates from the writer's baseline and suggests deception.

(1) Arrived LA dock 18:45 loaded 3 pallets to rental truck stack bed, 2 pallets airplane tires -1 pallet with 2 boxes. (2) Departed LA dock 19:30 for Lancaster. (3) About 21:00 between top of truck ramp from I–5 to the 14 Freeway and camper pulls along side of me and tell me that a pallet had fallen out of the back of my truck. (4) And just before that when I got to the top of the truck ramp had pulled over to check straps (strike) on trucks – all 3 pallets were still

aboard. (5) So when I got to Sand Canyon Rd pulled off to check load and both straps + chain was loose or off of pallets and there was only 2 pallets on truck, 1 pallet of 2 boxes + 1 pallet of 3 airplane tires. (6) So I (strikeout) turned around (strikeout) and went back toward LA looking for the missing pallet. (7) Found nothing. (8) Went onto Lancaster office. (9) Unloaded truck.

The driver omitted Personal Identifiers in Sentences 1 and 2. He used the Personal Identifier "me" and "I" in Sentences 3 through 6. The driver again omitted Personal Identifiers in Sentences 7 through 9. In this statement, the omission of Personal Identifiers is the baseline and the use of Personal Identifiers deviates from the baseline. In Sentence 3 the driver used the Present Tense "pulls" and "tell," which signal deception. Any deviation from the baseline signals deception. This statement will be examined in greater detail later in this book.

FUTURE IN THE PAST

Future in the Past expresses an idea or action that a person in retrospect did or thought might have happened given a specific set of circumstances. The speculative nature of Future in the Past allows people to make conjectures as to what might have happened in retrospect; however, the conjecture need not be true. Liars often tell people what they would have done and not what they actually did. Future in the Past is a clever way to lie because interviewers do not know if interviewees are stating what occurred in the past or merely speculating as to what might have occurred. The Truth Bias complicates the detection of deception when liars use Future in the Past because interviewers tend to believe interviewees and assume that what they conjectured is the truth. The following deposition excerpt demonstrates the use of Future in the Past.

> **INTERVIEWER:** Tell me what you were doing just prior to the accident.
> **INTERVIEREE:** I was driving north on Main Street. I wanted to go to the super market so I had to change lanes. I did what I normally would'da done. I looked in my rear view mirror and if I didn't see any cars, I'd look over my shoulder to check my blind spot. If everything was clear, I'd turn on my blinker and change lanes. The next thing I knew this other car hits me.

The interviewer must keep in mind that the interviewee's statement may or may not be true. The interviewee may have described what he did or conjectured as to what he might have done in similar circumstances. If the interviewee lied to avoid taking responsibility for the accident, then he gave the illusion that he looked in his rear view mirror for cars, looked over this shoulder to check his blind spot, activated his turn signal, and changed lanes when, in fact, this was not what he actually did. Future in the Past is sometimes difficult to catch in verbal speech, especially when the word "would" is combined with other words to form contractions. To counter Future in the Past, interviewers should respond, "I didn't ask what you would have done. I asked you what you actually did. What did you actually do?" If the interviewee is telling the truth, he should clarify what he did using simple past tense.

At the conclusion of one of my lectures, a CIA case officer challenged my assertion that even when liars know PNA principles, they have a difficult time lying. I accepted the challenge. I asked the case officer where he had lunch. He told me that he went to McDonalds. I instructed him to omit the fact that he went to McDonalds for lunch. I asked the case officer to describe everything he did from the time he arrived at the training facility to the time he approached me at the end of my presentation. The case officer successfully answered every question I asked him without revealing any verbal indicators of deception. I was about to concede but decided to try one more technique. I summarized the case officer's activities as he described them to me. At the end of my summary, the case officer said, "Yeah, that's what I would have done." Gottcha! I responded, "Yeah, that's what you would have done, but that's not what you did!" The case officer sighed in disbelief. He knew in his mind that the summary of activities I presented was not accurate. His mind automatically selected the grammar structure Future in the Past to accurately describe the truth. Since PNA techniques rely on how people construct sentences using grammar structures, and it is very difficult to defeat.

ARTICLES

The Articles "a" and "the" are small but powerful words. The Article "a" generally identifies one person or thing that is among many people or things. The Article "the" specifically identifies one person or thing to the exclusion of other people and things. Consider this example: "A man put a knife to my throat. He forced me into the alley, and raped me." This statement is consistent with a true statement because the rape victim used the Article "a," which indicates that the man was one of many men in the male population. The victim probably did not know her assailant. On the other hand, if a rape victim wrote. "The man put a knife to my throat, we went into the alley, and raped me," the sentence would not be consistent with a truthful statement. The rape victim used the Article "the" to describe her assailant, which suggests that she either knows her assailant or has seen her assailant prior to the rape. Additionally, the rape victim also used the pronoun "we," which suggests that the rape victim had a relationship, to some degree, with her assailant. The interviewer could exploit this knowledge by asking the alleged rape victim the presumptive question, "When did you first meet the man who raped you?

LOGICAL SEQUENCE OF EVENTS

Truthful people tell stories in chorological order and their narratives have coherent structures. Truthful people have little difficulty retrieving facts from their memories and relaying those facts using the past tense. Conversely, liars must make up facts or modify existing truthful memories. Liars tell their stories in what they perceive as logical sequence. However, at some point in the story, they realize that something they previously said or wrote requires support to maintain the illusion of truthfulness. They add support for what they previously said or wrote at the point in the narrative when they realize additional support is necessary.

The following statement cited earlier in this book was written by a truck driver who mysteriously lost a pallet of three airplane tires off the back of his truck while he was driving from Los Angeles to Lancaster, California. The use of the Personal Identifier "I" deviates from the writer's baseline and suggests deception.

(1) Arrived LA dock 18:45 loaded 3 pallets to rental truck stack bed, 2 pallets airplane tires – 1 pallet with 2 boxes. (2) Departed LA dock 19:30 for Lancaster. (3) About 21:00 between top of truck ramp from I-5 to the 14 Freeway and camper pulls along side of me and tell me that a pallet had fallen out of the back of my truck. (4) And just before that when I got to the top of the truck ramp had pulled over to check straps (strike) on trucks – all 3 pallets were still aboard. (5) So when I got to Sand Canyon Rd pulled off to check load and both straps + chain was loose or off of pallets and there was only 2 pallets on truck, 1 pallet of 2 boxes + 1 pallet of 3 airplane tires. (6) So I (strikeout) turned around (strikeout) and went back toward LA looking for the missing pallet. (7) Found nothing. (8) Went onto Lancaster office. (9) Unloaded truck.

Sentences 1, 2, and 3 are in Logical Sequence. Sentence 3, although in Logical Sequence up to this point in the narrative, contains the Present Tense words "pulls" and "tells," which signal deception. Sentences 4, 5, and 6 are

Out of Logical Sequence. The driver wrote, "And just before that…," meaning before the camper pulled alongside of him. One hypothesis posits that the driver wanted to ensure the reader that he checked the straps on his load before the driver of the camper notified him that the tires fell off the back of his truck. In other words, it was not my fault because I checked the straps on the tires just minutes before the camper pulled alongside me.

In summary, the driver's statement is Out of Logical Sequence, contains tense changes, and the use of Personal Identifiers that deviate from the baseline, which supports the hypothesis that the driver was deceptive. The driver's statement contains one Word Clue that provides the key to the truth. I challenge the readers to identify this Word Clue and develop a hypothesis as to what really happened. Some readers might want to develop some strategies to interview the driver.

Some additional facts in this investigation include: (1) Interstate 5 (I–5) and the 14 Freeway are heavily traveled roadways, especially in the early evening due to rush hour traffic; (2) No 911 calls were made to the police reporting debris in the roadway; (3) No accidents were reported due to the pallet of tires falling off the truck; (4) The California Highway Patrol (CHP) sent patrol cars to look for the pallet of tires, but they could not find the pallet, the tires, or any debris from the cargo falling off the truck; and (5) Residential housing overlooks Sand Canyon Road. The solution to this narrative and interviewing strategies, as well as a full PNA of the driver's statement is presented in Appendix A of this book.

Chapter 4

LYING BY OMISSION

Lying by omission is the preferred method to lie because liars need only remember the portion of the story they left out. Leaving out selected facts in an otherwise true story enables liars to express the appropriate emotions, display believable nonverbal cues, and experience less cognitive demand. The Truth Bias also helps liars because people tend to excuse one or two irregularities in an otherwise truthful story. Lying by omission is not only the preferred method to lie, but it is the most difficult lie to detect using nonverbal cues and paralinguistic indicators because lairs only fabricate a small portion of the story. Analyzing grammar structures more readily detects lies of omission because liars must use specific grammatical devices to circumvent withheld information. Based on my research and personal experiences, the Text Bridge is the most common grammatical device to evade detection.

TEXT BRIDGES

Most liars tell the truth up to the point where they want to conceal information, skip over the withheld information, and tell the truth again. Successful liars construct sentences that allow them to skip over withheld information, thus creating information gaps. Constructing a sentence to span the information gap replicates building a bridge across a river. A road stops at the river's edge, a bridge spans the river, and the road continues on the opposite bank. Bridges come in a variety of designs, but each design must adhere to specific construction standards or structural failure occurs. Likewise, sentence construction must follow certain grammar rules. Truthful people use the same grammar rules as do deceptive people to construct sentences. The only difference between a truthful narrative and a deceptive narrative is the deliberate obfuscation or omission of the truth. Isolating the

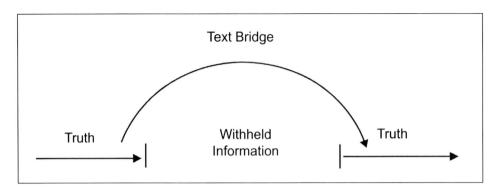

words or grammatical structures used to bridge information gaps identifies where in the narrative people intentionally or unintentionally withheld information. Text Bridges serve as markers that signal withheld information; however, withheld information does not always indicate deception.

Text Bridges comprise three categories: subordinating words, adverbial conjunctives, and transition words. Some Text Bridges overlap categories depending on the context of the sentence but, regardless of their grammatical function, they still act as Text Bridges. Subordinating words connect unequal but related ideas and create information gaps. Subordinating words include after, although, as if, as long as, because, before, even though, if, in order, that, since, so, than, through, unless, until, when, whenever, wherever, where, and while. For example, a husband suspected of killing his wife arrived home at 5:00 p.m. and made the following statement, "After I came home, I found my wife dead." The subordinating word "after" creates an information gap from the time the man came home until the time he found his wife dead. The murder suspect wanted to give the impression that he arrived home and immediately found his wife dead; however, this was not the case. The murder suspect arrived home at 5:00 p.m. but did not indicate what time he found his wife dead. An information gap exists from 5:00 p.m. until the suspect found his wife dead. During this information gap, the murder suspect got into an altercation with his wife and killed her. The murder suspect hid the physical altercation with his wife by using the Text Bridge "after."

Adverbial conjunctives connect two complete ideas. Adverbial conjunctives include accordingly, however, besides, nevertheless, consequently, otherwise, again, indeed, also, moreover, finally, therefore, furthermore, then, and thus. Adverbial conjunctives create information gaps. For example, a young boy told his parents "I was playing with my toys and then Tommy came over and hit me." The adverbial conjunctive "then" bridges the information gap. In reality, the young boy took the toy Tommy was holding when he approached. In retaliation, Tommy struck the young boy. The young boy instigated the attack by taking Tommy's toy but used a text bridge to make himself appear as if he were the victim.

Transitional words connect themes and ideas or establish relationships. Transitional words group into four basic categories: (1) time, (2) contrast, (3) result, and (4) addition. Transitional words indicating time include: after, afterward, before, during, earlier, eventually, finally, first, later, meanwhile, since, then, and until. Transitional words indicating contrast include: however, in contrast, indeed, instead, nevertheless, on the contrary, on the other hand, and yet. Transitional words indicating result include because, consequently, as a result, on account of, so, then, therefore, and thus. Transitional words indicating addition include also, and, besides, for example, furthermore, in addition, moreover, and too.

Grammar Function	*Text Bridges*
Subordinating Words	after, although, as if, as long as, because, before, even though, if, in order, that, since, so, than, through, unless, until, when, whenever, where, wherever, where, while
Transitional Words	
Time	after, afterward, before, during, earlier, eventually, finally, first, later, meanwhile, since, then, until
Contrast	however, in contrast, indeed, instead, nevertheless, on the contrary, on the other hand, yet
Result	because, consequently, as a result, on account of, so, then, therefore, thus
Addition	also, and, besides for example, furthermore, in addition, moreover, too
Adverbial Conjunctives	accordingly, however, besides, nevertheless, consequently, otherwise, again, indeed, also, moreover, finally, therefore, furthermore, then, thus

A motorist wrote the following description of his automobile accident:"I saw the stop sign. Before I entered the intersection, I looked both ways, drove into the intersection and was struck in the right passenger door by the other vehicle." A witness told the traffic investigator that the motorist did look both ways at the intersection, but he did not make a complete stop at the stop sign. In reality, the motorist did see the stop sign. He did look both ways before entering the intersection, and the other vehicle did strike the motorist's passenger side door; however, the motorist failed to write that he did not stop at the stop sign. The motorist used the Text Bridge "before" to conceal the fact that he did not stop at the stop sign before entering into the intersection.

For my dissertation, I conducted extensive research on Text Bridges. My research found that the most commonly used Text Bridge in the deceptive narratives is "then," which was used 57 percent of the time. The Text Bridge "so" was used 22 percent of the time. The Text Bridge "after" was used 7 percent of the time. The Text Bridge "when" was used 2 percent of the time. The Text Bridge "as" and "while" were each used 3 percent of the time and the Text Bridge "next" was used 1% of the time. These seven text bridges: then, so, after, when, as, while, and next were used in over 95% of the time in deceptive narratives. The remaining Text Bridges: once, finally, afterwards, and eventually occurred less than 1 percent of the time. The lack of Text Bridges does not mean the writer is truthful because not all of the study's participants used Text Bridges in their deceptive narratives. The most commonly used Text Bridges: then, so, after, when, as, while, and next are easily memorized and provide a powerful tool to identify where people withhold information during professional or social conversations.

Text Bridges allow people to transition from one topic to another topic without detailing lesser-included activities. For example, in the sentence "I got up, and then I took a shower, and then I ate breakfast," the Text Bridge "then" signals withheld information. The withheld information does not constitute deception. The writer did not want to bore the listener or reader with the lesser-included activities of taking a shower and eating breakfast. The omitted activities encompass turning on the water, soaping, rinsing, drying off, donning clothes, walking to the kitchen, taking a bowl from the cupboard, filling the bowl with cereal, going to the refrigerator to get milk, etc. However, Text Bridges used at critical times during interviews or interrogations may signal deception. The critical time in a statement or narrative is the point in the communication that addresses the main topic of the inquiry. For example, if a bank were robbed at 2 p.m., the critical time would begin at the point in the interviewee's narrative where the bank robbery is first mentioned and end with the last mention of the bank robbery. In the event the interviewee did not mention the bank, the critical time would begin from the event in the interviewee's narrative that occurs at the approximate time the bank was robbed until the time when the bank robbery ended. If investigators deem the missing information to have no value, then they can ignore the Text Bridge.

Narratives divide into three sections: the prologue, the incident, and the epilogue. The prologue begins with the first sentence and ends with the sentence before the writer first addresses the incident. The incident portion of the written statement begins with the first sentence that addresses the incident and ends with the last sentence that describes the incident. The epilogue begins with the sentence after the last sentence discussing the incident and continues until the end of the statement. The words and grammar structures in the prologue and the epilogue serve as a baseline against which to compare the words and grammar structures in the incident portion of the narrative.

Consider the following example. At the end of the day, Susie, a bank teller, was out of balance. Her drawer was short $2,000. Susie denied taking the money. A second teller, Jim, was the only other person who had access to Susie's cash drawer. The next day, a bank investigator came to investigate the loss. The bank investigator instructed Suzie and Jim to write statements regarding their activities on the previous day. Jim wrote:

> (1) On Tuesday the 2nd of February I arrived to work at 8:45 in the morning and worked till 5:45. (2) I took my breaks at 10:15–1:15–3:45. (Prologue) (3) I only had one transaction with Suzie. I remember that all of my transactions were balanced when I left. (4) I left before Suzie was balanced. (Incident) (5) I did not know she was out of balance until I came in this morning. (6) Other than that nothing was out of a normal day. (Epilogue)

Jim's narrative contained six sentences, two in the prologue, three in the incident, and one in the epilogue. All six sentences were written in the first-person and used simple past tense, which indicate no deception. The narrative contained no Text Bridges, which indicates that the teller did not intentionally withhold any information. Sentence 5, "I did not know she was out of balance until I came in this morning" is not a Spontaneous Negation. The teller answered the presumed question, Why is Susie out of balance?; the stated reason for writing the narrative. Spontaneous Negations will be discussed later in this book. In Sentence 6, Jim used the Push-Pull Word "normal." The word "normal" pushes off the word "not normal" or "abnormal." Within the context of this narrative, the use of the Push-Pull word "normal" does not signal deception. Jim did not know that Susie was out of balance until he arrived the next day; therefore, in retrospect, the abnormal thing that occurred during the previous day was Susie being out of balance. The use of the present tense word "remember" in the Sentence 4 does not signal deception. Jim wrote the narrative the day after the incident and, therefore, is presently remembering what occurred the previous day. The activities that occurred on the previous day should be referred to in the past tense. Jim subsequently used the past tense "balanced" and "left," which is consistent with a truthful narrative. A PNA of this narrative indicates no obvious deception.

Susie wrote:

(1) After I finished with my customer, I sold $1,000 in 20s to Pete because he needed 20s. (2) That was about 2 p.m. (Prologue) (3) I then sold more than $10,000 to Jim in large + twenties so he could run the branch as a sub-vault. (4) After that I did not have any hundreds, fifties, twenties or tens left. (5) I started balancing at about 4:30 and as soon as I knew that I was short $2,000 I started rechecking all my work, I also let Kim know that I was out of balance. (Incident) (6) She rechecked my cash and then we (Kim, and I) counted the entire branch under dual control. (7) When we were almost done we called our Branch Service Manager Deborah at home around 8:00 p.m. to let her know about the outage. (8) After we finished counting everyone we called the Regional Manager Tom Smith to let him know about the situation. (9) We locked up and left about 9:00 p.m. (10) I do not recall anything different about this day. (Epilogue)

Susie's narrative contained nine sentences, two in the prologue, three in the incident, and five in the epilogue. Susie used six Text Bridges, "after" in Sentence 1, "then" in Sentence 3, "after" in Sentence 4, "as soon as" in Sentence 5, "then" in Sentence 6; and "after" in Sentence 8. Of the six Text Bridges, one occurred in the prologue, three occurred in the incident, and two occurred in the epilogue. The Text Bridges that occurred in the prologue and epilogue are less significant because Susie did not have contact with money from the vault. When describing the incident, Susie used the Text Bridge "then" in Sentence 3, creating an information gap from the time she sold money to Pete at 2 p.m. until the time she sold money to Jim. In Sentence 4, the Text Bridge "after" created an information gap from the time she sold money to Pete at 2 p.m. until she balanced at 4:30. In Sentence 5, Susie the Text Bridge "as soon as," created an information gap from the time she sold money to Pete at 2 p.m. until she balanced at 4:30. Susie constructed a triple span Text Bridge to cover the information gap from the time she sold money to Pete at 2 p.m. until she balanced at 4:30, which coincidently covers the entire time period Susie had contact with the money at the teller station. Additionally, Sentences 2 and 10 were written in the Present Tense. In Sentence 2, the present tense word "recall" does not signal deception. Susie wrote the narrative the day after the incident and, therefore, is presently remembering what occurred the previous day. The activities that occurred on the previous day should be referred to in the past tense. Susie used the Past tense "sold "in Sentence 2, which is consistent with a truthful narrative. However, in Sentence 10, Susie referred to the activities that occurred on the day she wrote the narrative and not the activities of the previous day. The use of the present tense in this sentence signals the possibility of deception. Susie used the Stopped-Action Word "started" in Sentence 5, which indicates that some action prevented her from completing the act of balancing. Susie also used the Stopped-Action word "started" in Sentence 6, which indicates that some action prevented her from completing the act of rechecking her work. Susie used the Spontaneous Negation "I did not have any hundreds, fifties, twenties or tens left," which indicates that she had denominations of money other than the ones she named. Susie used the second Spontaneous Negation "I do not recall anything different about this day," which indicates a high probability that she does recall something about the day that was unusual. Spontaneous Negations will be discussed later in this book. Susie also used the Word Qualifier "more than" in Sentence 4, which indicates that she did now know how much money she sold to Jim. A PNA of this narrative indicates a high likelihood of deception. Not only does the PNA analysis indicate deception, but the interviewer can identify the places in Susie's narrative that she intentionally or unintentionally withheld information. The interviewer should develop an interviewing strategy that targets the areas of missing information.

The following illustration demonstrates how to exploit Text Bridges. A student wrote a statement in response to an allegation that she took $20 from her professor's office during the first class break. Pursuant to an informal investigation, the student wrote a narrative account of her activities from the time she entered the building until the end of the first break. The following is a copy of her statement:

(1) I arrived at 7:45 a.m. with Jenna. (2) I came into the room, put my bag at my desk and Jenna and I went to the little snack area to get some coffee. (3) I returned to the classroom and sat at my desk. (Prologue) (4) At 8:50 we went on a break. (5) Jenna and I went to the bathroom. (6) After that I came back to the classroom and Jenna stayed in the bathroom. (7) She came back to the classroom soon after. (Incident) (8) We sat at our desk and waited for our class to continue. (Epilogue)

The student's statement consists of eight sentences, three in the prologue, four in the incident, and one in the epilogue. The incident comprises Sentences 4 through 7. These sentences focus on the first break, the time during which the money was stolen. The section that addressed the break reads, "At

8:50 we went on a break. Jenna and I went to the bathroom. After that I came back to the classroom and Jenna stayed in the bathroom. She came back to the classroom soon after." The student used the Text Bridge "after," which created an information gap from the time she went to the bathroom and to the time she came back to the classroom. This information gap in the student's narrative was sufficient time for her to walk down the hall to the instructor's office and steal the $20. After conducting a Micro-Action Interview, the student admitted taking the $20. Micro-Action Interviews will be discussed later in this book. The Text Bridge "after" concealed the fact that after she went to the bathroom and before she came back to the classroom she walked down the hall to the instructor's office and stole $20. In addition to the Text Bridge, the student used Misdirection. The student was asked to provide an account of her activities not Jenna's activities. The student changed the focus from her activities during the break to Jenna's activities during the break as a substitute for the missing time when the money was stolen.

Parents should listen for Text Bridges when they question their teenagers. If their answers contain Text Bridges, further inquiry may be necessary. For example, I wanted to find out what my 17-year-old daughter did the previous evening with my car. This inquiry is delicate. If I push too hard, my daughter will contend that I do not trust her. If I do not push hard enough, she may get away with abusing her privilege to drive the family car. PNA techniques are benign and strike the perfect balance between these two positions. I asked my daughter the following question.

> **ME:** Where were you last night?
> **MY DAUGHTER:** I went to the library and then I came straight home.

The Text Bridge "then" indicates that my daughter consciously or unconsciously withheld information. She may have withheld lesser-included activities related to the library such as checking out books, leaving the library, getting into her car, driving home, etc. On the other hand, she may have used a Text Bridge to cover intentionally withheld activities. In addition to the Text Bridge "then," she used the Push-Pull Word "straight," which pushes off the word "crooked" or "not straight." The Push-Pull word "straight" suggests my daughter did not come straight home. The combination of the Text Bridge and the Push-Pull Word raises sufficient doubt to make further inquiries.

After conducting a Micro-Action Interview, my daughter admitted to her activities on the previous evening. The Micro-Action Interview will be discussed later in this book. My daughter did go to the library the previous evening for five minutes. I asked her why she even bothered going to the library. She told me that she knew I was a good lie catcher and if she went to the library for five minutes, she would evade detection. My daughter did come straight home, straight home from a party. If my daughter were telling me the truth the Text Bridge, "then" could be logically explained; however, the Push-Pull Word "straight" cannot be logically explained and betrayed her lie.

The earlier referenced statement written by the victim who was raped at a fraternity party demonstrates how Text Bridges can assist interviewers conduct complete and through interviews, obtaining the maximum amount of information as possible. In her statement, the victim used several Text Bridges. Text Bridges signal intentionally or unintentionally withheld information. The interviewer should identify the information gaps in her statements and conduct a Micro-Action Interview to extract the missing information.

(1) Gerry came over and started to massage my shoulders. (2) He then asked me if I wanted to see the house. (3) I said ok so we went inside. (4) We went through the kitchen and then down the hall to the foyer to a room that had a piano. (5) We stayed in that room for about 15 minutes. (6) We talked and I played the piano. (7) He said do you want to see the upstairs so I said alright. (8) We went upstairs and then he took me to Stan's bedroom. (9) He then started kissing me. (10) While we were kissing we made our way to the bed and laid down. (11) We kissed for a couple of minutes and he started to unbutton my blouse. (12) Then he pulled my blouse off, undid my bra and took it off. (13) He then undid my pants. (14) I started feeling uncomfortable and tried to button them back up. (15) I said I would like to go back to the party, I started to sit up and he said no the party is here. (16) My heart was pounding and I kept trying to get up and he kept pushing me down. (17) I said no, no, I want to go. (18) He then started to finger me and I went limp. (19) He said so that's the way you're going to be now. (20)He got off me and I got up and got dressed. (21) I went to the door, opened it to leave and he shut the light off and then grabbed me around the neck and pulled me back on the bed. (22) I pulled away and screamed loud. (23) He pushed my head on the bed so I couldn't scream. (24) He twisted my neck. (25) He said, "I swear to God I'll kill you, drop you in a body bag in Philly and no one would ever know. (26) He pulled my pants off. (27) I was just crying and saying no, please don't hurt me. (28) He punched me about four times. (29) I told him I couldn't breathe. (30) Then he rolled me on my back and I felt him push his penis against me. (31) Then he put it in me and I started crying oh God, oh God.

In Sentence 2, the victim used the Text Bridge "then" creating an information gap from the time Gerry massaged her shoulders to the time he asked her if she wanted to see the house. In Sentence 4, the victim used the Text

Bridge "then," creating an information gap from the time they went through the kitchen to the time they went down the hall. In Sentence 8, the victim used the Text Bridge "then" creating an information gap from the time they went upstairs to the time Gerry took her to Stan's room. In Sentence 12, the victim used the Text Bridge "then" creating an information gap from the time he started to unbutton her blouse to the time Gerry pulled her blouse off. In Sentence 13, the victim used the Text Bridge "then" creating an information gap from the time Gerry took the victim's blouse off to the time he undid her pants. In Sentence 18, the victim used the Text Bridge "then" creating an information gap from the time the victim said she wanted to go to the time when Gerry started to finger her. In Sentence 20, the victim used the Text Bridge "then" creating an information gap from the time Gerry shut the light off to the time he grabbed the victim around her neck. In Sentence 23, the victim used the Text Bridge "so" creating an information gap from the time Gerry pushed the victim's head on the bed to the time she could not scream. In Sentence 30, the victim used the Text Bridge "then" creating an information gap from the time the victim told Gerry that she could not breathe to the time he rolled her on her back. In Sentence 31, the victim used the Text Bridge "then," creating an information gap from the time the victim felt Gerry push his penis against her to the time Gerry put his penis inside the victim.

The victim's extensive use of Text Bridges does not necessarily indicate deception. For whatever reason, she edited her story. Text Bridges indicate where in the victim's story she intentionally or unintentionally withheld information. The interviewer could now go back and conduct a Micro-Action Interview to fill in the missing information. Clearly, the interviewer could obtain significantly more information from the victim using Text Bridges and the Micro-Action Interview, information that may have otherwise not come to light. The victim reported her rape to the police. Gerry was later arrested for rape, found guilty, and was sentenced to nine years in prison. When I was writing my comments on the rape victim's statement, (refer to the challenge I posed to the readers on page 64.) I initially used the word "alleged" to avoid creating the Primacy Effect in the readers' minds. Thereafter, I referred to the writer as a victim because I knew that she told the truth and that Gerry was sentenced to prison. The Word Clue "victim" signaled to the readers that I considered the writer to be a victim and that her written statement was truthful. To maintain neutrality, I should have referred to the writer of the statement as "the writer." I subconsciously referred to the writer as a victim because I knew the outcome of the case. The Word Clue "victim" unbeknownst to me revealed my true thoughts.

The following example demonstrates how Text Bridges revealed that a person who the police thought was a witness was really a codefendant in the brutal rape and murder of Teresa Halbach. Brendan Dassey, a 16-year-old boy from Wisconsin, was invited by his uncle, Steven Avery, to go to his trailer to help him burn some refuse in an open pit in his uncle's back yard, which was adjacent to a junkyard owned by his uncle. While burning the refuse, Dassey saw a toe protruding from the pile of burning trash. The toe belonged to Halbach. Avery later confessed that he invited Halbach to his trailer to photograph a vehicle for a car-advertising magazine. When Halbach arrived, Avery restrained her in his bedroom and raped and murdered her. Shortly thereafter, Avery invited Dassey to the trailer to help him burn some refuse.

On February 27, 2006, police investigators interviewed Dassey. At this point, they considered Dassey a witness. Dassey provided the following written statement.

> (1) I got off the bus at 3:45 and seen her Jeep. (2) Then I went in my house and played PlayStation 2 for about three hours and then I eat at 8:00 and I watch TV and then got a phone call from Stephen, if I wanted to come over to have a fire and I did and he told me to bring the golf cart, and I did. (3) So then we went driving around the yard and got to pick up the stuff around the house. (4) Then we dropped the seats by the fire and went to get the wood and the cabinet and then went back to throw the seat on the fire and then we waited for it to go down and throw on the wood and cabinet. (5) Then I seen the toes before we throw the wood and the cabinet on the fire. (6) When we did that he seen me and I seen the toes. (7) He told me not to say anything and he told me that he stabbed her in the stomach in the pit and he took the knife and put it under the seat in her Jeep.

Based on Dassey's use of Text Bridges, he created information gaps in the following places:

1. In Sentence 2 from the time saw he saw Halbach's Jeep until the time he went into the house;
2. In Sentence 2 from the time he played PlayStation 2 until he ate;
3. In Sentence 2 from the time he watched TV until the time Stephen Steven telephoned;
4. In Sentence 3 from the time he arrive at Stephen's trailer until the time he went driving around the backyard;
5. In Sentence 3 from the time they picked up the stuff around the house until they dropped the seats by the fire;
6. In Sentence 4 from the time they went to get the wood and cabinet until they threw the seat on the fire;
7. In Sentence 4 from the time they throw the seat on the fire until the fire went down;

8. In Sentence 4 from the time they throw the wood and cabinet on the fire until he saw Halbach's toes;
9. In Sentence 5 from the time he saw Halbach's toes until the time they threw the wood and cabinet on the fire;
10. In Sentence 5 from the time they threw the wood and cabinet on the fire until the time Steven saw Dassey looking at Halbach's toes; and
11. In Sentence 6 from the time they throw the wood and the cabinet on the fire to the time Steven put the knife under the seat of Halbach's Jeep.

Text bridges signal missing information. If Dassey was, in fact, a witness, the investigator would have known where in Dassey's written statement he intentionally or unintentionally withheld information. The investigator could have conducted a Micro-Action Interview to obtain the missing information. The combination of Text Bridges and the Mirco-Action Interview allows investigators to obtain information they might not have otherwise obtained. In this case, a Micro-Action Interview would have revealed Dassey's complicity in the rape and murder of Halbach. In addition to the Text Bridges, a tense change occurred in the second sentence. Dassey used the present tense "eat" and "watch" instead of the past tense "ate" and "watched," which signals deception.

Based on subsequent evidence, the investigators determined that Dassey was an accomplice in Halbach's murder. Dassey was interviewed several times. During these interviews, Dassey admitted his guilt. The prosecutor offered Dassey a plea agreement that included testifying against his uncle. Dassey initially agreed to cooperate with the prosecution. On May 13, 2006, investigators reinterviewed Dassey to obtain additional information to support a search warrant. During this interview, Dassey provided the following verbal statement. Based on Dassey's use of Text Bridges in his truthful statement, he still intentionally or unintentionally withheld information. Again, the investigator could have obtained full disclosure using the combination of Text Bridges and the Micro-Action Interview. Dassey's verbal narrative was transcribed as follows:

Well, I came home off the bus and then walked home into the house and I played PlayStation 2 until five o'clock, called, called my friend and watched TV and then at 6:00 o'clock I got a phone call from Blaine's boss and I told him that Blaine was going trick-or-treating and at 7:00 o'clock I got a phone call from Steven to see if I wanted to come over to the bonfire. I had told him I would and then while I was getting ready, he called again and seein' when I was, what was taking me so long and so I went over there. He went to go pick up some stuff around the yard, and then after that we, he asked me to come in the house cuz he wanted to show me somethin'. And he showed me that she was laying on the bed . . . her hands were roped up to the bed and that her legs were cuffed. And then he told me ta have sex with her, and so I did because I thought I was not gonna to get away from 'em cuz he was too strong, so did what he said and after that, he untied her and uncuffed her and then he brought her outside and before he went outside, he told me to grab her clothes in her shoes. So we went inta the garage and before she before she went out, when before he took her outside, he tied up her hands and feet and then was in the garage and he stabbed her and then he told me to. And, after that he wanted to make sure that she was dead or somethin' so he shot her five times, and while he was doing that I wasn't looking because I can't watch that stuff. So I was standing by the big door in the garage, and then after that, he took her outside and we put her on the fire and we used her clothes to clean up the some of the blood. And, when we put her in the fire, and her clothes, we were standing right by the garage, to wait for it to get down so we threw some of that stuff on it after it went down. And then, 'bout 9:00 o'clock my mom came home and she called Steven on his cell phone to tell him that I was supposed to be home by 10:00 o'clock, and she asked Steven if I had a sweater on. So while we waited for the fire to go down, by the time it did get down, it was probably close to 10 o'clock so he told me to go home, so I did, and then got in the house and I talked to my mom for a little bit, then went to bed.

A side-by-side comparison of Dassey's written statement provided on February 27, 2006 and his verbal statement on May 13, 2006 reveals that he lied by omission and used Text Bridges to circumvent the information gaps. The facts in both statements are consistent. The only difference is the information Dassey deliberately withheld. Text Bridges are in bold. Information mentioned in the first statement that was not mentioned in second statement is in parentheses and information provided in the second interview but not provided in the first interview is in parentheses. Note the large information gap in the first statement. Dassey used a series of Text Bridge to cover up his participation in the rape and murder of Halbach.

Text Bridges are difficult to defeat because grammar rules are ingrained in the human psyche, and speaking and writing become automatic responses. People typically do not think about grammar rules when they communicate, especially when they speak. Liars use most of their cognitive capacity to control their nonverbal behaviors, remember what they said or did not say, and to monitor the target of the line, but give little or no thought to the grammar structure of their sentences.

Statement of Brendan Dassey (Written) Mishicot High School February 27, 2007	Statement of Brendan Dassey (Verbal) Sheboygan County Sheriff's Department May 13, 2006
I got off the bus (at 3:45 and seen her Jeep.) **Then** I went in my house and played Play Station 2 for about three hours and **then** I eat at 8:00 and I watch TV and **then** got a phone call from Stephen, if I wanted to come over to have a fire (and I did and he told me to bring the golf cart, and I did.) **So then** we went driving around the yard and got to pick up the stuff around the house. **Then**	Well, I came home off the bus and **then** walked home into the house and I played Play Station 2 until five o'clock, (called, called my friend) and watched TV and **then** (at 6:00 o'clock I got a phone call from Blaine's boss and I told him that Blaine was going trick-or-treating and) at 7:00 o'clock I got a phone call from Stephen to see if I wanted to come over to the bonfire. (I had told him I would and) **then while** (I was getting ready, he called again and seein' when I was, what was taking me so long and) **so** (I went over there.) He went to go pick up some stuff around the yard, and **then after that** (we, he asked me to come in the house

cuz he wanted to show me somethin'. And he showed me that she was laying on the bed, ta her hands were roped up to the bed and that her legs were cuffed. And)

then

(he told me ta have sex with her, and)

so

(I did because I thought I was not gonna to get away from 'em cuz he was too strong,)

so

(did what he said and)

after that,

(he untied her and uncuffed her and)

then

(he brought her outside and)

before

(he went outside, he told me to grab her clothes in her shoes.)

So

(we went inta the garage and)

before she before

(she went out,)

when before

(he took her outside, he tied up her hands and feet and)

then

(was in the garage and he stabbed her and)

then

(he told me to. And,)

after that

	(he wanted to make sure that she was dead or somethin')
	so
	(he shot her five times, and)
	while
	(he was doing that I wasn't looking because I can't watch that stuff.)
	So
	(I was standing by the big door in the garage, and)
	then after that,
	(he took her outside and we put her on the fire and we used her clothes ta clean up the some of the blood. And,)
	when
	(we put her in the fire, and her clothes, we were standing right by the garage, to wait for it to get down)
	so
we dropped the seats by the fire and went to get the wood and the cabinet and	
then	
went back to throw the seat on the fire and	we threw some of that stuff on it
then	
(we waited for it to go down and throw on the wood and cabinet.)	**after**
Then	
(I seen the toes)	(it went down. And)
before	**then,**
(we throw the wood and the cabinet on the fire.)	

<table>
<tr>
<td>

When

(we did that he seen me and I seen the toes. He told me not to say anything and he told me that he stabbed her in the stomach in the pit and he took the knife and put it under the seat in her Jeep.

</td>
<td>

('bout 9:00 o'clock my mom came home and she called Stephen on his cell phone to tell him that I was supposed to be home by 10:00 o'clock, and she asked Steven if I had a sweater on.)

So while

(we waited for the fire to go down, by the time it did get down, it was probably close to 10 o'clock)

so

(he told me to go home,)

so

(I did, and)

then

(got in the house and I talked to my mom for a little bit,)

then

(went to bed.)

</td>
</tr>
</table>

SPONTANEOUS NEGATIONS

When people respond to open-ended questions, they should describe the actions they took rather than the actions they did not take. A Spontaneous Negation occurs when people report activities that they did not do rather than activities that they did. Spontaneous Negations differ from negations in that negations are in response to direct questions. For example, "Did you rob the bank?" a deceptive person as well as a truthful person would answer, "No, I did not rob the bank." Spontaneous Negations occur during narrative answers or in response to open-ended questions. In the earlier referenced grand jury testimony of President Clinton, he used the Spontaneous Negation "I wasn't trying to give you a cute answer to that," which indicates the high probability that he was trying to provide a cute answer to the question.

In the interview of the rape and murder suspect referenced earlier in the book, the suspect used a Spontaneous Negation.

> **INTERVIEWER:** Did you want to kiss her?
> **SUSPECT:** I . . . I . . . I didn't feel . . . I didn't remember feeling any attraction towards her, so…

The interviewer asked a yes or no question, but the suspect did not give a yes or no answer. If the suspect answered, "I did not want to kiss her," the answer would not be a Spontaneous Negation because the answer would have been a direct response to a direct question. However, the suspect did not provide a direct answer. Instead, he answered with two Spontaneous Negations, "I didn't feel and I didn't remember."

My research showed that the use of Spontaneous Negations indicate a high probability of deception. The study examined the predictive value of grammar structures to differentiate truthful written narratives from deceptive written narratives. Native English speakers watched a digital presentation of a person shoplifting an item from a convenience store and wrote truthful and deceptive narratives regarding the shoplifting event. Of the 608 truthful and deceptive narratives collected in the study, 60 percent contained Spontaneous Negations and 90 percent of those were used in deceptive narratives. In other words, in nine out of ten times when Spontaneous Negations were used, they were used in deceptive narratives. Therefore, the presence of a Spontaneous Negation in open narrative statements or answers indicates a high probability that the speaker or writer is being deceptive.

The following exchange took place between an FBI Special Agent and a Russian exchange student attending a Southern California University.

> **SPECIAL AGENT:** I see that you've been in the United States for eight months. I hope you had time to do some sightseeing.
> **STUDENT:** Yes, I did. I visited California, Utah, and Texas, but I never went to New York.

The use of the Spontaneous Negation "I never went to New York" indicates a high probability that the student, in fact, visited New York. Of the 47 states the student did not visit, he singled out New York as a state he did not visit for a reason. A follow-up investigation revealed that the student went to New York and met with a Russian KGB officer. The KGB officer directed the exchange student to collect information about the super computer at the university where he attended. The student betrayed his intelligence gathering activities by the use of a Spontaneous Negation.

Chapter 5

THE MICRO-ACTION INTERVIEW

Text Bridges locate withheld information. If the interviewer deems the withheld information important, the Micro-Action Interview closes the information gap by methodically accounting for all the interviewee's time and behaviors. Interviewers can use the Micro-Action Interview to extract more detailed information from witnesses and reveal deception in both social and professional settings. The Micro-Action Interview differs from other interviewing techniques in that interviewers ask the simple question, "What happened next?" Innocent people convey their stories; guilty people put themselves in the psychological vise.

The systematic narrowing of the information gap acts like a psychological vise. The unique feature of the Micro-Action Interview is that honest people do not experience stress because they tell the truth; however, liars place themselves in a self-tightening vise. The psychological pressure increases to the point where liars cross the fight/flight threshold. Crossing the fight/flight threshold causes physiological changes, which are difficult to control. Consequently, guilty people leak nonverbal and paralinguistic indicators of deception. These nonverbal and paralinguistic cues provide interviewers with immediate feedback as to the veracity of interviewees. Deceptive indicators signal the interviewer to continue the interview. Conversely, innocent people remain relatively calm and answer the questions as presented. Although innocent people may find the line of questioning tedious, they will not typically emit verbal or nonverbal indicators of deception. The psychological vise provides interviewers with immediate feedback as to the veracity of the interviewees. Truthful interviewees simply relate facts while deceptive interviewees become nervous and try to convince the interviewers of the "truth."

The Micro-Action Interview begins at the point just before the first Text Bridge. The interviewer should anchor the interviewee. Anchoring simply means having the interviewee describe his or her position just prior to the Text Bridge. After anchoring the interviewee, the interviewer should ask the

100

simple question "What happened next?" The interviewee will typically provide additional information and use another Text Bridge to circumvent the withheld information. The interviewer should go back to just before the newly added Text Bridge, anchor the interviewee, and ask, "What happened next?" The interviewer should continue this process until the information gap closes or until the interviewee shows signs of deception. If deception is indicated, the interviewer can either continue closing the information gap or use alternate interviewing techniques. Eventually, the information gap becomes so small that guilty people can no longer find words in the English language to bridge the gap. At this point, the interviewer should pose a Presumptive Statement. A Presumptive Statement merely affirms the obvious. For example, a suspect was questioned regarding the mysterious disappearance of his wife. The interviewer could make the Presumptive Statement, "So, you were pretty angry with your wife." The interviewer could also make a more aggressive Presumptive Statement, "I can understand why you didn't want your wife around anymore." In most instances, guilty people admit their guilt at this juncture. In the event guilty people remain steadfast, interviewers can employ additional interviewing techniques.

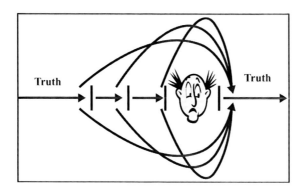

Repeatedly asking the question, "What happened next" can detract from the interviewing process, so investigators should intersperse some self-deprecating remarks such as: "I'm sorry. I zoned out for a second. Let's go back to (the point just prior to the last Text Bridge);" "My brain is not processing as fast as you are talking, Can we back up to (the point just prior to the last Text Bridge)?;" or "I'm confused; you said you were (refer to the action just prior to the last Text Bridge).

In the previously described illustration, police recovered a woman's body several years after she disappeared. A detective interviewed the dead woman's husband. The following exchange took place during an interview between the detective and the suspect:

DETECTIVE: Tell me about the last time you saw your wife?
SUSPECT: (1) I recall that, ah, it was one evening probably 11 o'clock.

(2) We were both in bed and we had not gone to sleep yet and she got out of bed. (3) I, ah, thought she was probably going to the bathroom and then I hear the, ah, front door close and I waited for a minute to see what she was doing and then I hear the car start and I look out the window and see the car disappearing around the corner and that's the last time I ever saw her.

The suspect used the Text Bridge "then" two times in Sentence 3. The first Text Bridge created an information gap from the time his wife got out of bed until the time the suspect heard the front door close. The second Text Bridge created an information gap from the time the suspect heard the door close until the time he heard the car start. These two Text Bridges form a double span Text Bridge from the time the suspect's wife got out of bed until he heard the car start, which creates a large information gap during a critical time. The sentence just before the Text Bridge reads, "I, ah, thought she was probably going to the bathroom and then I hear the, ah, front door close." Note also that the interviewee used the present tense in this sentence, adding another indication of deception at a critical point in his statement. The interviewer should begin the Micro-Action Interview at the point when the suspect and his wife got into bed. Intuitively, this is a good place to begin the Micro-Action Interview because if something happened to cause the suspect's wife to get out of bed other than her need to use the bathroom, then that would be a significant event. The interviewer should ask the suspect to describe his and his wife's actions from the time they got into bed until the time she got out of bed. The interviewer should obtain details such as were they sitting up or lying down on the bed. If they were lying down, what side of the bed did each of them occupy. Were they under the covers or lying on top of the bedspread? Once the interviewer establishes the suspect and his wife's physical orientation, the interviewer should ask the question, "What happened next?" The suspect will likely provide a few details and then use a Text Bridge to bridge the shrinking information gap. The interviewer should go back to just before the second text bridge and ask the suspect, "What happened next?" The interviewer should continue this process until the suspect accounts for all of his time and all of his actions from the time he and his wife got into bed until the time she got out of bed.

The following excerpt from a transcript of an interview between an accident investigator and a driver demonstrates the application of the Micro-Action Interview:

INVESTIGATOR: Describe what happened.
DRIVER: I looked up saw the car coming toward me and then I tried to avoid hitting the car.

(The Push-Pull Word "looked up" indicates that the driver was not looking at the road when the accident happened.)

INVESTIGATOR: You saw the car coming toward you. What happened next?

DRIVER: I put both hands on the wheel and then tried to avoid hitting the car.

(The Word Qualifier "both hands" indicates that the driver did not have both hands on the wheel when the accident occurred. "Tried" is a Stopped-Action Word that indicates something prevented the driver from avoiding hitting the other car.)

INVESTIGATOR: Let's back up. You put both your hands on the wheel. What happened next?

DRIVER: I put my foot on the brake and then the car went out of control.

INVESTIGATOR: I'm sorry. I must have missed something. You put your foot on the brake. What happened next?

DRIVER: The brake didn't work and then I pushed harder but the car didn't slow down.

INVESTIGATOR: I'm a little confused. You pushed harder on the brake but the car didn't slow down. What happened next?

DRIVER: I tried to kick the cell phone out of the way. It must have fallen down when I grabbed the wheel.

INVESTIGATOR: So, you were talking on your cell phone when the accident occurred.

(Based on the information gained from the Micro-action interview in conjunction with Push-Pull Words, a Stopped-Action Word, and Word Qualifiers, the investigator tested his hypothesis using a presumptive statement.)

DRIVER: Yeah.

INVESTIGATOR: You dropped your cell phone, tried to retrieve it, and lost control of the car?

(The Investigator followed the driver's admission with a follow-up Presumptive Statement.)

DRIVER: I just took my eyes off the road for a second. I thought it was safe to pick up my phone.

(The Micro-Action Interview forced the driver to reveal the real cause of the accident.)

Chapter 6

TESTING FOR DECEPTION

Several techniques signal the possibility of deception. The following is a short review of some of those techniques. These techniques are not 100 percent successful at detecting deception, but they do provide investigators with some indication of truthfulness or deception.

POOR MAN'S POLYGRAPH

The Poor Polygraph consists of several techniques that indicate deception. The Poor Man's Polygraph provides indicators of deception, not proof of deception. Detecting deception is difficult because truthful people sometimes emit verbal and nonverbal cues that indicate deception, and deceptive people sometimes emit verbal and nonverbal clues that indicate truthfulness. Investigators must exercise discretion when using the Poor Man's Polygraph.

WHY SHOULD I BELIEVE YOU?

Investigators should ask interviewees, "Why should I believe you?" This forces interviewees to articulate the reasons why investigators should believe the story. Truthful people reply, "Because I'm telling the truth" or some derivation thereof. Liars experience difficulty saying "Because I am telling the truth" and, instead, offer various other responses. The following exchange demonstrates this technique.

INTERVIEWER: You said you were not responsible for cooking the books?

INTERVIEWEE: I did not cook the books.
INTERVIEWER: Sir, believe it or not people have lied to me in the past. I really don't know who you are so why should I believe you?
INTERVIEWEE: Why would I lie?
INTERVIEWER: Sir, I didn't ask you why you would lie. I asked you why I should believe you. Why should I believe you?
INTERVIEWEE: I don't know.
INTERVIEWER: If you don't know why I should believe you, then I can only assume that you are lying.

The investigator called the interviewee a liar. If the interviewee is telling the truth, he should object and go on the offensive. Deceptive people will typically go on the defensive.

PARALLEL LIE

A follow-up to the "Why Should I Believe You?" technique is the Parallel Lie technique. Investigators do not repeat the same question as in the "Why Should I Believe You?" technique but rather, ask the interviewees about their responses.

> **INTERVIEWER:** Sir, when you told me that you didn't cook the books, were you lying?

Truthful people have no problem processing this type of question, but liars often hesitate because they not only have to think about how the question was asked but they must also take time to formulate the appropriate answer. When interviewees hesitate, investigators should make the presumptive, "I knew you were lying." or a more benign presumptive such as, "I didn't think you were being truthful." Indirectly, investigators tell interviewees that their stories are not believable. Honest people will protest to some degree after being called liars and often display emphatic gestures such as finger pointing or slapping a table. Dishonest people tend not to protest after being called liars. Observing the interviewees' responses to the question is more important than their answers.

YOU CHOOSE

Investigators can test for veracity by posing the question, "Do you really want to get away with this?" If the interviewee answers "Yes," the investigator should respond, "That's why I'm here, to stop you from getting away with this." If the interviewee answers, "No," the investigator should respond, "That's why I'm here, to stop you from getting away with this." Liars, when faced with two choices, tend to pick one of the choices presented because it is easier to pick one of the choices rather than coming up with an alternate answer. Truthful people do not feel restricted to the two choices provided and typically respond, "Get away with what?"

DIRECT QUESTIONS

Asking a Yes or No question can test veracity. If interviewees choose not to answer "Yes" or "No," then they must go to the Land of Is, which suggests deception. A "Yes" plus mitigating information is a Yes answer and a "No" plus mitigating information is a No answer.

INVOKING SECONDARY SOURCES

Liars often feel the need to employ a Secondary Source to bear witness to their testimony. Secondary Sources are often inanimate objects incapable of testifying on the behalf of the interviewee. Liars will also invoke God's name to bear witness to their story. Rarely do liars invoke the names of real people who can be interviewed by investigators. For example:

INTERVIEWEE: I swear on a stack of bibles.
INTERVIEWEE: I swear on my mother's grave.
INTERVIEWEE: As God is my witness.

WELL . . .

Beginning an answer to a direct question with the word *well* indicates that the person responding is going to provide an answer that the person who asked the question is not expecting. Interviewers should allow interviewees to complete their answers to prevent them from discovering this technique and altering their subsequent responses.

PARENT: Did you brush your teeth?

The child knows the parent expects the answer, "Yes." Since the child did not brush his teeth, he knows he cannot provide the expected "Yes" answer, so he begins his response with the word *well.*

> **CHILD:** Well . . . .
> **PARENT:** Go brush your teeth.

Consider the following example:

> **EMPLOYEE:** Did I get the promotion?
> **EMPLOYER:** Well . . . .

There is a high probability that the employee did not get the promotion because the employer began his answer with the word "Well." The employee expected the answer "Yes." The employer is about to give an answer to the employee that the employer knows the employee is not expecting.

Chapter 7

WRITTEN COMMUNICATIONS

Written and oral communications differ; nonetheless, the writer or speaker must use the same grammar structures to communicate. Written communications are more precise because the written word lacks the nonverbal cues that attend oral exchanges. Writers cannot monitor the reader for nonverbal cues that indicate the reader's understanding or acceptance of the written communication. Delayed feedback slows the communication process because a reader must seek out the writer to render an opinion or obtain clarification. What is written is written. Sarcasm and humor are more difficult to communicate in written correspondence because written messages lack nonverbal and paralinguistic cues. Evidence of this is the widespread use of emotive symbols that accompany text messages and emails. These emotive symbols insure against miscommunication. The written word is permanent. Writers cannot dispute what they wrote. Consequently, written communications are more formal. Writers have more time to think about what they write and often make corrections or deletions.

Readers can analyze written documents more carefully because they have the luxury of rereading the documents as often as necessary to understand the message. Readers can develop hypotheses, set the documents aside, think about what was written and, at a later time, could return to the documents for clarity or affirmation of hypotheses. Although nonverbal cues are not available to readers, punctuation and formatting provide valuable insights into a person's age, education level, behavioral characteristics, and socioeconomatic level.

PUNCTUATION

Punctuation represents the nonverbal cues for written documents. The lack of punctuation or the misuse of punctuation could signal level of education, age, or foreign heritage. The overuse of exclamation points, capitalization, or underlining could indicate the writer's emotional state. Angry writers will often begin a document using correct grammar and punctuation. The closer they get to the heart of their anger, punctuation becomes erratic and words are often missing because the writer's mind is working faster than he can write. Sentences that do not make sense or violate grammar rules indicate the possibility that the writer has a mental deficiency or speaks English as a second language. Extensive writing in the margins of the paper is another measure of mental stability. Smaller marginal notes might also indicate that the writer left something out of the narrative that must be inserted to support an earlier assertion. Refer to Logical Sequence of Events discussed earlier in this book.

CAPITALIZATION

Capitalization or lack of capitalization of words can be significant. Writers typically capitalize entire words to emphasize the meaning of those words or to express emotion. Words that are initially capitalized but later in the written narrative are written without being capitalized usually indicate that the writer diminished the status of the word. For example, if a person writes, "I went to the baseball game with my brother Robert. I enjoyed the game, but robert disagreed with the outcome of the game." The writer initially capitalized Robert's name but later did not capitalize his name. Within the context of the sentence, the writer diminished the status of Robert because he disagreed with the outcome of the game. Diminishing people or places often signals a Change in Perspective (refer to *Change in Perspective* discussed earlier in this book – see index).

STRIKEOUTS

Strikeouts can reveal the writer's true intentions. A writer jots something down, changes his mind, strikes it out, and revises his sentence. For some reason, the writer thought what he wrote was inappropriate, sent the wrong message, or created the wrong impression. In many instances, the strikeout reveals the writer's true intentions or thoughts, especially if the writer is being deceptive. Strikeouts should be examined closely.

FEWER WORDS

Research has shown that liars use fewer words and their statements contain less relevant information when they deceive. Liars tend to use fewer words when describing fabricated events because a story with fewer words is easier to remember than a story with a large number of words. Liars tend to keep descriptors to a minimum because they did not experience the event firsthand and possess fewer facts about the topic of their deception. In the event liars are asked to repeat their stories, fewer facts are easier to command than stories filled with a large amount of fabricated details.

EXTRANEOUS DETAILS

Liars typically include Extraneous Details in their written narratives. Extraneous Details can be used as filler to make up for the lack of details the liar has regarding the topic she is talking about. Extraneous Details can be used to cover for information the liar wants to withhold. Extraneous Details can also be used to manage the perception of the reader. In this instance, liars usually shout their message in an effort to convince the reader of something rather than merely conveying information.

FIRST SENTENCE

People begin their narratives where they logically think the incident occurred, which is often a different place from where the interviewer thinks the incident began. Investigators should instruct interviewees to begin their narratives from the beginning. An investigator should say something to the effect: "Tell me everything that you did on that day from the time you got up this morning until the time you went to sleep" or "Tell me everything you did from the time you got up this morning until now." Writers often ask, "Where should I begin?" The investigator should respond, "At the beginning, of course." Directing the writer to write about everything he did on the day of the incident, allows the writer to establish a baseline before the incident and after the incident against which to compare the description of the incident. Establishing a baseline is yet another means to measure veracity. Writers often begin their statements after the incident occurred. This allows the writer to write the truth without having to obfuscate or omit information.

A bank teller's drawer was $1,000 short when she balanced on Monday evening. The bank investigator asked the teller to write a statement regarding the missing money. The first sentence in the teller statement was:

Starting Saturday December 6, 2003, I was cashing a lot of check and cash withdrawals for large amount [sic] of money, and customers didn't want small bills which I told them at that time I only have 20's first they would say it's ok, then they would change their minds: so I was doing a lot of cash exchange between teller and I also got some from the vault.

The second sentence from the teller's statement read, Then On Monday Dec. 8, 2003 I was depositing the night drops. . . . The teller began her statement with "Starting Saturday December 6, 2003" because in her mind that was the beginning of the sequence of events that lead to the missing money. The teller's activities starting Saturday were important to her and should be explored in detail by the interviewer. The investigation revealed that on Saturday, the teller gave her boyfriend, who was posing as a customer, an extra $1,000 when he cashed a $100 check. The money was not missing on Monday as the bank investigator thought but, rather, on Saturday.

The second sentence supports the hypothesis that the teller stole the money on Saturday. In the second sentence, the teller used the crossed out Text Bridge "Then" creating an information gap from the time she conducted transactions on Saturday until the time she deposited night drops on Monday. Logically, the second sentence in the teller's statement should have been the first sentence in her statement if she stole the money on Monday. The writer began her story on Saturday because in her mind she knew that there was a connection between the events that occurred on Saturday and the discovery of the missing money on Monday evening. She attempted to cover her crime with the inadvertent use of the Text Bridge "then." The writer provided the clues that lead to the resolution of the investigation.

In the following example, the writer began his statement after the incident occurred to avoid addressing his whereabouts when the incident occurred. The writer was on a cruise ship. He met a woman in the lounge and stuck up a conversation. At the end of the evening, the writer made sexual overtures, which the woman spurned. She left the lounge, and walked on deck to get some fresh air. The woman was never seen again. After a thorough search of the ship, the ship's captain presumed that the woman either accidently fell overboard or committed suicide. The writer was the last known person to see the woman alive and was asked to write a statement. The first sentence read: "When I first went on the deck at 2200 on 08 FEB 2006, I noticed the security camera covered, an empty overturned glass on the deck, the purse, and scattered papers."

The writer used the Text Bridge "When" creating an information gap from an unknown point before he went on deck to the time he went on deck and noticed the items. The writer also used the Push-Pull Word *first.* In order to have a first, there must be a second, which suggests the writer went on deck at least two times. The subsequent investigation revealed that the first time the writer went on deck he strangled the woman, threw her body overboard, and scattered her personal items on the deck to make her disappearance look like a suicide. The combination of the Text Bridge "When" and the Push-Pull Word "first" alerted the investigator to the possibility that the writer withheld information and began his statement after the murder occurred to cover the fact that he killed the woman.

SOCIAL INTRODUCTIONS

A writer's first reference to a person in a written statement is similar to a social introduction. If the writer does not properly introduce a person, then the likelihood increases that problems exist between the writer and the person he introduced. Avinom Sapis states that "before the reader would be able to say 'Lisa' is the writer's wife, the writer has to refer to her as 'my wife'" in his written statement. If the writer does not do so, then Lisa may be the writer's wife in reality but not a wife in language. In this example, the relationship between the writer and his wife should be further explored to determine why the writer did not properly introduce Lisa.

OBTAINING WRITTEN STATEMENTS

Obtaining written statements typically presents greater resistance than obtaining oral interviews. An interviewee can always deny what he said during an oral interview because there is no permanent record of the exchange. For the reasons stated earlier, written statements are easier to analyze. Several techniques provide an incentive for the interviewee to write a statement prior to the interview.

SEND A FAX/EMAIL

Interviewees are more likely to provide written statements if they are permitted to have as much time as they want to write their statements and can write their statements in the comfort and privacy of their own homes. To further motivate the interviewees to write statements the interviewer could say, "I'll fax/email you a few questions I would like you to answer. Take as much time as you want and fax/email me your answers. If you thoroughly answer the questions, you may not have to come to my office for a personal interview." If the interviewee is guilty, he or she will be more likely to write a statement to avoid a face-to-face interview. The guilty person may feel that given unlimited time, he or she can construct a deceptive statement that will go undetected. Even if the interviewee engages a friend or a lawyer to review the statement, the truth cannot be obfuscated or omitted because friends and lawyers must use the same grammar structures as does the interviewee.

IN PERSON

When an interviewee arrives, ask him to write a statement describing the circumstances surrounding the incident. Instruct the interviewee to write down everything that he did from the time that he woke up on the day of the incident until the time he went to sleep that evening. When the interviewee completes the statement, allow him to take a break. During the break, the interviewer can conduct a PNA of the written narrative and use the newly acquired information to exploit the interviewee during the subsequent interview. Some interviewees will ask the interviewer where to start the statement. The interviewer should respond, "Write down everything that happened. Start from the beginning."

EDUCATIONAL LEVEL

A writer's educational level can be determined by correct punctuation, spelling, and word usage. An uneducated person will often misspell words and incorrectly punctuate sentences. Uneducated writers often use words incorrectly in an effort to appear more educated. A more precise method of determining a writer's educational level is to scan the written document into a word processing program with a grammar checker feature. Most grammar checker features evaluate the narrative to determine the grade level of the writer. One common scale is the Flesch-Kincaid Grade Level Scale. The Flesch-Kincaid Grade Level Scale rates text on a standard U.S. grade level. Most educated people write at the seventh to eighth grade level.

Chapter 8

ORAL COMMUNICATIONS

Oral communications are more difficult to analyze because the spoken word is fleeting. Interviewers must train themselves to quickly identify the grammar structures and words that signal the probability of deception. Once deception is suspected, interviewers must immediately identify the appropriate techniques to uncover the truth. This skill is acquired through practice. Fortunately, people can practice their PNA skills every time they communicate with another person, listen to politicians speak, or simply watch television or movies. The key to analyzing oral communications is listening. During conversations, people attend more to what they just said or what they are about to say than to what the other person said or is saying. A person cannot determine the veracity or others if he does not even know what the other person said.

The Communication Loop serves as a blueprint for communication in both personal and professional settings. During practice sessions, interviewers should deliberately go through each step in the Communication Loop. At first, sequencing through the Communication Loop will seem slow and awkward but with practice, sequencing speeds will increase until it becomes an automatic response. When sequencing becomes an automatic response, interviewers will increase the probability of detecting deception and understanding the behavioral characteristics of the people with whom they speak.

COMMUNICATION LOOP*

Interviewers require good listening skills, but good listening skills alone do not guarantee success. Successful interviewers listen to what people say, analyze what they said, and exploit the newly acquired information within the context of the interviewee's world. These principles provide the framework

---

* The Communication Loop concept was developed by Randy Marcoz and further refined during conversations with the author.

for the Communication Loop. The Communication Loop, initially designed for law enforcement use, also serves as a blueprint for effective communication in social and professional settings. The Communication Loop consists of four basic components: Objective, Lead, Above the Line Actions, and Below the Line Thinking. Good interviewers can cycle through the Communication Loop in nano seconds.

Objective

Truth is the primary objective for criminal investigators. Nonlaw enforcement communication goals include information, entertainment, persuasion, and influence. The Communication Loop operates the same way during interviews and interrogations.

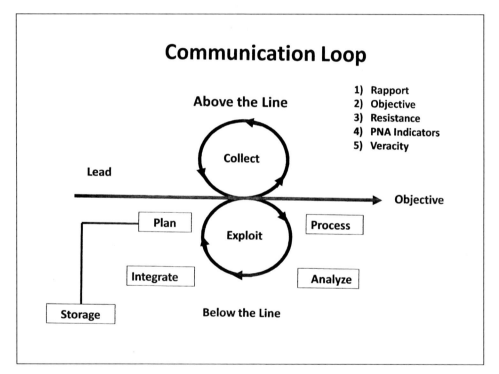

During some interviews, interviewers reach a decision point when sufficient evidence indicates that the interviews should transition to interrogations. The objective for interrogation is a confession or actionable intelligence. Conversely, in the nonlaw enforcement arena, the objective of inquiries is information. Everything the interviewer says or does should direct the interview toward the truth. Interviewers should not introduce anything into the interview that does not move the interview closer to the interview objective.

Lead

The Lead introduces the topic of the inquiry or conversation by posing an initial question or statement, which sets the tone, the direction, and the framework for the interview or conversation. The Lead plays a critical role in the interview because all else that follows hinges on the interviewee's response to the Lead question or statement. A well thought out Lead question or statement initiates the interview process and sets the course of the interview toward the interview objective.

Above the Line Actions

Interviewers collect information from Above the Line Actions. The type of information collected depends on the type of actions assigned to Above the Line Actions. The basic Above the Line Actions for most interviews include rapport, movement toward the objective, resistance, nonverbal cues, verbal cues (PNA), and veracity.

Rapport

Rapport serves as the foundation for interviews and interrogations. Interviewees provide information more readily when they like the people to whom they are speaking. Interviewers should continually monitor rapport and take time to reinforce rapport as needed. Some interviewers hesitate to ask hard questions for fear of losing rapport. Rapport functions like a savings account. Accumulated rapport allows interviewers to ask hard questions, which, in turn, depletes saved rapport. When rapport levels diminish, interviewers can discontinue asking hard questions and replenish rapport by using rapport-building techniques. After accumulating additional rapport, the interviewer can resume asking hard questions again.

Objective

Objectives vary depending on the context of the communication. Most interviews seek information or confessions. Interviewers should recognize movement toward the objective no matter how slight. Interviewers should recognize this movement and use the appropriate techniques to continue momentum toward the interview objective.

Resistance

Interviewers should monitor interviewees to determine the weakening or strengthening of their resistance to provide information. When resistance weakens, interviewers can adjust their interviewing techniques to continue to weaken resistance. When resistance increases, interviewers can strengthen rapport or try a different technique to reduce resistance. Nonverbal cues provide feedback to determine the status of rapport building and veracity. Nonverbal cues should agree with the words visitors speak.

PNA Indicators

Words mirror people's thoughts. Some mirrors reflect perfect images of what people think while others reflect distorted perceptions of a person's thoughts. To lessen distorted perceptions of an interviewee's thoughts, an interviewer must integrate himself into the interviewee's world.

Veracity

Discerning the truthfulness of interviewees is critical. When interviewees provide information, interviewers must have some degree of confidence that interviewees are truthful. Interviewers often have to rely solely on their "gut instinct" to determine veracity. While instinct is important, this book provides observable indicators of truthfulness and techniques to test veracity.

Below the Line Thinking

Below the Line Thinking allows interviewers to exploit information collected from Above the Line Actions and allows interviewers to monitor the interview to keep the interview aligned with the interview objective. Below the Line Thinking consists of four parts: Process, Analyze, Integrate, and Plan.

Process

Process simply means carefully listening to what interviewees say. Failing to Process is typically the first critical weakness in an interview. Instead of listening to what the interviewees say, most interviewers use this time to formulate their next question or statement. If interviewers do not know what the interviewees said, interviewers cannot develop effective follow-up questions or statements. Interviewers who fail to Process often lose key information that could result in the exploitation of all the available facts and information that interviewees possess.

To be more effective, interviewers should wait one to two seconds before presenting their next question or statement. Silence serves several purposes.

First, silence allows time for interviewers to Process. Second, the time lapse allows interviewees the opportunity to provide additional information, which they might not have provided had the interviewers immediately followed up with a question or statement. Witnesses and suspects alike often feel the need to fill silence gaps, especially if the interviewers nod their heads and use verbal encouragers such as "uh huh," "interesting," or "go on." Third, time lapses provide interviewers the opportunity to observe nonverbal cues. Liars often display signs of relief after they believe they successfully lied. Liars may also display nonverbal cues indicating anxiety if they think the interviewers do not believe their lies. Skepticism from interviewers often enhances this phenomenon.

Analyze

Analyze, the second step in Below the Line Thinking, requires interviewers to evaluate the information gleaned in the Process step. During the Analysis step, interviewers monitor Above the Line Actions. For example, do the interviewee's responses signal growing or diminishing rapport? Do the interviewee's verbal and nonverbal cues comport with what they said? Liars sometimes nod their heads up and down while making denials—an indication of deceit. Does an interviewee show signs of comfort or discomfort? Do the interviewee's responses move the interview closer to the stated objective? How does the information provided by the interviewee fit in with the information he or she previously provided? Does the information provided follow in logical order? Liars often relate information that does not follow in logical sequence because they often must provide support for something they previously stated.

During the Analyze step, interviewers also develop hypotheses and Competing Hypotheses about interviewees' behavioral characteristics and the information they have provided. Interviewers should seek information that either supports or contradicts newly developed hypotheses. Additionally, interviewers should develop Competing Hypotheses to avoid the "Primacy Effect." This phenomenon creates biased filters through which interviewers view interviewees. For example, if an interviewer initially believes that an interviewee is guilty, then the interviewer will tend to interpret everything that the interviewee says or does as evidence of guilt when, in fact, the evidence suggests the opposite. A Competing Hypothesis offsets the hypothesis of guilt, reducing the Primacy Effect. Competing hypotheses allow interviewers to view the words and actions of interviewees from a more neutral perspective.

Integrate

Integration, the third step in Below the Line Thinking, integrates the information derived from the Analyze step into the interviewee's world. Interviewers often view the information gained through analysis of their own world and not from the interviewee's perspective. The second critical weakness in the interview is the failure to integrate the information obtained in the Analyze step. The interviewer's perspective may significantly differ from the interviewee's perspective, especially if an interviewee possesses guilty knowledge. Other misperceptions can occur if interviewees come from one generation or culture and the interviewers represent another generation or culture. Values, morals, conduct, and a sense of right and wrong can change from one generation to the next. These differences, especially over several generations, often result in miscommunication between interviewers and the interviewees. As often as possible, interviewers should interpret the information gleaned through analysis from the interviewee's perspective. What makes sense in the interviewer's world may not make sense in the interviewee's world.

Interviewers often fall into the trap of "egocentrism" if they cannot make sense of the behaviors of the interviewees or information provided by them. Egocentrism prevents officers from viewing life from the interviewee's perspective, making an interviewee's words and actions ring false. However, the same behaviors or information when viewed from the interviewee's perspective may make sense and provide a vista from which to view their world. Incorporating analyses into the interviewee's perspective allows interviewers to form good follow-up questions or statements and to understand that the behaviors and information that once seemed disjointed now make perfect sense.

Interviewers should also consider what pressures interviewees might be experiencing. These pressures could give interviewers insights into what motivates the interviewees. If interviewers can identify an interviewee's primary and secondary motivations, the interviewer can either increase or decrease those pressures to achieve the interview objectives.

Plan

The Plan represents the final step in Below the Line Thinking. During the Plan step, interviewers select the appropriate tool to accomplish one or more of the Above the Line Actions. For example, if the analysis and integration of what the interviewee said signals diminishing rapport, then the interviewer should select the appropriate rapport-building technique to bolster rapport. If the analysis and integration of the interviewee's verbal and nonverbal cues suggests deception, then the interviewer could select a technique to test the interviewee's veracity. If the interviewer determines that rapport exists between the interviewer and the interviewee, then the interviewer should choose an interviewing tool that moves the interview toward the interview objective. In some cases, the synthesized information can be placed in Storage for future use. For example, confronting the veracity of the interviewee could be exploited more effectively later in the interview.

The Communication Loop not only serves as a good instructional model but also functions as a good tool to evaluate interviews. Instructors can use the Communication Loop as a model to teach interviewers effective interviewing and interrogation techniques. Additionally, the Communication Loop can be used to evaluate not only what went wrong during the interviews but also where the interviewers went wrong. Typically, failure occurs when interviewers only engage Above the Line Actions precluding them from exercising Below the Line Thinking. Below the Line Thinking failures most often occur in the Process and Integration steps. Simply listening to what interviewees say increases the probabilities of success. Integrating the information culled from the analysis of what the interviewees said into the interviewees' world further increases the probability of success. Interviewers can correct interview deficiencies using the Communication Loop.

The transcript of Senator Larry Craig's police interview will be examined from two perspectives. First, as an example of how interviewers can continually monitor live interviews by using the Communication Loop and second, as an example of how instructors could conduct interview postmortems to determine what went right in the interview, what went wrong in the interview, and what techniques interviewers need to learn or hone. Senator Craig allegedly engaged in misconduct while using a restroom at the Minneapolis-St. Paul International Airport. The interviewer arrested Senator Craig and subsequently interviewed him. The Above the Line Actions will focus on Rapport, Objective (Confession), Resistance, and Veracity. Below the Line Thinking is difficult to measure because a person's thoughts are private. If Below the Line Thinking is evident, the interviewer's response will be evaluated. If not, then Below the Line Thinking will be evaluated from an instructor's perspective. A PNA of Senator Craig's interview will be examined later in this book. The interview lasted approximately 10 minutes. The Senator's demeanor throughout the interview was not confrontational but was somewhat contentious.

INTERVIEW WITH LARRY CRAIG (LC) CASE 07002008

LC: Am I gonna have to fight you in court?

INTERVIEWER: No. No. I'm not gonna go to court unless you want me there.

LC: Cause I don't want to be in court either.
INTERVIEWER: Ok. I don't either. (inaudible) Um, here's the way it works, um, you'll, you'll be released today, okay.
LC: Okay.

Above the Line Actions

Rapport: Good
The interviewer told Senator Craig that he would be released later that day. People become more relaxed when they know what is going to happen to them. Additionally, interviewees tend to cooperate if they know they will not be going to jail.
Objective: Toward Objective
Resistance: Low
Veracity: Truthful

Below the Line Thinking

Process: Good
The interviewer processed what Senator Craig said and began to establish rapport. The interviewer continued to build rapport by telling the Senator what was going to happen to him in the future.
Analyze: Instructor's Perspective
Senator Craig did not want the case to go to court. One hypothesis posits that the Senator knew what he did was wrong and did not want his actions revealed to the public. A Competing Hypothesis posits that the Senator's actions coincidently mirrored the actions of a criminal and he did not want the case to go to court because he would be wrongly identified as a criminal, which would damage his reputation.
Integration: Instructor's Perspective
If the Senator's actions were deliberate, then he would be embarrassed and might take extreme measures to keep his case out of the court system. The interviewer should save this information and possibly use it as leverage in the event the Senator's resistance increases.
Plan: Instructor's Perspective
The interviewer should psychologically prepare the Senator for rights advisement.

INTERVIEWER: All right. I, I know I can bring you to jail, but that's not my goal here, okay? (inaudible)
LC: Don't do that. You, You . . .
INTERVIEWER: I'm not going to bring you to jail.

LC: You solicited me.
INTERVIEWER: Okay. We're going to get, we're going to get into that. (inaudible)
LC: Okay.

Above the Line Actions

Rapport: Good going Poor
The interviewer exercised his power over the Senator by telling him that he could still go to jail. The interviewer's credibility could be damaged because he previously told the Senator that he would be released later the same day. The Senator's response clearly demonstrated that rapport diminished. The interviewer should have suspended his ego in order to maintain rapport with the Senator.
Objective: Away from objective
Instead of moving toward the objective, the interviewer exerted his power by telling the Senator that he could go to jail at the interviewer's discretion. The interviewer refocused the interview on himself instead and away from the Senator.
Resistance: Medium
Veracity: Truthful

Below the Line Thinking

Process: Poor
The interviewer failed to recognize that he needed to continue to build rapport with the Senator to prepare him for the advisement of rights.
Analyze: Instructor's Perspective
The Senator became anxious about the renewed possibility of going to jail. Since the Senator did not demonstrate resistance, the interviewer should put the theme of going to jail in *Storage*. This theme could always be renewed in the event the Senator's resistance increased.
Integration: Instructor's Perspective
Because the interviewer did not process what the Senator said, he missed the opportunity of using jail avoidance as a means to build rapport. The interviewer may have wanted to use the theme of going to jail as motivation for the Senator to tell the truth, but the risk of losing credibility with the Senator outweighs the benefit of the technique, especially if the Senator's resistance was low.
Plan: Instructor's Perspective
The interviewer could repair the damage to rapport by using an empathic statement such as, "Going to jail is not one of the things on your agenda today."

INTERVIEWER: But there's the, there, there's two ways, yes. You can, you can, ah, you can go to court. You can plead guilty.

LC: Yep.

INTERVIEWER: There'll be a fine. You won't have to explain anything. (inaudible) I know.

LC: Right.

INTERVIEWER: And you'll pay a fine, you be (inaudible), done. Or if you want to plead not guilty, ah, and I, I can't make these decisions for you.

LC: No, no. Just tell me where I am (inaudible) I need to make this flight.

Observation: The interviewer used a technique referred to as *Closing Up Front.* The Senator affirmed that he could plead guilty, pay a fine, and not explain his actions. Innocent people typically do not make these types of affirmations. The Senator's series of affirmations also indicates that he knew what he did was wrong.

INTERVIEWER: Okay. Okay. And then I go to people that are not guilty, then I would have to come to court and end up testifying. So those are the two things, okay. Did I explain that part?

LC: Yes.

INTERVIEWER: Okay Um, ah, I'm just going to read you your rights real quick, okay?

INTERVIEWER: You got it on? (talking to a second interviewer referencing the tape recorder) Second Interviewer: Yep.

INTERVIEWER: Okay.

INTERVIEWER: Ah, the date is 6/11/07 at 1228 hours. Um, Mr. Craig?

LC: Yes.

INTERVIEWER: Sorry about that. (ringing phone)

INTERVIEWER: You have the right to remain silent. Anything you say can and will be used against you in court of law. You have the right to talk to a lawyer now or have a present, a lawyer present now or anytime during questioning. If you cannot afford a lawyer, one will be appointed to you without cost. Do you understand each of these rights the way I have explained them to you?

LC: I do.

INTERVIEWER: Do you wish to talk to us at this time?

LC: I do.

Above the Line Actions

Rapport: Poor going Good
Objective: Toward objective
Resistance: Low
Veracity: Truthful

Below the Line Thinking

Process: Good

The Senator said, ". . . just tell me where I am." The interviewer asked the Senator if he understood what was said and then read him his rights.

Analyze: Good

The interviewer moved forward toward reading the Senator his rights after he acknowledged that he understood what the interviewer had explained to him.

Integration: Instructor's Perspective

The interviewer could have added to the Senator's sense of urgency by saying, "I don't want you to miss your flight, so why don't I read you your rights and then you can tell me what happened and hopefully you can catch your flight."

Plan: Instructor's Perspective

Ask the Senator to tell his side of the story from the beginning. Instructing interviewees to begin their stories from the beginning is important because the interviewees begin the stories where they know the story starts and not from where the interviewer thinks the stories begin. This technique may yield additional information.

> **INTERVIEWER:** Okay, Um, I just wanna start off with a your side of the story, okay. So, a . . .
>
> **LC:** So, I go into the bathroom here as I normally do, I'm a commuter too here.
>
> **INTERVIEWER:** Okay.
>
> **LC:** I sit down, um, to go to the bathroom and ah, you said our feet bumped. I believe they did, ah, because I reached down and scooted over and um, the next thing I knew, under the bathroom divider comes a card that says Police. Now, um, (sigh) that's about as far as I can take it, I don't know of anything else. Ah, your foot came toward mine, mine came towards yours, was that natural? I don't know. Did we bump? Yes. I think we did. You said so. I don't disagree with that.
>
> **INTERVIEWER:** Okay. I don't want to get into a pissing match here.
>
> **LC:** We're not going to.
>
> **INTERVIEWER:** Good. Um . . .

Above the Line Actions

Rapport: Poor going Good going Poor

The Senator agreed with the interviewer's supposition but the interviewer failed to acknowledge the Senator's admission. The interviewer's caustic response increased the Senator's anxiety. Increased anxiety increases the probability that the Senator will engage his fight/flight response and terminate the interview.

Objective: Away from objective

Veracity: No deception

Resistance: Low

Below the Line Thinking

Process: None

The interviewer did not process what the Senator said. After the Senator described his activities in the bathroom stall, he concluded that he did not disagree with the interviewer's supposition. The interviewer's response clearly indicated that he did not process what the Senator said. The failure to process caused rapport to go from good to poor.

Analyze: Instructor's Perspective

The Senator reiterated the interviewer's question, "Did we bump?" and then answered the question, "Yes, I think we did. You said so. I don't disagree with that." The Senator agreed that his feet and the interviewer's feet bumped; however, he went through an elaborate thought process before he could vocalize the answer, "Yes." The Senator equivocated his "Yes" answer with the follow-up response, "I think we did." He firmed up his "Yes" answer with the response, "You said so." The Senator again equivocated his "Yes" answer with the negative assertion, "I don't disagree with that." One hypothesis posits that the question he spontaneously posed, ". . . was that natural?" and his answer, "I don't know." may have been the cause of his anxiety. The Senator may be wrestling with his sexual identity. Another hypothesis posits that the Senator's actions in the bathroom were random and his random actions coincidently mimicked the behaviors of the type of criminals sought by the police.

Integration: Instructor's Perspective

The Senator questioned whether his actions were natural, which suggests that he thought that his actions were, to some degree, not natural. The Senator experienced dissonance between his actions in the restroom and his definition of natural behaviors. The Senator may have also felt dissonance due to his prominent status in the community. The Senator has an image of how a senator should conduct himself, which did not comport with his behavior in the restroom.

Plan: Instructor's Perspective

The interviewer can reduce the Senator's anxiety by using an empathic statement. The use of empathic statements is a powerful rapport building technique. Empathic statements capture the essence of what people say and reflect the same idea back to the person using parallel language. For example, "So you are not happy with the way you behaved in the restroom."

> **LC:** I don't, ah, I am not gay, I don't do these kinds of things and . . .
> **INTERVIEWER:** It doesn't matter, I don't care about sexual preference or anything like that. Here's your stuff back sir. Um, I don't care about sexual preference.
> **LC:** I know you don't. You're out to enforce the law.
> **INTERVIEWER:** Right.
> **LC:** But you shouldn't be out to entrap people either.
> **INTERVIEWER:** This isn't entrapment.
> **LC:** All right.

Above the Line Actions

Rapport: Poor

The interviewer cut the Senator off when he said he was not gay and missed an opportunity to obtain additional information. By returning the Senator's "stuff" midsentence, the interviewer dismissed what the Senator said.

Objective: Away from objective
Veracity: Truthful
Resistance: Low

Below the Line Thinking

Process: None

The interviewer failed to process what the Senator said. The Senator said, "I don't do these kinds of things . . . .," which suggests that the senator was familiar with the activities he conducted in the bathroom stall. The senator tacitly admitted that he knew what he did in the stall. The interviewer failed to recognize the movement toward the interview objective. Additionally, the Senator revealed something very personal about his life. Based on the interviewer's response, he focused on returning the Senator's personal belongings and did not focus on what he said.

Analyze: Instructor's Perspective

The Senator struggled to rationalize his behavior. The Senator acknowledged that the interviewer was not interested in his personal struggle but rather enforcing the law. The interviewer missed an opportunity to obtain additional information by not recognizing the Senator's personal struggle. One hypothesis posits that the Senator knew what he did was wrong, struggled with his sexual identity, and felt guilty because his secret life was revealed.

Integration: Instructor's Perspective

The Senator experienced ambivalent feelings about his sexual identity. The Senator did not protest when the interviewer told him that what occurred was not entrapment. The Senator did not protest that he engaged in solicitation but, rather, that he was caught unfairly. This is was a tacit admission of guilt.

Plan: Instructor's Perspective

The interviewer could use an empathic statement such as, "So, you don't normally engage in this activity and it's embarrassing to get caught" or "You say you're not gay because you're married and that's why you feel guilty about what you did in the restroom."

> **INTERVIEWER:** Um, you you're skipping some parts here, but what, what about your hand?
> **LC:** What about it? I reached down, my foot like this. There was a piece of paper on the floor. I picked it up.
> **INTERVIEWER:** Okay.
> **LC:** What about my hand?
> **INTERVIEWER:** Well, you're not being truthful with me, I'm kinda disappointed in you Senator. I'm real disappointed in you right now. Okay. I'm not, just so you know, just like everybody, I, I, I, treat with dignity, I try to pull them away from the situation.
> **LC:** I, I . . .
> **INTERVIEWER:** . . . and not embarrass them.
> **LC:** I appreciate that.
> **INTERVIEWER:** And I . . .
> **LC:** You did that after the stall.

Above the Line Actions

Rapport: Poor going Good

The interviewer told the Senator that he was a liar and then mitigated this accusation by telling the Senator that he was treating him with dignity.

Objective: Toward the objective

Resistance: Increasing

The Senator became more resistant when he asked the questions, "What about my hand?" and "What about it?" and made the statement "But you shouldn't be out to entrap people either."

Veracity: Deceptive

Below the Line Thinking

Process: Yes

The interviewer told the Senator that he did not believe him and was disappointed by his actions. Anticipating the Senator's reaction, the interviewer followed up by telling him that he treated everybody with dignity. The Senator agreed with the interviewer but noted that he embarrassed him in the bathroom.

Analyze: Partial

The interviewer confronted the Senator, correctly anticipated his reaction, and used a good technique to maintain rapport. The interviewer called the Senator a liar and he did not protest. Truthful people who are called liars, typically protest. The interviewer called the Senator a liar; however, he focused on the fact that the interviewer treats people with dignity. The Senator's response supports the hypothesis that he is deceptive.

Integration: Yes

The interviewer induced dissonance. The Senator viewed himself as an honest man and the interviewer described him as less than truthful. Dissonance motivates people to live up to the expectations of other.

Plan: Instructor's Perspective

Encourage the Senator to continue his story. The Senator will likely tell the truth because he wants the interviewer to see him as an honest person.

> **INTERVIEWER:** I will say every person I've had so far has told me the truth. We've been respectful to each other and then they've gone on their way. And I've never had to bring anybody to jail because everybody's been truthful to me.
>
> **LC:** I don't want you to take me to jail and I think.
>
> **INTERVIEWER:** I'm not gonna take you to jail as long as you're cooperative, but I'm not gonna lie. We . . .
>
> **LC:** Did my hand come below the divider? Yes. It did.
>
> **INTERVIEWER:** Okay, sir. We deal with people that lie to us everyday.
>
> **LC:** I'm sure you do.
>
> **INTERVIEWER:** I'm sure you do too, sir.
>
> **LC:** And gentleman so do I.

INTERVIEWER: I'm sure you do. We deal with a lot of people that are very bad people. You're not a bad person.

LC: No, I don't think I am.

INTERVIEWER: Okay, so, what I'm telling you, I don't want to be lied to.

LC: Okay.

Above the Line Actions

Rapport: Good going Poor

The dialogue between the interviewer and the Senator reduced to a power struggle. The Senator became defensive, especially when the interviewer brought up the topic of going to jail again.

Objective: Away from objective

Resistance: Increasing

Veracity: Truthful

Below the Line Thinking

Process: None

The interviewer used the theme of going to jail, which prompted an admission from the Senator; however, the interviewer did not process what the Senator said. The Senator said, "Did my hand come below the divider? Yes. It did." The Senator agreed with the interviewer's supposition and based on the interviewer's response, "Okay, sir. We deal with people that lie to us everyday" demonstrated that that he did not process what the Senator said. The Senator tacitly admitted to engaging in the activity alleged by the interviewer, but the interviewer failed to process this information. The interviewer's responses significantly diminished rapport.

Analysis: Instructor's Perspective

The Senator said that he did not think that he was a bad person. The interviewer responded, "I don't want to be lied to." According to Miller's Law, the Senator did not lie to the interviewer. He told the truth, but the truth about what? The interviewer failed to analyze what the Senator said he missed an opportunity to obtain additional information without becoming more confrontational.

Plan: Instructor's Perspective

The interviewer should reassure the Senator that he will not go to jail if he tells the truth and refocus the interview toward the Objective.

INTERVIEWER: Okay. So, we'll start over, you're gonna get out of here. You're gonna have to pay a fine and that will be it. Okay. I don't call media, I don't do any of that type of crap.

LC: Fine.
INTERVIEWER: Okay.
LC: Fine.
INTERVIEWER: All right, so, let's start from the beginning. You went in the bathroom.
LC: I went in the bathroom.
INTERVIEWER: And what did you do when you . . .
LC: I stood beside the wall, waiting for a stall to open. I got in the stall, sat down, and I started to go to the bathroom. Ah, did our feet come together, apparently they did bump. Well, I won't dispute that.

Above the Line Actions

Rapport: Poor going Good
    The interviewer agreed to start over and reminded the Senator that he would be allowed to leave and that he would not call the media, two issues that were important to the Senator.
Objective: Toward the objective
Resistance: Low
Veracity: Truthful

Below the Line Thinking

Process: None
    The Senator agreed with the interviewer's supposition. Again, the interviewer missed an opportunity to move toward a confession because he failed to process what the Senator said.
Analyze: Instructor's Perspective
    The Senator agreed with the interviewer's suppositions for a second time in this interview. The Senator wanted to tell the truth but he was worried about his public image and the ambivalence he felt about his activities in the restroom.
Plan: Instructor's Perspective
    The interviewer should acknowledge the Senator's admission that their feet touched and continue movement toward the Objective.

    INTERVIEWER: Okay. When I got out of the stall, I noticed other, other stalls were open.
    LC: They were at the time. At the time I entered, I, I, at the time I entered, I stood and waited.
    INTERVIEWER: Okay.

LC: They were all busy, you know?

INTERVIEWER: Were you (inaudible) out here while you were waiting? I could see your eyes. I saw you playing with your fingers and then look up. Play with your fingers and then look up.

LC: Did I glance at your stall? I was glancing at a stall right beside yours waiting for a fella to empty it. I saw him stand up and therefore I thought it was going to empty.

INTERVIEWER: How long do you think you stood outside the stalls?

LC: Oh, a minute or two at the most.

INTERVIEWER: Okay. And when you went in the stall, then what?

LC: Sat down.

INTERVIEWER: Okay. Did you do anything with your feet?

LC: Positioned them, I don't know. I don't know at the time. I'm a fairly wide guy.

INTERVIEWER: I understand.

LC: I had to spread my legs.

INTERVIEWER: Okay.

LC: When I lower my pants so they won't slide.

INTERVIEWER: Okay.

LC: Did I slide them too close to yours? Did I, I looked down once, your foot was close to mine.

INTERVIEWER: Yes.

LC: Did we bump? Ah, you said so, I don't recall that, but apparently we were close.

INTERVIEWER: Yeah, well your foot did touch mine, on my side of the stall.

LC: All right.

Above the Line Actions

Rapport: Poor going Good

The interviewer's responses indicated that he engaged in active listening, which is a good rapport building technique.

Objective: Toward the objective

Resistance: Medium

Veracity: Truthful

Below the Line Thinking

Process: Yes

The interviewer finally recognized that the Senator agreed with the interviewer's supposition.

Analyze: Instructor's Perspective

The Senator spent several minutes inside the bathroom before entering the stall. One hypothesis posits that based on what the Senator previously said, he may have felt ambivalence about soliciting and finally decided to make a solicitation.

Integration: None

Plan: Instructor's Perspective

The interviewer could have used the following empathic presumptive, "You stood there deciding whether or not you wanted to solicit. A part of you wanted to, yet another part of you felt uncomfortable."

> **INTERVIEWER:** Okay. And then with the hand. Um, how many times did you put your hand under the stall?
> **LC:** I don't recall. I remember reaching down once. There was a piece of toilet paper back behind me and picking it up.
> **INTERVIEWER:** Okay. Was your . . . was your palm down or up when you were doing that?
> **LC:** I don't recall.
> **INTERVIEWER:** Okay. I recall your palm being up. Okay.
> **LC:** All right.

Above the Line Actions

Rapport: Poor
Objective: Toward the Objective
Resistance: Medium
Veracity: Truthful

The Senator was deceptive at first, but when the interviewer asked him a direct question, he agreed with the interviewer's supposition.

Below the Line Thinking

Process: None

The interviewer failed to process. The Senator agreed to the interviewer's supposition, but he did not listen to what the Senator said.

Analyze: Instructor's Perspective

The Senator had a difficult time explaining his actions in the stall because he was embarrassed.

Integration: Instructor's Perspective

Since the Senator was embarrassed, the interviewer could have increased rapport and get the Senator to make smaller, incremental admissions.

Plan: Instructor's Perspective

The interviewer could have used an empathic presumptive to increase rapport and elicit additional information not only about what the Senator did but what he was thinking when he did it.

> **INTERVIEWER:** When you pick up a piece of paper off the ground, your palm would be down, when you pick something up.
>
> **LC:** Yeah, probably would be. I recall picking the paper up.
>
> **INTERVIEWER:** And I know it's hard to describe here on tape, but actually what I saw was your fingers come underneath the stalls, you're actually touching the bottom of the stall divider.
>
> **LC:** I don't recall that.
>
> **INTERVIEWER:** You don't recall?
>
> **LC:** I don't believe I did that. I don't.
>
> **INTERVIEWER:** I saw, I saw . . .
>
> **LC:** I don't do those things.
>
> **INTERVIEWER:** I saw your left hand and I could see the gold wedding ring when it when it went across. I could see that. On your left hand, I could see that.
>
> **LC:** Wait a moment, my left hand was over here.
>
> **INTERVIEWER:** I saw there's a . . .
>
> **LC:** My right hand was next to you.
>
> **INTERVIEWER:** I could tell it with my, ah, I could tell it was your left hand because your thumb was positioned in a face-ward motion. Your thumb was on this side, not on this side.
>
> **LC:** Well, we can dispute that. I'm not going to fight you in court and I, I reached down with my right hand to pick up the paper.
>
> **INTERVIEWER:** But I'm telling you that I could see that so, I know that's your left hand. Also I could see a gold ring on this finger, so that's obvious it was the left hand.
>
> **LC:** Yeah, okay. My left hand was in the direct opposite of the stall from you.

Above the Line Actions

Rapport: Poor
Objective: Away from the Objective
Resistance: High
Veracity: Leaning truthful

Below the Line Thinking

Process: None

The interviewer and the Senator argued about which hand came under the divider. This is the first time that the Senator protested the interviewer's suppositions.

Analyze: Instructor's Perspective

The Senator protested, which is an indication of truthfulness. One hypothesis posits that the Senator reached under the divider with his right hand not his left hand.

Integration: Instructor's Perspective

The Senator may have focused on this point because the interviewer got this fact wrong. The Senator argued from a strong position because he knew he reached with his right hand. The Senator protested this point because he stood firmly on the truth.

Plan: Instructor's Perspective

The interviewer could have used the presumptive, "So, you reached under the divider with you right hand and not your left hand." The Senator faces a dilemma. If he agrees, he admits to placing his right hand under the divider and if he disagrees, he admits he placed his left hand under the divider.

> **INTERVIEWER:** Okay. You, you travel through here frequently correct?
> **LC:** I do.
> **INTERVIEWER:** Um . . .
> **LC:** Almost weekly.
> **INTERVIEWER:** Have you been successful in these bathrooms here before?
> **LC:** I go to that bathroom regularly.
> **INTERVIEWER:** I mean for any type of other activities.
> **LC:** No. Absolutely not. I don't seek activity in bathrooms.

Above the Line Actions

Rapport: Poor
Objective: Away from Objective
Resistance: High
Veracity: Deceptive

Below the Line Thinking

Process: None

The Senator said that he doesn't seek activities in bathrooms; however, the interviewer failed to process what the Senator said. If the Senator does not seek activities in bathrooms, where does he seek activities?

Analyze: Instructor's Perspective

The Senator tacitly admitted that he seeks activity in places other than the bathroom. One hypothesis posits that the Senator may solicit sexual activities in places other than the airport restroom.

Plan: Instructor's Perspective

The interviewer could have used a provocative empathic statement such as, "Yes, there are more appropriate places to conduct this activity." If the senator responds with "Yes" or "No," he tacitly admits that he engages in the activity.

INTERVIEWER: It's embarrassing.

LC: Well it's embarrassing for both . . . I'm not gonna fight you.

INTERVIEWER: I know you're not going to fight me. But that's not the point. I would respect you and I still respect you. I don't disrespect you, but I'm disrespected right now and I'm not tying to act like I have all kinds of power or anything, but you're sitting here lying to a police officer.

INTERVIEWER: It's not a (inaudible) I'm getting from somebody else. I'm (inaudible)

LC: (inaudible) (Talking over each other)

INTERVIEWER: I am trained in this and I know what I am doing. And I say you put your hand under there and you're going to sit there and . . .

LC: I admit I put my hand down.

INTERVIEWER: You put your hand and rubbed it on the bottom of the stall with your left hand.

LC: No. Wait a moment.

INTERVIEWER: And I, I'm not dumb, you can say I don't recall . . .

LC: If I had turned sideways, that was the only way I could get my left hand over there.

INTERVIEWER: It's not that hard for me to reach (inaudible) it's not that hard. I see it happen everyday out here now.

LC: (inaudible) you do. All right.

INTERVIEWER: I just, I just, I guess, I guess I'm gonna say I'm just disappointed in you sir. I'm just really am. I expect this from the guy that we get out of the hood. I mean, people vote for you.

LC: Yes, they do. (inaudible)

INTERVIEWER: unbelievable, unbelievable.

LC: I'm a respectable person and I don't do these kinds of . . .

INTERVIEWER: And (inaudible) respect right now though.

Above the Line Actions

Rapport: None
Objective: Away from objective
Resistance: High
Veracity: Truthful

Below the Line Thinking

Process: None
  The Senator did not like being compared to a person from the hood. The interviewer could have used an empathic statement to increase diminishing rapport. Again, the Senator objected when the interviewer said the Senator put his left hand under the divider.
Analyze: Instructor's Perspective
  The Senator sees himself as a respectable person but the interviewer told him that he was not a respectable person causing the Senator to become anxious. The Senator again protested having put his left hand under the divider, which supports the hypothesis that he is truthful. The Senator said "If I had turned sideways, that was the only way I could get my left hand over there." Earlier in the interview, the Senator said, ". . . I sit down, um, to go to the bathroom and, ah, you said our feet bumped. I believe they did, ah, because I reached down and scooted over and, um, the next thing I knew, under the bathroom divider comes a card that says Police." Based on the Senator's earlier statement he could have used his left hand because he admitted that he scooted over. This supports the hypothesis that the Senator is lying.
Observation: In many interviews, there is information and facts that support the hypothesis that the interviewee is telling the truth and information and facts that support the hypothesis that the interviewee is lying. This interview fits that scenario. The preponderance of evidence suggests that the Senator told the truth when he said he did not use his left hand to reach under the divider. The established pattern throughout the interview is that the Senator did not protest when the interviewer made an accusation or supposition that the Senator engaged in solicitation activities. The use of the left hand to reach under the divider was the only time the Senator objected, which lends support to the hypothesis that he told the truth notwithstanding the fact that he scooted over making it possible for him to use his left hand.
Integration: None
  The interviewer's lack of integration refocused the interview on the interviewer and away from the interviewee.
Plan: None

The interviewer could have taken this opportunity to rebuild some rapport with the Senator by reinforcing the idea that he is a respectable person.

LC: But I didn't use my left hand.
INTERVIEWER: I thought that you . . .
LC: I reached down with my right hand like this to pick up a piece of paper.
INTERVIEWER: Was your gold ring on your right hand at anytime today.
LC: Of course not, try to get it off, look at it.
INTERVIEWER: Okay. Then it was your left hand, I saw it with my own eyes.
LC: All right, you saw something that didn't happen.
INTERVIEWER: Embarrassing, embarrassing. No wonder why we're going down the tubes. Anything to add?
SECOND INTERVIEWER: Uh, no.
INTERVIEWER: Embarrassing. Date is 6/11/07 at 1236 interview is done.

Above the Line Actions

Rapport: None
Objective: Away from the objective
Resistance: High
Veracity: Deceptive

Below the Line Thinking

Process: Yes
   The interviewer recognized that he did not have rapport with the Senator, but did not elect to take any steps to improve rapport.
Analysis: None
Integration: None
Plan: Yes
   Terminate the interview.
Interview Postmortem
   The interview lasted approximately 10 minutes. In most interviews, 10 minutes is not sufficient time to develop rapport and obtain a confession. The interviewer should have taken more time to develop rapport, especially since the interviewee was a Senator.
   Using the Communication Loop to evaluate Senator Craig's interview showed where the interview failed. This interviewer failed to engage Below

the Line Thinking. One pivotal point in the interview was when Senator Craig agreed with the interviewer's supposition that their feet touched. Had the interviewer engaged Below the Line Thinking the interview might have looked like this:

Process: (Just listen to what the interviewee says)

> **LC:** I sit down, um, to go to the bathroom and ah, you said our feet bumped. I believe they did, ah, because I reached down and scooted over and, um, the next thing I knew, under the bathroom divider comes a card that says Police. Now, um, (sigh) that's about as far as I can take it, I don't know of anything else. Ah, your foot came toward mine, mine came towards yours, was that natural? I don't know. Did we bump? Yes. I think we did. You said so. I don't disagree with that.

Analyze (Evaluate what the interviewee said and develop Competing Hypotheses)

The Senator reiterated the interviewer's question, "Did we bump?" and then answered the question, "Yes, I think we did. You said so. I don't disagree with that." The Senator agreed that his feet and the interviewer's feet bumped; however, the Senator went through an elaborate thought process before he could vocalize the answer, "Yes." Senator equivocated his "Yes" answer with the follow-up response, "I think we did." He firmed up his "Yes" answer with the response, "You said so." The Senator again equivocated his "Yes" answer with the negative assertion, "I don't disagree with that."

One hypothesis posits that the Senator's "Yes" response caused him some degree of anxiety. The question he spontaneously posed, ". . . was that natural?" and his answer, "I don't know." may be the cause of his anxiety. The Senator questioned whether his actions were natural, which suggests that he thought that his actions were, to some degree, not natural. A Competing Hypothesis posits that the Senator's actions in the bathroom were random and his random actions coincidently mimicked the behaviors of the type of criminals sought by the police.

Integration

The Senator experienced dissonance between his actions, which he perceived as unnatural to some degree, and his prominent status in the community. If the interviewee had not been a senator, he may have felt less anxious because he would not have felt the urgency to protect his public image.

Plan

The Senator admitted to his actions in the stall; however, he felt anxiety because he perceived his actions as unnatural to some degree and his actions did not comport with his position in society. Increased anxiety increases the probability that the Senator will engage his fight/flight response and terminate the interview. Reducing the Senator's anxiety would be the best course of action to ensure his continued cooperation. The best tool to reduce anxiety is the empathic statement. For example, "You feel anxious talking about your actions in the bathroom." The Communication Loop begins anew and the interviewer again collects information pursuant to Above the Line Actions. The interviewer repeats the Communication Loop until the interview/interrogation objective is met or until the interviewee asks for an attorney or refuses to talk.

Much of the interview focused on the interviewer instead of the interviewee. The interviewer's failure to integrate into the Senator's world precluded the interviewer from taking full advantage of the information the Senator provided. The use of empathic statements is an effective technique to integrate into the interviewee's world. Empathic statements keep the focus of the interview on the interviewee.

Based on the pattern of the interviewer's approach, he formulated a universal interview approach that probably worked most of the time, but for whatever reasons, did not work with the Senator. Had the interviewer used the Communication Loop, he would have discovered early in the interview that the approach he was using was not effective and would have had time to implement a more suitable approach.

Using the Communication Loop to evaluate interviews not only shows where the interviews fail but also allows interviewers to identify their weaknesses and practice techniques to strengthen their interview techniques. For example, The Senator said:

> **LC:** I don't, ah, I am not gay, I don't do these kinds of things.

Interview Response Options:

> **INTERVIEWER:** You're not gay and you don't solicit in bathrooms.

This empathic statement builds rapport by letting the Senator know the interviewer is listening.

> **INTERVIEWER:** You're struggling with your sexual identity and you don't usually solicit in bathrooms.

This presumptive empathic statement builds rapport by letting the Senator know the interviewer is listening and presumes that he made a solicitation in the stall. If the Senator agrees with this statement, he moves closer to a confession admitting to soliciting in places other than the bathroom.

INTERVIEWER: You are having a hard time admitting to yourself that you are gay and getting caught brings this inner conflict to the surface.

This provocative empathic statement builds rapport by letting the Senator know the interviewer is listening and compels the Senator to provide an affirmation, denial, or explanation for his action.

Role-playing with other interviewers is the best way to practice possible responses. The role player presents a series of answers or statements to which the interview must respond. Role-playing forces the interviewer to go through the Communication Loop with increasing speeds. With practice, the Communication Loop becomes second nature.

Initially, interviewers should methodically go through the Communication Loop to ensure that they engage Above the Line Actions as well as Below the Line Thinking. At first, interviewers will cycle through the Communication Loop at slower speeds. Interviewers often observe that by the time they process what the interviewee said, analyze, integrate, and plan, the opportunity to use the planned technique has passed. Cycling speed increases with practice and eventually becomes a high-speed habitual process. Using the Communication Loop serves as a model for interviewers to emulate and will, once mastered, significantly increase the probability of successful interviews.

Appendix A

PNA OF WRITTEN COMMUNICATIONS

The following examples illustrate the use of PNA techniques to analyze written statements. Each written narrative is analyzed line-by-line to demonstrate the full capabilities of PNA. The statements are derived from actual investigations or situations. The names and locations have been changed to protect the identity of the people and locations involved. The hypotheses and Competing Hypotheses developed by the author were based on extant PNA indicators in each written narrative, but are, by no means, the only plausible alternatives. PNA is flexible because it allows investigators to develop their own hypotheses based on their unique perspectives and experiences. However, investigators must seek support for each of the hypotheses they posit. If the evidence to support a particular hypothesis is lacking, then the hypothesis must be discarded and another hypothesis should be developed to take its place. No matter which hypothesis investigators start with, in the end, each investigator should arrive at a general conclusion as to which hypothesis is supported by the preponderance of the evidence. As you read each example, feel free to develop your own Competing Hypotheses.

BABY SHAKER CASE

The writer took his son Dan to the babysitter's house on his way to work. Later that day, the babysitter noticed that Dan was lethargic and took him to the hospital. The physical examination of Dan determined that his injuries were likely due to violent shaking. The case was referred to the local police department. Detectives contacted the writer and asked him to write down everything he did from the time he got up until the time he dropped Dan off at the babysitter's house. The writer's statement was transcribed from his original hand-written narrative.

141

I woke up this morning at 6:50 took a shower, shaved and got my boxers on. I went downstairs to prepare Dan's meal, which consists of 3 tablespoons of rice cereal and 7 ounces of breast milk. I went upstairs to wake Dan up and feed him. Sometimes he's awake when I go to get him. Today he was asleep. When I wake him up by rubbing his belly, he looked up and gave me a big smile. I took him downstairs to feed him at 7:20. First I gave him his rice cereal, which is the 3 tablespoons plus 1 of the 7 ounces mixed together in a small bowl. I feed him this with a syringe. He finished the rice cereal with no fuss and then went to the bottle he ate 4 1/2 ounces of the 6 that were in the bottle. This was for a total of 5 1/2 ounces. Usually he eats 7 ounces so he had a lot less than normal today. After he is done eating, I burp him and hold him for about 20 minutes after meal time today, he slept almost the entire time. This was also about usual as he is usually awake for at least a portion of that time. After 20 minutes, I took him upstairs to his room and put him on the changing table. I then woke him up and as usual in the morning, he was in a great mood. I changed his diaper and got him dressed. I then took him into my room and put him on the bed. While Dan was on the bed I got dressed for work. Usually I wear a suit jacket today I wore jeans, tennis shoes, and a polo shirt because I was meeting some of fellow Lions Club members to help move grills for our members steak dinner night. Once I was dressed I got a suit and shirt and tie to take with me so that I could change after moving the grills. Once I had my things together I picked up Dan and took him downstairs and put him in his car seat, which was on our coffee table. Once he was in the seat I put my suit, shoes and a name plate (for real estate yard signs) in my car. I then went back in and got Dan and put him in the car. I then drove him to Kristine Layton's (our babysitter) house. I arrived at her house at about 8:35, got Dan out of the car and took him up to the front door. I knocked on the door. Kristine let me in and I sat dan down, still in his car seat, on the living room carpet. Kristine got him out of the car seat, he was awake and was in a good mood the whole time since changing him after his feeding. I gave him a kiss on the forehead; said goodbye, and drove to Wadsworth. That was the last time I saw him before getting a call that he was in the hospital. I got that call from Kristine at 12:38 but did not hear it. I called her back at 12:44 but got no answer. I then called my wife, Helen, and she told me to get to the hospital.

PNA of the Writer's Written Statement

1) I woke up this morning at 6:50 took a shower, shaved and got my boxers on.
   a) The writer used the First Person-Simple Past Tense, which indicates he is committed to the activity in this sentence.
   b) The writer provided a time reference of 6:50 for the beginning of his story.
   c) The Word Clue "got my boxers on" suggests that he did not dress completely.

2) **I went downstairs to prepare Dan's meal, which consists of 3 table-spoons of rice cereal and 7 ounces of breast milk.**
   a) The writer used the First Person-Simple Past Tense, which indicates he is committed to the activity in this sentence.
   b) The Push-Pull Word "downstairs" indicates that the writer lives in a 2-story house and that his bedroom is on the second story.
   c) The Word Clue "breast milk" indicates that Dan is breast fed and that Dan's mother was not present in the house because the breast milk was extracted and premeasured.

3) **I went upstairs to wake Dan up and feed him.**
   a) The writer used the First Person-Simple Past Tense, which indicates he is committed to the activity in this sentence.
   b) The writer used the present tense "feed." The use of the present tense within the context of this sentence is appropriate because the present tense is often used to describe actions repeated on a regular basis. The writer probably feeds Dan on a regular basis.
   c) The Push-Pull Word "upstairs," which supports the writer's use of the Push-Pull Word "downstairs" in Sentence 2. The complimentary use of the Push-Pull Words "downstairs" and "upstairs" supports the hypothesis that the writer is probably telling the truth about these activities.
   d) The writer used the present tense "wake." The use of the present tense within the context of this sentence is appropriate because the present tense is often used to describe actions repeated on a regular basis. The writer probably wakes Dan on a regular basis.

4) **Sometimes he's awake when I go to get him.**
   a) The writer used the Simple present tense "is" and "go." The use of the present tense within the context of this sentence is appropriate because the present tense is often used to describe actions repeated on a regular basis. The writer probably gets Dan on a regular basis.
   b) The Text Bridge "when" creates an information gap from the time he went upstairs until the time he got Dan.
   c) The Word Qualifier "sometimes" suggests that Dan is not always awake when the writer entered the bedroom.

5) **Today he was asleep.**
   a) The writer used the Simple past tense "was," which suggests he retrieved this information from his memory.
   b) The Word Qualifier "today" supports the Word Qualifier "sometimes" used in Sentenced 4, which indicates the writer probably told the truth about this activity.

6) **When I wake him up by rubbing his belly, he looked up and gave me a big smile.**
   a) The writer used the present tense "wake." Within the context of the statement, the use of the present tense is not appropriate because the

writer referenced this particular occasion when he woke Dan. This is not a reference to when the writer wakes Dan up on an ongoing basis. The inappropriate use of the present tense indicates deception.

b) The past tense "he looked up and gave me a smile" suggests that the writer retrieved this information from his memory.

c The Text Bridge "when" creates an information gap from the time the writer entered Dan's room until the time he rubbed Dan's belly.

d) The Word Clue "he looked up and gave me a big smile" suggests the writer focused on Dan's emotional status and not on his health status, the reason why he was hospitalized.

e) The Word Qualifier "big" suggests the writer wanted to emphasize Dan's emotional status.

f) The Extraneous Information "he gave me a big smile" indicates the possibility of deception.

7) I took him downstairs to feed him at 7:20.

a) The writer used the First Person-Simple Past Tense, which indicates he is committed to the activity in this sentence.

a) The writer used the present tense "feed." The use of the present tense within the context of this sentence is appropriate because the present tense is often used to describe actions repeated on a regular basis. The writer probably feeds Dan on a regular basis.

a) The writer provided a time reference of 7:20. Thirty minutes lapsed from the time the writer got up until he took Dan downstairs to feed him. Based on the activities the writer described, the time lapse is appropriate.

a) The Push-Pull Word "downstairs" supports the writer's use of the Push-Pull Words "downstairs" and "upstairs" in Sentences 2 and 3. The complimentary use of the Push-Pull Words "downstairs" and "upstairs" supports the hypothesis that the writer told the truth about these activities.

8) First I gave him his rice cereal, which is the 3 tablespoons plus 1 of the 7 ounces mixed together in a small bowl.

a) The writer used the First Person-Simple Past Tense, which indicates he is committed to the activity in this sentence.

b) The Article "the" indicates the rice and cereal were specifically identified by the writer setting those items apart from all other rice and cereal. The possibility exists that Dan's mother set those items out separately for the writer to mix and feed to Dan.

c) The Word Qualifier "first" suggests that the he engaged in at least one additional activity during the time he fed Dan. The writer should mention at least one other activity during the time he fed Dan or the writer is likely withholding information.

9) I feed him this with a syringe.

a) The writer used the present tense "feed." Within the context of the statement, the use of the present tense is not appropriate because the writer referenced this particular occasion when he fed Dan and not when he feeds him on an ongoing basis. The use of the present tense "feed" indicates deception. A Competing Hypothesis posits that from the writer's perspective, the used of the present tense "feed" may be appropriate. Since the writer feeds Dan on a regular basis, he may have considered the act of feeding Dan as an ongoing activity; thus, the use of the present tense would be appropriate.

10) **He finished the rice cereal with no fuss and then went to the bottle he ate 4 1/2 ounces of the 6 that were in the bottle.**

   a) The Spontaneous Negation "He finished the rice cereal with no fuss" indicates a high probability or deception. If Dan did not fuss when the writer fed him, the writer would have simply stated, "He finished the rice cereal." There is a high probability that Dan fussed when the writer fed him.

   b) The Word Clue "Dan ate 4 1/2 ounces of the 6" indicates that he did not finish his breakfast; however, the writer did not provide a reason why Dan did not finish his breakfast.

   c) The Text Bridge "then" creates an information gap from the time Dan finished the rice cereal until the time he went to the bottle. The combination of the Spontaneous Negation and the Text Bridge indicates the writer withheld information. This is a critical part of the narrative in that many baby shaking incidents occur during feeding time. One hypothesis posits the writer became frustrated because Dan would not eat properly and out of this frustration shook him. The writer used the Text Bridge "then" to bridge over the fact that he shook Dan. The writer used the Spontaneous Negation to give the illusion that feeding Dan was not problematic. The fact that Dan only consumed 4 1/2 ounces of the usual 6 ounces indicates Dan did not eat properly. Dan's abnormal eating behavior further supports the hypothesis that the writer shook Dan during feeding time.

11) **This was for a total of 5 1/2 ounces.**

   a) The past tense "was" indicates that he retrieved the information from his memory.

   b) The Word Clue "Dan ate a total of 5 1/2 ounces" indicates that he did not finish his breakfast, which supports the activities in Sentence 10. The total of 5 1/2 ounces comports with what the writer wrote in Sentences 8 and 10. The writer mixed 1 ounce of breast milk with the cereal and Dan drank 4 1/2 ounces of breast milk from the bottle for a total of 5 1/2 ounces. This supports the hypothesis that the writer told the truth about how much Dan consumed for breakfast.

12) **Usually he eats 7 ounces so he had a lot less than normal today.**

   a) The past tense "had" suggests that the writer retrieved this information from his memory.

b) The Push-Pull Word "usually" indicates that something unusual happened on this day.

c) The Push-Pull Word "normal" indicates that this day was not a normal day. The writer supported this hypothesis when he wrote "he had a lot less than normal;" however, he did not offer any reasons why this was an unusual day.

d) The Push-Pull Words "usually" and "normal" support the hypothesis that the writer experienced some degree of difficulty feeding Dan.

e) The Text Bridge "so" creates an information gap across time from the times in the past when Dan eats 7 ounces to this day when he ate less than 7 ounces.

13) **After he is done eating, I burp him and hold him for about 20 minutes after meal time today, he slept almost the entire time.**

a) The Present Tense "is," "burp" and "hold" suggests that the writer did not retrieve this information from his memory. The inappropriate use of the present tense is one indicator of deception.

b) The past tense "slept" suggests the write retrieved this activity from his memory.

c) The Text Bridge "after" creates an information gap from the time Dan is done eating until the time the writer burps Dan.

d) The second Text Bridge "after" creates an information gap from meal time to 20 minutes after meal time.

e) The Word Qualifier "today" indicates that the writer did not typically hold Dan nor did Dan typically sleep after he ate breakfast. The writer did not offer any reasons why Dan slept almost the entire time "today" as compared to other days. The fact that both the writer and Dan's behaviors were out of the ordinary supports the hypothesis that Dan's feeding was problematic and out of frustration, the writer probably shook him.

f) The Word Qualifier "almost" suggests that Dan was awake for some of the time.

14) **This was also about usual as he is usually awake for at least a portion of that time.**

a) The Push-Pull Word "usual" suggests that something unusual occurred. The writer used the Push-Pull Word "unusual" a second time, which reinforces the notion that something unusual occurred. The previous sentence ". . . he slept almost the entire time" reinforces the notion that something unusual occurred with respect to Dan sleeping.

b) The Word Qualifier "about" suggests that Dan slept almost the entire time is not entirely usual; however, the writer did not offer any reasons why this is not entirely usual.

c) The writer tried to justify the fact that Dan slept after he was fed instead of merely conveying facts. Liars tend to convince people that something occurred; truthful people simply convey information.

15) **After 20 minutes, I took him upstairs to his room and put him on the changing table.**
   a) The writer used the First Person-Simple Past Tense, which indicates he is committed to the activity in this sentence.
   b) The Text Bridge "After" creates an information gap from the time Dan fell asleep until the time the writer took him upstairs.
   c) The Push-Pull Word "upstairs" supports the sequence of Push-Pull Word in Sentences 2, 3, and 7. The complimentary use of the Push-Pull Words "downstairs" and "upstairs" supports the hypothesis that the writer is truthful about these activities.

16) **I then woke him up and as usual in the morning, he was in a great mood.**
   a) The writer used the First Person-Simple Past Tense, which indicates he is committed to the activity in this sentence.
   b) The Text Bridge "then" creates an information gap from the time he put Dan on the changing table until the time he woke Dan up.
   c) The Push-Pull Word "usual" indicates that something out of the ordinary occurred.
   d) The Word Qualifier "great" indicates Dan was in high spirits and did not cause any problems for the writer. The other instances in the narrative where the writer emphasized Dan's good behavior occur in sentence 6, ". . . he looked up and gave me a big smile" and in sentence 10, "He finished the rice cereal with no fuss." The writer overemphasized the fact that Dan was in high spirits. The writer tried to convince the reader that Dan was in high spirits instead of just conveying information. Liars tend to shout their message to ensure that the reader comprehends the liar's message.
   e) The Extraneous Information "he was in a great mood" indicates the possibility of deception.
   f) The writer focused on the emotional status of the Dan and not his health status, the reason for his hospitalization.

17) **I changed his diaper and got him dressed.**
   a) The writer used the First Person-Simple Past Tense, which indicates he is committed to the activity in this sentence.

18) **I then took him into my room and put him on the bed.**
   a) The writer used the First Person-Simple Past Tense, which indicates he is committed to the activity in this sentence.
   b) The Text Bridge "then" creates an information gap from the time he got Dan dressed until the time he took Dan to the bedroom.
   c) The Article "the bed" instead of the Possessive Pronoun "my bed," suggests that the writer did not take possession of the bed.

19) While Dan was on the bed I got dressed for work.

a) The writer used the First Person-Simple Past Tense, which indicates he is committed to the activity in this sentence.

b) The Text Bridge "while" creates an information gap from the time he put Dan on the bed until the time he dressed for work.

c) The Word Clue "got dressed" supports the hypothesis that the writer was only wearing his boxers.

d) The Article "the bed" instead of the Possessive Pronoun "my bed," suggests that the writer did not take possession the bed.

20) Usually I wear a suit jacket today I wore jeans, tennis shoes, and a polo shirt because I was meeting some of fellow Lions Club members to help move grills for our members steak dinner night.

a) The writer used the First Person-Simple Past Tense, which indicates he is committed to the activity in this sentence.

b) The Push-Pull Word "usually" suggests that this day was different from other days, but, unlike the previous instances in sentences 12, 14, and 16, he explained why the day was unusual.

c) The Word Clue "fellow" and the Personal Identifier "our" suggests that the writer feels a closeness with members of the Lions Club.

d) The writer used the present tense "wear." The use of the present tense within the context of this sentence is appropriate because the present tense is often used to describe actions repeated on a regular basis.

e) The Extraneous Information about moving grills for the Lions Club was out of the scope of the narrative and has no relationship to the story he was telling about Dan. One hypothesis posits that the writer may have been in a hurry this morning and pushed Dan to eat quickly. When Dan balked, the writer became frustrated and shook him.

21) Once I was dressed I got a suit and shirt and tie to take with me so that I could change after moving the grills.

a) The writer used the First Person-Simple Past Tense, which indicates he is committed to the activity in this sentence.

b) The Text Bridges "once" creates an information gap from the time he got dressed until the time he got a suit.

c) The Text Bridge "so" creates an information gap from the time he got his suit, shirt, and tie until the time he would have changed from his blue jeans into his suit.

d) The Text Bridge "after" creates an information gap from the time he would have finished moving the grills until the time he would change into his suit.

22) Once I had my things together I picked up Dan and took him downstairs and put him in his car seat, which was on our coffee table.

a) The writer used the First Person-Simple Past Tense, which indicates he is committed to the activity in this sentence.

b) The Text Bridge "once" creates an information gap from the time he got his things together until the time he picked Dan up.

23) **Once he was in the seat I put my suit, shoes and a name plate (for real estate yard signs) in my car.**

a) The writer used the First Person-Simple Past Tense, which indicates he is committed to the activity in this sentence.

b) The Text Bridge "once" creates an information gap from the time he put Dan in the car seat until the time he put his suit, shoes, and name plate in his car.

c) The Word Clue "name plate (real estate yard signs)" indicates that the writer is connected to the real-estate business and is probably an agent.

24) **I then went back in and got dan and put him in the car.**

a) The writer used the First Person-Simple Past Tense, which indicates he is committed to the activity in this sentence.

b) The Text Bridge "then" creates an information gap from the time he put the items in his car until the time he went back in and got Dan.

c) The writer did not capitalize Dan's name, suggesting that the writer distanced himself from Dan. One hypothesis posits that the writer distanced himself from Dan because he knew he was injured. If this is the case, then the writer demonstrated a degree of guilt because he shook Dan.

25) **I then drove him to Kristine's (our babysitter) house.**

a) The writer used the First Person-Simple Past Tense, which indicates he is committed to the activity in this sentence.

b) The writer properly introduced Kristine. A proper introduction is an indicator of truthfulness.

c) The Text Bridge "then" creates an information gap from the time he put Dan in the car until the time he drove him to Kristine's house.

26) **I arrived at her house at about 8:35, got Dan out of the car and took him up to the front door.**

a) The writer used the First Person-Simple Past Tense, which indicates he is committed to the activity in this sentence.

b) The writer provided the time reference of 8:35.

27) **I knocked on the door.**

a) The writer used the First Person-Simple Past Tense, which indicates he is committed to the activity in this sentence.

28) **Kristine let me in and I sat dan down, still in his car seat, on the living room carpet.**

a) The writer used the First Person-Simple Past Tense, which indicates he is committed to the activity in this sentence.

b) The writer did not capitalize Dan's name, suggesting that the writer distanced himself from Dan. This supports the hypothesis that the writer may have felt some degree of guilt because he shook Dan.

29) **Kristine got him out of the car seat, he was awake and was in a good mood the whole time since changing him after his feeding.**

   a) The writer used the First Person-Simple Past Tense, which indicates he is committed to the activity in this sentence.

   b) The Text Bridge "since" creates an information gap from the time he fed Dan to the time prior to feeding Dan.

   c) The Text Bridge "since" also serves as a Word Qualifier. The Word Qualifier "since" divides the written narrative into two sections, the time before changing Dan after he finished his feeding and the time after changing him after his feeding.

   d) The Word Qualifier "whole time" describes the time after Dan finished his feeding and does not include the time before he finished his feeding. The writer used the Word Qualifier to give the impression that Dan was in a good mood both before and after he finished his feeding, but this was probably not the case. This provides even more support for the hypothesis that Dan was problematic during feeding and, out of frustration, the writer shook him.

   e) The Word Qualifiers "awake" and "good mood" emphasize the fact that Dan was conscious and in a good mood to ensure the reader gets the message that Dan's was not problematic that morning. The writer asserted this theme in Sentences 6 and 16. The writer, yet again, shouted the message that Dan was in high Spirits.

30) **I gave him a kiss on the forehead, said goodbye, and drove to Wadsworth.**

   a) The First Person-Simple Past Tense, which indicates he is committed to the activity in this sentence.

   b) The Word Clue "I gave him a kiss on the forehead," continues the theme that the writer did not experience any problems with Dan that morning and that he is a loving father.

   c) The Extraneous Information "I gave him a kiss of the forehead, said goodbye" is an indicator of deception.

31) **That was the last time I saw him before getting a call that he was in the hospital.**

   a) The writer used the First Person-Simple Past Tense, which indicates he is committed to the activity in this sentence.

   b) The Text Bridge "before" creates an information gap from the last time the writer saw Dan until he got a call that he was in the hospital.

   c) The Word Qualifier "That was the last time I saw him" is unusual. One hypothesis posits that the writer may have tried to present an alibi or justification as to why he could not have been the person who shook Dan.

32) **I got that call from Kristine at 12:38 but did not hear it.**

   a) The writer used the First Person-Simple Past Tense, which indicates he is committed to the activity in this sentence.

b) The Spontaneous Negation "but I did not hear it" indicates a high probability of deception. A Competing Hypothesis posits that the writer may have asked himself the question to himself, "Why didn't I answer the phone the first time it rang?" and wrote the answer, "Because I did not hear it." In this instance, "but I did not hear" is a negation and not a Spontaneous Negation.

c) The writer provided a time reference of 12:38.

33) **I called her back at 12:44 but got no answer. I then called my wife, Jenny, and she told me to get to the hospital.**

a) The writer used the First Person-Simple Past Tense, which indicates he is committed to the activity in this sentence.

b) The Text Bridge "then" creates an information gap from the time he called her back and got no answer until the time Jenny answered the telephone.

c) The writer provided a time reference of 12:44.

Observations

Time Line
- 6:50–The writer woke up, took a shower, shaved, got his boxers on, and went downstairs to prepare Dan's meal.
- 7:20–The writer took Dan downstairs to feed him.
- 20 Minutes–The writer held and burped Dan after he finished eating.
- 8:35–The writer dropped Dan of at the babysitter's house.
- 12:38–The writer received a telephone call from Kristine.
- 12:44–The writer called Kristine but got no answer.

The police investigators suspected the writer of shaking Dan; therefore, any time that the writer and Dan shared the same space should be examined in great detail. The writer got up a 6:50, showered, shaved, put on his boxers, and went downstairs to prepare Dan's food. The writer went upstairs to feed Dan. Up to this point, the writer and Dan were not proximal, so this information is not critical. From the beginning of the written narrative until now, the writer used the First Person-Simple Past Tense, which indicates that he committed to the activities he described. The first physical contact the writer had with Dan was when he rubbed his belly to wake him. The critical area begins here. The Text Bridge "when," which created an information gap from the time the writer first saw Dan until the time the writer rubbed Dan's belly. This information gap is not significant because Dan was asleep. What is significant is the fact that the writer added the Word Qualifier "gave me a big smile" to send the message that Dan was happy when he woke. This Extraneous Information may have been an attempt by the writer at perception management. The writer wanted to ensure the reader that Dan was in a good mood and was not a source of frustration. Adults typically shake babies when the babies are noncompliant. The writer took Dan downstairs and fed him. The writer use the present tense "feed," the Text Bridge "then," and the Spontaneous Negation "He finished the cereal with no fuss." The combination of the present tense, the Text Bridge, and the Spontaneous Negation indicates deception. If the syringe feeding was uneventful, then the writer would have simply written, "He finished his cereal and went to the bottle." The writer's use of a Spontaneous Negation strongly suggests that he had trouble syringe feeding Dan. This may have been a source of frustration to the writer. Additionally, the writer may have been in a hurry that morning because he had to help move some items at the Lions Club. The writer used the Text Bridge "then," which created an information gap from the time he finished syringe feeding Dan to the time he started drinking from the bottle. This is a critical area because the writer wrote that Dan ate less than he normally did, which could be the source of the writer's frustration. The Push-Pull Word "normal" suggests that something not normal happened that morning. The writer used the Text Bridge "so," which created an information gap from the time Dan ate 4 1/2 ounces to the time when he would have eaten 7 ounces. Something occurred to cause Dan not to eat his normal serving of breakfast; however, the writer did not provide a reason for Dan's underperformance. The writer used the Text Bridge "after," which created an information gap from the time Dan finished his cereal to the time the writer burped Dan. The writer also used the present tense, "is," "burp," and "hold," which indicates that the writer may have fabricated this portion of the story. The writer used the Word Qualifier "today," which suggests that the writer did not normally hold Dan for 20 minutes. The writer used the Text Bridge "after," which created an information gap from the beginning of meal time to the time when the writer held Dan. The writer used the Word Qualifier "about," which suggests that Dan being asleep after breakfast was unusual; however, the writer did not indicate what was unusual that day. The writer used the Text Bridge "after," which created an information gap between the time the writer first held Dan until the time he took Dan upstairs and put him on the changing table. The writer used the Text Bridge "then," which created an information gap from the time the writer put Dan on the changing table to the time he woke Dan up. The writer again wrote that Dan was in a great mood. This is the third time that the writer mentioned that Dan was in a good mood and did not fuss during feeding. The writer wanted to ensure that the investigator got the message that Dan was not a source of frustration for the writer. The Text Bridge "then" created an information gap from the time he changed Dan's diaper until the time he put Dan on the bed. The writer added the Extraneous Information that he was a Lions Club member, which may be an attempt by the writer to manage the perception of the investigator by introducing the notion that he is an active member of the Lions Club and could not have possibly lost his temper and shaken Dan.

One hypothesis posits that the writer was in a hurry that morning because he had to move grills for the Lions Club and rushed through Dan's feeding. When Dan fussed, the writer became frustrated. The writer shook Dan out of frustration. The writer realized that he may have hurt Dan and consoled him for 20 minutes. When Dan stopped crying, the writer continued his normal activities. The writer supports this hypothesis when he wrote "he was awake and was in a good mood the whole time since changing him after his feeding." This statement divides the writer's activities with Dan into two segments, the time before he finished feeding and changing him and the time after he finished feeding him and changing him. In this sentence, the writer described Dan's mood after his feeding. When the writer wrote the "whole time," he referred only to the segment after Dan's feeding. The writer used the Word Qualifier "whole time" to give the reader the illusion that Dan was in a good mood the entire morning, when this was probably not the case. If Dan was in a good mood since his feeding, then he was in a less than a good mood before he finished feeding. The writer's use of Text Bridges, Word Qualifiers, Push-Pull Words, and a Spontaneous Negation during his description of the segment before Dan finished feeding suggests deception. The writer began his written narrative using the First Person Simple Past Tense. He took the reader to the Land of Is when he described his activities while feeding Dan and after feeding Dan, the writer returned to the use of the First Person Simple Past Tense. The writer's deviation from his baseline further supports the Hypothesis that the writer shook Dan out of frustration. Additionally, the writer shouted his message by telling the reader several times that Dan was in a good mood. If Dan was always in a good mood, then his being in a good mood this morning would be usual and the writer would not have to keep reminding the reader.

RAPE CASE

The writer accused a police officer of raping her during a traffic stop. She reported this incident to the police internal affairs division. The investigating officer asked the woman to make a written statement of the alleged crime. Her statement reads as follows:

> I was on my way home from my boyfriend's house when I was pulled over by a police officer. I ask him what I did he told me to stay in my car then he came

back and told me to get out of my car he walk me to his car told me to turn around a his handcuff my hand behind my back and put me in the back seat of his car then he got in the car a drove the car turned around the corner and went down a little way then he turned the car off and got in the back seat with me then he put tape across my mouth and eyes than he uncuff me took off my sweater then put the cuff back on me then be began to take off my pant's then he started to play with my virgina then he starte to grab my breast then he stop I could hear him grabbing a bag then after that he began to stick he pensis in me and evertime he kept saying you deserve this you deserve this when his was done I heard him open the door

I could see me pull his pant's he closed the door when the door open agained and he pulled me out of the car and told me to stand up then told me to start walking forward I rember hearing a lot of dunking and water then he told me to stop then I heard boy's and then he un-cuffed my hand's and told me not to move I could here him walking away from me and that his when I thought he was going to shoot me I just stay there than I heart a door close and the car being started I just stay and did move for a while then I finally removed the tape from my mout's and eye's seen my clothe put them on began to walk forward's I saw piscince beach and then I look to the other side and saw my car 11) I got into my car and went home This statement is ture and coreect

1) I was on my way home from my boyfriend's house when I was pulled over by a police officer,
   a) A comma was used instead of a period. This was the only time the writer used sentence punctuation, which suggests the writer received little formal education.
   b) The formula First Person Simple Past Tense indicates the writer is commitment to the action in this sentence.
   c) The use of the Article "a" to describe the police officer is nonspecific suggesting the writer was unfamiliar with the police officer. The appropriate identification cue should have been the Article "the" police officer, indicating the writer was already familiar with the police officer, which would have been the case if the writer was recalling the incident from memory. However, if the writer was fabricating the story, she would have been thinking in the present tense, which is an indicator of deception. Another hypothesis posits that the writer experienced a traumatic event and she is reliving the incident as she is relating the story in the Present Tense, which is an indicator of truthfulness.

2) I ask him what I did
   a) No sentence punctuation.
   b) The present tense "ask" suggests the writer fabricated the story as she was writing the statement. When a story is recalled from memory, the past tense is typically used because the activity or action recalled is seen in the writer's mind as having been previously completed. When a story

is fabricated, the events are visualized in the present tense and the writer often neglects to frame the activity or event in the past tense.

c) The Personal Identifier "him" replaced "a police officer." The writer continued to use the Personal Identifier "him" throughout the rest of the statement. The writer's attempt to distance herself from the police officer is either due to the writer's contempt for the person who raped her or is due to the writer's attempt to avoid further description of a nonexistent police officer.

3) **he told me to stay in my car then he came back and told me to get out of my car**

a) The first word in the sentence is not capitalized.

b) No sentence punctuation.

c) The Communication Word "told" suggests a one-way conversation. Within context, the use of the Communication Word "told" is appropriate.

d) The Push-Pull Word "he came back" indicates the police officer approached her car, left, and returned to her car. The writer did not provide any information about the first time that the police officer approached her car. The initial exchange between the officer and the writer is critical and should be explored in more detail.

e) The Text Bridge "then" creates an information gap from the time the police officer told the writer to stay in her car to the time he came back and told her to get out of the car.

4) **he walk me to his car told me to turn around a his handcuff my hand behind my back and put me in the back seat of his car then he got in the car a drove the car turned around the corner and went down a little way then he turned the car off and got in the back seat with me then he put tape across my mouth and eyes than he uncuff me took off my sweater then put the cuff back on me then he began to take off my pant's then he started to play with my virgina then he started to grab my breast then he stop**

a) The first word in the sentence is not capitalized.

b) No sentence punctuation.

c) The present tense "walk" and "handcuff" suggests the writer fabricated the story as she was writing the statement. When a story is recalled from memory, the past tense is used because the activity or action recalled is seen in the writer's mind as having been previously completed. When a story is fabricated, the events are visualized in the present tense and the writer often neglects to frame the activity or event in the past tense.

d) The Communication Word "told" suggests a one-way conversation. Within context, the use of the Communication Word "told" is appropriate.

e) The writer used the singular "hand" instead of the plural hands.

f) A disjunction exists between the actions "told me to turn around" and "a his handcuff my hand behind my back." The omission of the conjunction *and* suggests these two actions were not connected in the same action. The grammar structure used in this sentence is faulty, which suggests the possibility that the writer is uneducated or may have diminished mental capacity.

g) The writer used the Article "the" to describe a specific car not the Article "a" as she did when she described the police officer in the first sentence. The appropriate use of the Article "the" in this sentence supports the hypothesis that the use of the Article "a" in the first sentence indicates that the writer may have fabricated the encounter with the police officer.

h) The Text Bridge "then" creates an information gap from the time the police officer went down a little way to the time he turned the car off.

i) The word "turned" is misspelled.

j) The Word Clue "got in the back seat with me" suggests a relationship between the writer and the police officer. Typically, when a man approaches a woman to rape her, the woman does not describe the man as being with her but is more likely to report something to the effect, "He got in the back and put tape on my mouth and eyes."

k) The Text Bridge "then" creates an information gap from the time the police officer got into the back to the time he put tape across the writer's mouth and eyes.

l) The present tense "uncuff" suggests the writer fabricated the story as she was writing the statement. When a story is recalled from memory, the past tense is used because the activity or action recalled is seen in the writer's mind as having been previously completed. When a story is fabricated, the events are visualized in the present tense and the writer often neglects to frame the activity or event in the past tense.

m) The Text Bridge "then" creates an information gap from the time the police officer took off the writer's sweater to the time the police officer put the cuff back on.

n) The writer used the singular word "cuff" instead of the plural "cuffs." The writer used the singular "hand" to describe the first time she was handcuffed, and in this sentence, she used the singular word "cuff."

o) The Text Bridge "then" created an information gap from the time the police officer put the cuffs back on the writer until the time he began to take off the writer's pants.

p) The Stopped-Action Word "began" indicates that some action prevented the police officer from completing the action of taking the writer's pants off.

q) The writer wrote "pant's" instead of "pants."

r) The Text Bridge "then" creates an information gap from the time the police officer began to pull the writer's pants off until the time he started to play with writer's vagina.

s) The Stopped-Action Word "started "indicates that some action prevented the police officer from completing the action of playing with the writer's vagina.

t) The writer misspelled the word "vagina."

u) The Text Bridge "then" creates an information gap from the time the police officer played with the writer's vagina until the time he started to grab the writer's breast.

v) The Stopped-Action Word "started" indicates that some action prevented the police officer from completing the action of grabbing her breasts.

w) The Text Bridge "then" creates an information gap from the time the police officer started to grab the writer's breast until the time he stopped.

x) The present tense "stop" indicates deception.

y) The writer used the singular form to describe her body parts (e.g., hand and breast).

z) When the writer described the rape sequence, she described it as though she was going through the steps that she thought were logical for a rapist to take and not the actions of the rapist. For example, the writer stated, "then he uncuff me took off my sweater then put the cuff back on me." A rapist would not logically uncuff his victim to take her sweater off and then replace the cuffs. The nature of rape suggests the woman is not a willing participant so, why would the rapist risk uncuffing his victim when he could easily access the victim's breasts by sliding his hand under her sweater. Either the writer was a willing participant or the possibility exits that she is fabricating the rape sequence.

aa) This long run-on sentence suggests the writer received little formal education.

5) **I could hear him grabbing a bag then after that he began to stick he pensis in me and evertime he kept saying you deserve this you deserve this**

a) The first word in the sentence is not capitalized.

b) No sentence punctuation.

c) The Text Bridge "then" and "after" creating an information gap from the time she could hear the police officer grabbing a bag until the time the police officer began to stick his penis in the writer.

d) The writer used the Word Clue "bag." Bag is the slang for condom. Younger people use the term bag. The writer is probably in her late teens or early twenties.

e) The word "penis" is misspelled.

f) The Stopped-Action Word "began" indicates that some action prevented the police officer from completing the action of sticking his penis into the writer.

g) The present tense "stick" indicates deception.

h) The writer used the Personal Identifier "he" to describe the rapist's penis instead of the possessive pronoun "his." The Personal Identifier "his" attaches the penis to the police officer. By omitting the pronoun "his," the writer separated the police officer from his penis suggesting it was not the police officer's penis that was used to rape her.

i) The Word Clue "you deserve this you deserve this" indicates the writer felt as though something she did caused the rape.

6) when his was done I heard him open the door

a) The first word in the sentence is not capitalized.

b) No sentence punctuation.

c) The writer used the Personal Identifier "his" instead of the pronoun "he."

d) The Word Clue "when his was done" suggests she focused on the action of rapist's penis not the rapist, himself. In conjunction with the Word Clue in Sentence 5 "you deserve this you deserve this," the writer might associates the male penis as a means to punishment her.

7) I could see me pull his pant's

a) No sentence punctuation.

b) The writer used the Personal Identifier "me" instead of "his."

c) The Word Clue "I could see me pull his pant's" suggests the writer may have fantasized about having sex with the police officer.

d) The writer stated earlier that the police officer put tape over her eyes making it impossible for her to physically see anything except in her mind's eye. This supports the hypothesis that the writer fantasized about having sex with the police officer.

8) he closed the door when the door open agained and he pulled me out of the car and told me to stand up then I he told me to start walking forward

a) The first word in the sentence is not capitalized.

b) No sentence punctuation

c) The writer misused the word "again(ed)."

d) The Present Tense "open" indicates deception.

e) The writer used the Strikeout "I" and wrote "he" suggesting the writer had control of her actions and therefore she was not under the control of the police officer. She may not have been handcuffed as she indicated earlier.

9) **I rember hearing a lot of (dunking) and water then he told me to stop then I heard key's and then he un-cuffed my hand's and told me not to move**
   a) No sentence punctuation.
   b) The word "remember" is misspelled.
   c) The present tense "remember" which indicates deception. A Competing Hypothesis posits that while the writer is writing the statement, she is remembering back to the incident. In this context the use of the present tense "remember" may be appropriate.
   d) The writer used the plural "hands."
   e) The writer placed the word "dunking" in parenthesis, which separates this activity from the other activity in the sentence.
   f) The writer used past tense "told," "heard," and "uncuffed."
   g) The Text Bridge then creates an information gap from the time she heard water until the time the police officer told her to stop.
   h) The Text Bridge "then" creates an information gap from the time she heard keys until the time the police officer uncuffed her.
   i) The Text Bridge "then" creates an information gap from the time she heard keys until the time the police officer uncuffed her. The writer used two Text Bridges to span this information gap.
   j) The writer used the word "key's" instead of "keys."

10) **I could here him walking away from me and that his when I thought he was going to shoot me**
   a) No sentence punctuation.
   b) Writer misused the word "hear."
   c) The writer used the word "his" instead of the word "is." If this was the case, then the writer used the present tense, which suggests deception. A Competing Hypothesis posits that the writer used the Hanging Word "his," but did not finish the describing "his what."

11) **I just stay there than I heart a door close and the car being started**
   a) No sentence punctuation.
   b) The writer misused the word "heart."
   c) The Word Qualifier "just" minimizes this action.
   d) The present tense "stay" indicates deception.
   e) The Passive Language "being started" suggests the writer distanced herself from this activity.

12) **I just stay and did move for a while then I finally removed the tape from my mout's and eye's seen my clothe put them on began to walk forward's**
   a) The first word in the sentence is not capitalized.
   b) No sentence punctuation.
   c) The writer used the present tense "stay."

d) The Word Qualifier "did move for awhile" suggests that the writer had some freedom of movement. A competing hypothesis posits that the writer omitted the word "not."

e) The Push-Pull Word "finally" pushes off the word not finally, which suggests that the writer engaged in some activities prior to removing the tape from her mouth and eyes. This supports the hypothesis that the writer had some freedom of movement as discussed in the previous comment.

13) **I saw (piscince beach) and then I look to the other side and saw my car**

a) The first word in the sentence is not capitalized.

b) No sentence punctuation.

c) The present tense "look" indicates deception.

d) The writer placed the words "piscince beach" in parenthesis, which separates this activity from the other activities in the sentence.

e) The writer wrote that she saw piscince beach. In the town where the rape allegedly occurred there are no beaches or water bodies. There are no landmarks, streets, or buildings called piscince beach. A Competing Hypothesis posits that the writer may have used a personal nickname for some landmark in the area. Knowledge of the area where the activity occurred can provide crucial information to support or reject a hypothesis or competing hypotheses.

f) The Text Bridge "then" creates an information gap from the time the writer saw piscince beach to the time she looked to the other side.

g) The Word Qualifier "look to the other side and saw my car" suggests the car was in the writer's direct line of sight. In sentence 4, the writer wrote, ". . . put me in the back seat of his car then he got in the car and drove the car turned around the corner and went down a little way . . ." If this activity occurred, the writer's car would not have been in her direct line of sight.

14) **I got into my car and went home**

a) The first word in the sentence is not capitalized.

b) No sentence punctuation.

c) The Word Clue "went home" suggests that the writer did not call the police or seek medical assistance.

15) **This statement is ture and coreect**

a) The first word in the sentence is not capitalized.

b) No sentence punctuation.

c) The writer misspelled the word "True."

d) The writer misspelled the word "correct."

Observations

Based on the abundance of PNA indicators, the writer's story is suspect. The investigator should conduct a Micro-Action Interview beginning from the time the police officer first made contact with the writer.

MISSING AIRPLANE TIRES

The following is a PNA of the written statement by the truck driver who mysteriously lost a pallet of three airplane tires off the back of his truck while he was driving from Los Angeles to Lancaster, California. If you have not yet identified the word that reveals what really happened, look for it as you read through the PNA analysis. The word will be identified at the end of analysis as well as the outcome of the case.

Arrived LA dock 18:45 loaded 3 pallets to rental truck stack bed, 2 pallets airplane tires–1 pallet with 2 boxes. Departed LA dock 19:30 for Lancaster. About 21:00 between top of truck ramp from I-5 to the 14 Freeway and camper pulls along side of me and tell me that a pallet had fallen out of the back of my truck. And just before that when I got to the top of the truck ramp had pulled over to check straps (strike) on trucks–all 3 pallets were still aboard. So when I got to Sand Canyon Rd pulled off to check load and both straps + chain was loose or off of pallets and there was only 2 pallets on truck, 1 pallet of 2 boxes + 1 pallet of 3 airplane tires. So I (strikeout) turned around (strikeout) and went back toward LA looking for the missing pallet. Found nothing. Went onto Lancaster office. Unloaded truck.

1) **Arrived LA dock 18:45 loaded 3 pallets to rental truck stack bed, 2 pallets airplane tires, 1 pallet with 2 boxes. (Sequential)**
   a) The driver provides the time reference 18:45.
   b) The driver used the military notation for the time.
   c) The driver omitted the Pronoun "I."
   d) The driver did not use the First Person Simple Past Tense, which indicates the driver is not committed to the activities in this sentence.
   e) The driver used the Word Clue "LA," which suggests that he lives in the greater Los Angeles area. LA is commonly used instead of Los Angeles by people who live in or near LA.
   f) The driver used the Word Clue "loaded to rental truck." This word usage is not normal. Things are loaded on, onto, or in trucks not to trucks. "To trucks" is typically used when transferring items from one truck to another truck.

g) The Word Clue "rental truck," suggests the driver does not routinely ship goods. If he shipped goods on a regular basis, he would probably own his own truck. If he did ship goods on a regular basis and had a long-term rental or lease, he would have referred to the vehicle as a truck.

h) The Word Clue "stack bed" lends support to the hypothesis that the driver does not ship goods on a regular basis. The correct term for the type of truck the writer referred to is "stake bed" not "stack bed."

2) **Departed LA dock 1930 for Lancaster. (Sequential)**
   a) The driver omitted the Pronoun "I."
   b) The driver did not use the First Person Simple Past Tense, which indicates the driver is not committed to the activities in this sentence.
   c) The driver provided a time reference of 1930.

3) **About 2100 between top of truck ramp from I-5 to the 14 Freeway and camper pulls along side of me and tell me that a pallet had fallen out of the back of my truck. (Sequential)**
   a) The driver provided a time reference.
   b) The driver used the Present Tense "pulls" and "tell," which indicates deception.
   c) The driver used the Possessive Pronoun "my truck" in this sentence but used the word rental to describe the same truck in Sentence 2. One hypothesis posits that the driver already transferred the missing pallet to another waiting truck. Since the theft already occurred, the driver felt comfortable claiming the truck as his. A Competing Hypothesis posits that since the driver had been driving the truck for about an hour and a half, he psychologically taken possession of the truck.

4) **And just before that when I got to the top of the truck ramp had pulled over to check straps (strikeout) on trucks–all 3 pallets were still aboard. (Out of Sequence)**
   a) The driver used the First Person Simple Past Tense, which suggests he committed to the activities in this sentence.
   b) This sentence is Out of Logical Sequence. In sentence four, the truck driver wrote that a camper pulled alongside and told him that a pallet had fallen out of the back of his truck. In sentence 5, the truck driver wrote that just before the camper came along side his truck, he stopped at the top of the truck ramp and pulled over to check straps on all three pallets.
   c) The driver used the Text Bridge "when" creating an information gap from the time the camper pulled alongside him to the time he got to the top of the truck ramp.
   d) The writer used the Word Qualifier "all." The driver wanted to ensure the reader that all three pallets were still on the back of the truck.
   e) The driver used the plural "trucks" instead of the singular "truck," indicating that he checked more than one truck.

f) The driver omitted the Article "the straps" and "the trucks." In sentence 3, the driver used the possessive pronoun "my" to describe the truck. The Change in Language suggests the driver distanced himself from the truck.

g) The Strikeout was unintelligible.

5) **So when I got to Sand Canyon Rd pulled off to check load and both straps + chain was loose or off the pallets and there was only 2 pallets on truck−1 pallet of 2 boxes + 1 pallet of 3 airplane tires.**

a) The driver used the Personal Identifier "I got to Sand Canyon", but omitted the Personal Identifier "I" when he pulled off, indicating that the he is committed to getting to Sand Canyon but he is not committed to pulling off.

b) The driver used the First Person Simple Past Tense "I got to Sand Canyon," which indicates he is committed to this activity. The driver did not use the First Person Simple Past Tense, in the rest of the sentence, which indicates the driver is not committed to the activities in the rest of the sentence.

c) The driver used the Word Qualifier "straps + chains." In Sentence 4, the driver wrote that he checked the straps. The driver may have used the Word Qualifier "straps" to give the reader the impression that the load was very secure because there were straps and chains.

d) The driver used the Text Bridge "So" creating an information gap from the time there was only two pallets on the truck to the time he turned around.

6) **So I (Strikeout) turned around (Strikeout) and went back toward LA looking for the missing pallet. (Return to Sequential)**

a) The driver used the First Person Simple Past Tense, which indicates he is committed to the activities in this sentence.

b) The driver used the Text Bridge "so" creating an information gap from the time the driver noticed one pallet missing to the time when he turned around.

7) **Found nothing. (Sequential)**

a) The driver omitted the Pronoun "I."

b) The driver did not use the First Person Simple Past Tense, which indicates the driver is not committed to the activities in this sentence.

8) **I went to the Lancaster office. (Sequential)**

a) The driver used the First Person Simple Past Tense, which suggests he committed to the activities in this sentence.

9) **Unloaded truck. (Sequential)**

a) The driver omitted the Pronoun "I."

b) The driver did not use the First Person Simple Past Tense, which indicates the driver is not committed to the activities in this sentence.

Sentences 1, 2, and 3 are in logical sequence. Sentence 4 is out of sequence. The writer wrote "a camper pulls along side of me and tell me that a pallet had fallen out of the back of my truck" and then the writer wrote about what he did right before the camper pulled alongside him. The driver used the past tense in Sentences 1 and 2 and changed to the Present tense in Sentences 3. The driver changes back to Past Tense in Sentences 5 through 9 and used the past tense for the remainder of the statement. The change in tense signals the possibility of deception. The writer used Change of Language from truck in Sentences 1, 4, 7, and 12 to trucks in Sentence 5, which indicates the possibility that he checked the straps on more than one truck. The lack of the First Person Simple Past Tense suggests the driver is committed to some parts of his story but not to other parts of his story. This is normal because most people mix the truth with lies to make detection more difficult.

One hypothesis posits the driver exited at Sand Canyon Road, met an awaiting truck, transferred one pallet of airplane tires from his truck to the awaiting truck, checked the chains on his truck and the straps on the other truck, and drove off. The driver wrote the plural "trucks" which supports the hypothesis that he transferred the tires from his truck to another truck. If this is the case then, the driver would have had to check the straps on his truck as well as the straps on the second truck. The driver fabricated the camper notifying him of the missing pallet to make his story more believable. Knowing this information before interviewing the driver gives the interviewer an advantage. The interviewer must develop one or more Competing Hypothesis to avoid the Primacy Effect.

When the investigator interviewed the driver, he told the driver that the facts of the case were odd in that no one reported the incident to 911 nor were the tires found on or near the road, so he conducted a neighborhood canvass of the houses located on the ridge above Sand Canyon Road. The investigator told the driver that he found the neighborhood snoop and she reported that she saw two trucks in the isolated area just off Sand Canyon Road. They transferred big tires from one truck to the other truck and drove off. The investigator created the Primacy Effect that someone witnessed the transfer of the tires. The driver faced a volatile conundrum. He does not know if the investigator made up the story about the nosey neighbor or if someone really saw the transfer of the tires. If the driver did transfer the tires as suggested by the PNA indicators in of his statement, he may admit to the theft or, at least, try to explain why the other truck was there. If the driver did not steal the tires, then the investigator lost nothing by the ruse. He could always say, "You know how those nosey neighbors can be."

The one word in this statement that revealed what really happened is the word "trucks." The driver pulled off the highway at Sand Canyon Road, transferred the tires to a waiting truck. The driver admitted that he checked the straps on both trucks before driving off and thus correctly used the plural "trucks." The driver was arrested for theft of government property, served a short prison sentence, and was on probation for five years.

Appendix B

PNA OF ORAL COMMUNICATIONS

Using PNA indicators to analyze oral narratives is more difficult than analyzing written narratives because words are fleeting. A line by line analysis of oral narratives is not possible. Interviewers should practice listening for PNA indicators and recognize that that the interviewee is telling the truth, going to the Land of Is, or omitting information. The use of parenthetical comments in the following examples serves to demonstrate how to quickly recognize PNA indicators during oral communication.

JOB APPLICANT

Consider the following exchange between a job applicant and a human resource person.

> **HR PERSON:** I see in your resume that you have a bachelor's degree in business administration.
> **JOB APPLICANT:** I attended the University of Illinois and majored in business administration. I also minored in psychology. Minoring in psychology helped me increase sales numbers in my previous position. Does your company offer a continuing education program? I'm thinking about going after my MBA.

(The job applicant used the Word Qualifiers attended and "majored in business administration" to give the impression that he received a degree from the University of Illinois. The job applicant stated that minoring in psychology increased his sales numbers in his previous position. This statement accomplishes two goals. First, it supports the illusion that the job applicant received a bachelor's degree and second, it creates the illusion that the job applicant was successful in his previous position. The Job Applicant used Misdirection to change the focus of the question from earning a bachelor's degree to his ambition of earning a MBA. This Misdirection achieved two goals. First, it supports the illusion that the job applicant received a bachelor's degree and second, creates the illusion that the job applicant is ambitious. The interviewer recognized the job applicant's non-answer and asked a direct question for clarification. The job applicant told the truth, but the truth about what?)

> **HR PERSON:** What year did you graduate?
> **JOB APPLICANT:** I attended the University of Illinois from 1978 to 1982. I really enjoyed my college years. Don't you wish life was that simple again?

(The job applicant used the Word Qualifier "attended." The job applicant used the Word Qualifiers "1978 to 1982" to give the illusion that he graduated in 1982. Many students attend universities but do not graduate. The job applicant used Misdirection to change the focus of the question from the year he graduated to his quality of life at college. The job applicant further used Misdirection "Don't you wish life was that simple again?" to redirect the conversation from the year he graduated to the interviewer's quality of life at college. The interviewer recognized the job applicant's non-answer and asked a direct question for clarification. The job applicant told the truth, but the truth about what?)

> **HR PERSON:** So, you received your bachelor's degree in 1982?
> **JOB APPLICANT:** Yes, that's when I left the University of Illinois.

(The Word Qualifier "left" indicates that he may have left the university without receiving a degree. The interviewer recognized the job applicant's nonanswer and asked a direct question for clarification. The job applicant told the truth, but the truth about what?)

> **PERSON:** Did you leave with a bachelor's degree?
> **JOB APPLICANT:** I had to leave college for a while because my mom got sick and I had to care for her. I would have had a bachelor's degree except for a few classes I have to take.

(The job applicant used Future in the Past "I would have had a bachelor's degree." The job applicant told the interviewer what he would have had not what he actually has. The job applicant used the Word Qualifier "except for a few classes" to continue the illusion that has a bachelor's degree within the framework of Future in the Past. The job applicant introduced an emotional component to his response by stating, "I had to leave college for a while because my mom got sick and I had to care for her." The job applicant used the Word Qualifier "for a while" to give the illusion that he returned to complete his degree.

> **HR PERSON:** So, you don't have your bachelor's degree yet, but you are taking classes to complete the degree. It takes a person with a lot of determination to work and go to school at the same time.
> **JOB APPLICANT:** Yes sir, it does.

(The HR Person forced the job applicant to admit that he does not have a college degree while, at the same time, putting a positive spin on the job applicant's oversight by telling him that it takes a determined person to work and go to school at the same time. The HR Person will not likely hire the job applicant because he lacks candor, which is not a good trait in a potential employee.)

ROGER CLEMENS

Roger Clemens is a professional baseball player who was accused of using human growth hormones (HGH) to enhance his performance on the baseball field. The following is an excerpt from the Congressional testimony of Roger Clemens regarding his use of Human Growth Hormone.

> **CHAIRMAN WAXMAN:** Under the previous unanimous consent agreement, we will control 15 minutes in the first round, and Mr. Davis, 15 minutes on his side. And I would like to yield at this time five minutes to Mr. Cummings. I would like to yield a full 15 minutes to Mr. Cummings.
> **MR. CUMMINGS:** Thank you very much, Mr. Chairman. And thank you, gentlemen, for being with us this morning. And I was very pleased to hear both of the witnesses talk about children, because that is what this was all about what we started, so many children trying to emulate their sports stars. I am going to ask you a few questions, Clemens, and I first want to make sure that you are very clear. You understand that you are under oath; is that correct?
> **MR. CLEMENS:** That's correct.
> **MR. CUMMINGS:** And you know what that means; is that correct?
> **MR. CLEMENS:** That's correct.

MR. CUMMINGS: Very well. First of all, Mr. Pettitte, Andy Pettitte, is one of the most respected players in the major leagues, and commentator after commentator said that he is one of the most honest people in baseball. Would you agree with that?

MR. CLEMENS: I would agree with that, yes, sir.

MR. CUMMINGS: In fact, this is what your own lawyer, Rusty Hardin, said about Mr. Pettitte in the New York Times, "We have nothing to fear about what Andy may testify to. Everyone says that Andy is honest. We have no reason to believe he will lie." Would you agree with the statement your lawyer made?

MR. CLEMENS: I would agree with that, yes.

MR. CUMMINGS: Very well. Now, Mr. Clemens, I want to ask you just one thing. In his deposition, Mr. Pettitte told the committee that he had a conversation with you in 1999 or 2000 in which you admitted that you used human growth hormones. Is that true?

MR. CLEMENS: It is not.

MR. CUMMINGS: And–but at the same time you just said that he is a very honest fellow; is that right?

MR. CLEMENS: I believe Andy to be a very honest fellow, yes.

MR. CUMMINGS: Very well. Let's continue. In his deposition, Mr. Pettitte was honest and forthcoming with the committee. He told us things that were embarrassing, that we had no way of knowing except through his own testimony. First, he confirmed that Mr. NcNamee injected him with HGH in 2002, which is in the Mitchell Report. You understand that, right?

MR. CLEMENS: I do.

MR. CUMMINGS: Then he told us that he injected himself, again, in 2004. We did not know about the 2004 injection, but he volunteered that information because he wanted the committee to know the entire truth. It was hard for Mr. Pettitte to tell the committee about the 2004 injections. The circumstances which he described in length were exceptionally personal and embarrassing. But it was even harder for him to talk about you, Mr. Clemens. He is friends with both you and Mr. McNamee, and he felt caught in the middle. During his deposition, he was asked how he would resolve the conflict between two friends. Here is what he said, "I have to tell you all the truth. And one day I have to give an account for, and not to nobody else, of what I have done in my life. And that is why I said and shared that stuff with y'all that I would now like to share with y'all. Now, Mr. Clemens, I remind you that you are under oath. Mr. Clemens, do you think Mr. Pettitte was lying when he told the committee that you admitted using human growth hormones?

(Cummings asked a Yes or No question. Yes or No questions deserve "Yes" or "No" answers. Clemens took Cummings to the Land of Is.

MR. CLEMENS: Mr. Congressman Andy Pettitte is my friend. He will–he was my friend before this. He will be my friend after this. And again, I think Andy has misheard.

(Clemens used the Word Qualifier "misheard." Clemens did not say that Pettitte was lying; he only misheard. The Word Qualifier "think," which means that Clemens was not sure that Pettitte misheard; therefore, the possibility exists that he heard correctly. Cummings should have pursued the possibility that Pettitte did not mishear.)

MR. CUMMINGS: I'm sorry, I didn't hear you.
MR. CLEMENS: I believe Andy has misheard, Mr. Congressman, on his comments about myself using HGH, which never happened.

(The Word Qualifier "believe"indicates that Clemens is not sure that Pettitte misheard. Again, the possibility exists that Pettette heard correctly. This sentence makes little sense when the extraneous words "Mr. Congressman" are removed. The sentence reads, "I believe Andy has misheard on his comments about myself using HGH, which never happened."

(response cont.) The conversation that I can recall, that I had with Andy Pettitte, was at my house in Houston, while we were working out. And I had expressed to him about a TV show something that I have heard about three older men that were using HGH and getting back their quality of life from that. Those are the conversations that I can remember.

(The Push-Pull Word "recall" indicates that other conversations took place; however, he cannot recall them. The Word Clue "expressed" indicates that he tried to give a formal answer using word he was not comfortable with. One hypothesis posits that Clemen's tried to give a formal answer. Clemens use of Pettitte's full name supports this hypothesis. The Word Qualifier "heard about" suggests that he did not actually see the TV show himself. The plural "conversations" indicates that he did recall more than one conversation. Cummings should have asked Clemens about those other conversations that he recalled.)

(response cont.) Andy and I's friendship and closeness was such that, first of all, when I learned when he was–when he said that he used

HGH, I was shocked and had no idea. When I just heard your statement and Andy's statement about that he also injected himself, I was
shocked. I had no idea that Andy Pettitte had used HGH.

(Clemens misused the Personal Identifier "I." He should have said "my." The
misuse of the Personal Identifier could support the hypothesis that Clemens
tried to make his answer sound formal by using words that he thought would
make his statement sound more formal. The Word Qualifier "also injected"
indicates that there is more than one method to ingest HGH. One hypothesis posits that Clemens was shocked by the fact that Pettitte injected HGH,
not that he used HGH, probably in another form when he was with
Clemens.)

> (**response cont.**) My problem with what Andy says, and why I think he
> misremembers, is that if Andy Pettitte knew that I had used HGH, or
> that I had told Andy Pettitte that I had used HGH, what have you, he
> would have come to me and asked me about it. That is how close our
> relationship was. And then when he did use it.

(Clemens used the If/Then Conditional ". . . if Andy Pettitte knew that I had
used HGH, or that I had told Andy Pettitte that I had used HGH, what have
you, he would have come to me and asked me about it." Clemens supported this If/Then Conditional with the fact that he and Pettitte were close
friends, a fact Clemens mentioned several times. Clemmons only related
what he thought Pettitte would do under the parameters of the If/Then
Conditional, not what Pettitte actually did. The Word Clue "he would have
come to me and asked me about it" suggests that Clemens saw himself as a
person with sufficient knowledge to councel Pettitte on the use of HGH.)

> (**response cont.**) And I say that for the fact that we also used a product
> called Hydroxycut and ThermaCore. It had ephedra in it, from what I
> understand to be a natural tree root. I believe ephedra was banned in
> 2004, something of that nature. A player in Baltimore passed away
> because of it. Andy and I talked openly about this product. And so
> there is no question in my mind that we would have talked, if he knew
> that I had tried or done HGH, which I did not, he would have come to
> me to ask me those questions.

(Clemens used the IF/Then Conditional "if he knew that I had tried or done
HGH, which I did not, he would have come to me to ask me those ques-
tions." Clemens supported this If/Then Conditional with the fact that he and
Pettitte were close friends. Clemens further supported the If/Then Con-

ditional by stating, "And so there is no question in my mind that we would have talked." Clemens related what Pettitte would have done not what he actually did. Ironically, Clemens set himself up. Pettitte testified that he had conversations with Clemens about his HGH use. In his response, Clemens stated, "And so there is no question in my mind that we would have talked." Clemens actually supported Pettitte's testimony. Cummings missed an opportunity to trap Clemens. Clemens used Misdirection to change the focus of the question from ". . . do you think Mr. Pettite was lying when he told the committee that you admitted using human growth hormones? to his use of Hydroxycut and ThermaCore and what Pettitte would have done under certain conditions. Clemens did not address the question and took Cummings to the Land of Is.)

> **MR. CUMMINGS:** Well, let's continue. In the deposition, we wanted to make absolutely sure, because we knew the significance of this, that Mr. Pettitte had a clear recollection. And let me read another excerpt from the deposition, and this was a question to Mr. Pettitte: "you recollect a conversation with Mr. Clemens. Your recollection is that he said he was taking human growth hormone?" Answer: "yes." "And you have no doubt about that recollection?" "I mean, no, he told me that." Now, Mr. Clemens, you know Mr. Pettitte well. You just again describe your relationship. You described him as a close friend in your deposition. Would he tell the Congress that one of his close friends was taking an illegal, performance-enhancing drug if there were any doubt in his mind about the truth of what he was saying.
> **MR. CLEMENS:** Mr. Congressman, once again, I believe . . .
> **MR. CUMMINGS:** Please.
> **MR. CLEMENS:** I am sorry.
> **MR. CUMMINGS:** No, I just want you to go ahead and answer that. Do you think he would do that?

(Yes or No question deserve "Yes" or "No" answers. Clemens took Cummings to the Land of Is.

> **MR. CLEMENS:** I think he misremembers-

(The Word Qualifier "think" which indicates that he does not know if Pettitte misremembered. The possibility exists that Pettitte did remember correctly. Mr. Cummings should have asked the question, "So, there is a possibility that Pettitte remembered correctly, right?"

> **MR. CUMMINGS:** Very well.

(Mr. Cummings became frustrated because he did not know how to prevent Clemens from going to the Land of Is.)

> **MR. CLEMENS:** [continuing] our conversation. And let me add, in 2006–in 2006, he and I had a conversation in Atlanta's locker room when this *L.A. Times* report became public about a Grimsley report, and they said that Andy's and my name were listed in that. And I remember him coming into that room, the coach's room, the main office there of the clubhouse attendant, and sitting down in front of me, wringing his hands and looking at me like he saw a ghost. And he looked right at me and said, 'What are you going to tell them?' And I told him that I am going out there and I am going to tell them the truth, I did not do this, I never worked out with Jason Grimsley, he was a teammate of mine, and I never worked out with him. And I am going to go out there and tell them the truth. That alone should have confirmed Andy's misunderstanding that I have ever told him that I used HGH.

(Clemens used Miller's Law. Pettitte asked Clemens, "What are you going to tell them?" Clemens responded he was going to tell the truth. Clemens further said, "I did not do this. I never worked out with Jason Grimsley, he was a teammate of mine, and I never worked out with him. The Tag Qualifier "this" indicates that some portion of what he is about to say is true. The Tag Qualifier also leaves open the possibility that if Clemens did not do this, he did something else. Clemens said that Grimsley was his teammate but he never worked out with him. This is probably true. The Word Qualifier "worked out" restricts his contact with Grimsley to exercising. Clemens may have had contact with Grimsley other than when he exercised. Clemens added, "And I am going to go out there and tell them the truth." If the truth is Grimsley is his teammate and he never worked out with him, Clemens would be telling the truth, but the truth about what? Next Clemens inferred that because he told the truth about Grimsley, that he told the truth about his conversations with Pettitte. Clemens established a False Premise, I am believable (premise) because I told the truth about Grimsley (argument); therefore, I told the truth about my conversations with Pettitte (inference); Cummings missed another opportunity to trap Clemens.)

> **MR. CUMMINGS:** Very well. Let's continue, because I want to make sure that I get through some . . .
> **MR. CLEMENS:** Yes, sir.
> **MR. CUMMINGS:** [continuing] very key points, Mr. Clemens, you have been very critical of Mr. McNamee's motives. You just did it a few minutes ago. What possible motive would Mr. Pettitte have to fabricate a story about you, his friend?

MR. CLEMENS: Andy would have no reason to.

MR. CUMMINGS: Very well. This was so important we went back to Mr. Pettitte a third time, a third time. We asked him to submit an affidavit to the committee. This gave him a chance to express his recollection clearly, without the pressures of a deposition. I want to read to you what he wrote. It says, "In 1999 or 2000, I had a conversation with Roger Clemens in which Roger told me that he had taken human growth hormones. This conversation occurred at his gym in Memorial, Texas, He did not tell me where he got the HGH or from whom, but he did tell me that it helped the body recover." It is not just Mr. Pettitte who recollects this conversation. During his deposition, Mr. Pettitte told us that he tells his wife everything. So we asked his wife to give us an affidavit about what she knew. And understand, this is under oath, Let me read to you what his wife said in her affidavit. "I, Laura Pettitte, do depose and state, in 1999 or 2000, Andy told me he had a conversation with Roger Clemens in which Roger admitted to him using human growth hormones." Mr. Clemens, once again I remind you. You are under oath. You have said your conversation with Mr. Pettitte never happened. If that was true, why would Laura Pettitte remember Andy telling her about the conversation?

MR. CLEMENS: Once again, Mr. Congressman, I think he misremembers the conversation that we had. Andy and I's relationship is close enough to know that if I would have known that he was–had done HGH, which I now know, that he–if he was knowingly knowing that I had taken HGH, we would have talked about the subject. He would have come to me to ask me about the effects of it.

(The Word Qualifier "think" leaves open the possibility that Pettitte did not misremember. Clemens used the Present Tense "misremembers "instead of the Past Tense "misremembered." The Word Qualifier "which I now know" to emphasize that he did not previously know about Pettitte's HGH use. Clemens tried to convince Cummings of the information provided versus conveying information, which suggests deception. Clemens Reaffirmed the False Premise that because he and Pettitte had a close personal relationship, Pettitte would have talked to Clemens. Clemens again stated the False Premise that he told the truth because he and Pettitte had a close personal relationship and, therefore, would have talked to Clemens. Clemens stated, "He would have come to me to ask me about the effects of it," which suggests that Clemens was not only knowledgeable about HGH but was recognized by his peers as knowledgeable about HGH. This statement begs the question, "Why was Clemens so knowledgeable about HGH if he did not consider using it?")

MR. CUMMINGS: Well, that fact is Mr. Clemens, that apparently now you know he knew it and he didn't tell you. Has your mind changed about his credibility?

MR. CLEMENS: Andy's a fine gentleman. I have no reason, again . . .

MR. CUMMINGS: Very well.

(Cummings is trapped in the Land of Is and appears to be frustrated.)

MR. CLEMENS: I think he misremembers.

(The Word Qualifies "think" leaves open the possibility that Pettitte could have remembered correctly. Clemens used the present tense "misremembers" instead of the past tense "misremembered.")

MR. CUMMINGS: Very well.

(Cummings' response supports the hypothesis that he is frustrated).

MR. CLEMENS: I know it. Again, our relationship was close enough that if I knew–if he knew that I had tried HGH, which I hadn't, he would have come to me and talked to me and discussed the subject.

(Clemens stated the False Premise that he is telling the truth because he and Pettitte have a close personal relationship. Clemens stated that because he and Pettitte had a close personal relationship, he would have talked to Clemens. Clemens' False Premise could have been used against him. Pettitte stated that he had a conversation with Clemens. Clemens stated that he would have come to Clemens to discuss HGH because of their close relationship. Clemens knows Pettitte to be an honest person. Therefore, according to Clemens' own words, Pettitte told the truth. Clemens would be faced with the volatile conundrum. He would have to discredit Pettitte and admit to Congress that he lied at the beginning of his testimony when he said that Pettitte was an honest person or admit that he and Pettitte did not have a close personal relationship and Pettitte did not have a conversation with Clemens about HGH. This would negate Clemens' False Premise that he is telling the truth because he had a close personal relationship with Pettitte.)

MR. CUMMINGS: I understand. The 1999 or 2000 conversation is not the only conversation that Mr. Pettitte remembers having with you about HGH. He also remembers a second conversation very clearly. This conversation took place in 2005. Let me read to you what he wrote about this conversation in his affidavit:

In 2005, around the time of the congressional Congressional hearings into the use of performance-enhancing drugs in baseball, I had a conversation with Roger Clemens in Kissimmee, Florida. I asked him what he would say if asked by reporters if he had ever used performance-enhancing drugs. When he asked what I meant, I reminded him that he had told me that he had used HGH. Roger responded by telling me that I must have misunderstood him. He claimed that it was his wife Debbie who used HGH; and I said "OK," or words to that effect, not because I agreed with him, but because I wasn't going to argue with him.

This conversation happened just 3 years ago, and it is the kind of conversation that most people would remember. It is hard for me to imagine that Mr. Pettitte made up this conversation. Did you have a conversation with him to this effect?

MR. CLEMENS: I don't believe I had a conversation in 2005 with him in Kissimmee, Florida. We would have been with the Houston Astros at the time. But I don't remember that conversation whatsoever.

(The Word Qualifier "believe" leaves open the possibility that he may have had a conversation with Pettitte. Clemens used the Word Qualifiers "2005 and Kissimmee, Florida," which restricts the time and location of the conversation. If Clemens and Pettitte had a conversation in any place other that Kissimmee, Florida and at any other time other that in 2005, Clemens told the truth when he stated, "But I don't remember that conversation whatsoever," but the truth about what? Clemens used the Tag Qualifier *that*, which indicates that other conversations took place.)

MR. CUMMINGS: Are you saying that you don't remember it, or are you telling us that you didn't have it? Do you know? And the reason why I am asking you that is because we are dealing with some serious matters here, and I want to give you–you wanted a fair chance to address this committee; and I am just wondering, are you telling us under oath that it didn't happen, or are you saying you just don't remember it?

MR. CLEMENS: I don't remember that. And again, I will address the –any conversation about my wife Debbie using HGH. I know that at one point she read a *USA Today* article about that. I don't know the year. It sure could have been 2005 when this article came about. And they just–it was just general talk . . .

(Clemmons used the Tag Qualifier "that." If any nuance of Cummings' description of the conversations between Clemens and Pettitte is not correct, then Clemens would be telling the truth, but the truth about what? Clemens used the Push-Pull "I don't remember," which indicates that the memory of a conversation with Pettitte exists, but Clemens cannot retrieve it. Cummings should have asked, "What conversations do you remember having with Pettitte about HGH?" Clemens used Misdirection refocusing from his conversation with Pettitte to his wife's use of HGH.)

> **MR. CUMMINGS:** All right.
> **MR. CLEMENS:** [continuing] about HGH.
> **MR. CUMMINGS:** Let me go on. Laura Pettitte also has a clear recollection of being told about this conversation by her husband. Let me read what she wrote:

A few years, later, I believe in 2005, Andy again told me of a conversation with Roger Clemens about HGH. Andy told me that he had been thinking that if a reporter asked him, he would tell the reporter of his own use of HGH in 2002. He said that he told Roger Clemens this and asked Roger what he would say, if asked. Andy told me that in the 2005 conversation Roger denied using HGH and told Andy that Andy was mistaken about the earlier conversation. According to Andy, Roger said that it was his wife Debbie who used HGH.

Now, the timeline is very important here. According to Mr. Pettitte, his first conversation with you, Mr. Clemens, occurred in 2003. That makes it impossible that you could have been referring to your wife's use of HGH in the first conversation. There aren't the only relevant conversations that Mr. Pettitte told us about. He told us that after his first conversation with you, Mr. Clemens, he spoke with Mr. McNamee. Let me read what–let me read to you again that affidavit:

Shortly after my conversation with Roger, I spoke with Brian McNamee. Only he and I were parties to the conversation. I asked Roger about HGH, and told him that Roger said he had used it. Brian McNamee became angry. He told me that Roger should not have told me about his use of HGH because it was supposed to be confidential." Mr. McNamee do you remember that conversation?

> **MR. McNAMEE:** Yes, sir.
> **MR. CUMMINGS:** Did it happen?
> **MR. McNAMEE:** Yes, sir.
> **CHAIRMAN WAXMAN:** Mr. Cummings, your time has expired.
> **MR. CUMMINGS:** Thank you very much.

SHOELESS JOE JACKSON

The 1919 World Series spawned the most famous scandal in baseball history. Eight players from the Chicago White Sox were accused of taking money to throw the World Series against the Cincinnati Reds. The 8 players included "Shoeless" Joe Jackson, pitchers Eddie Cicotte and Claude "Lefty" Williams; infielders Buck Weaver, Arnold "Chick" Gandil, Fred McMullin, and Charles "Swede" Risberg; and outfielder Oscar "Happy" Felsch. The following is a copy of "Shoeless" Joe Jackson's testimony before the Cook County grand jury on September 28, 1920. Jackson waived immunity and testified. His testimony is a good example of how a truthful person answers questions. In contrast to Clemens testimony before Congress, Jackson did not take the prosecutor to the Land of Is. He simply told the truth. A transcript of Jackson's transcript is as follows:

JOE JACKSON, called as a witness, having been first duly sworn, testified as follows:

Examination by
Mr. Replogle

Q: Mr. Jackson, you do understand that any testimony you may give here can be used in evidence against you at any future trial;   you know who I am, I am State's Attorney, and this is the Grand Jury, this is the Foreman of the Grand Jury. Now I will read this immunity waiver to you so you will know just what it is:

Chicago, Illinois, September 28, 1920. I, Joe Jackson, the undersigned, of my own free will make this my voluntary statement and me willing to testify and do testify before the Grand Jury with full knowledge of all the facts and of my legal rights, knowing full well that any testimony I may give might incriminate me and might be used against me in any case of prosecution or connected with the subject matter of my testimony, and now having been fully advised as to my legal rights, I hereby with said full knowledge waive all immunity that I might claim by reason of my appearing before the Grand Jury and giving testimony concerning certain crimes of which I have knowledge. (Whereupon the witness signed the foregoing document)

Q: What is your name?
A: Joe Jackson.
Q: Where do you live, Mr. Jackson?
A: You mean in the city here?
Q: Where is your home?
A: Greenville, South Carolina.

Q: What is your business?

A: Baseball player

Q: How long have you been playing professional baseball?

A: Since 1908.

Q: Where have you played professional baseball?

A: Why, I started out in Greenville, South Carolina; went there to Philadelphia, Philadelphia Americans.

Q: How long were you with them?

A: I went in the fall of 1908, and went to Savannah, Georgia.

Q: How long were you there?

A: Finished the season there, and I was called back by the Athletics; from there went to New Orleans, in 1910; 1910 in the fall I came to Cleveland and stayed with Cleveland until 1915, and I have been here ever since.

Q: Did you play with the White Sox from 1915?

A: About the middle of the season I was there.

Q: Are you married or single?

A: Married.

Q: How long have you been married?

A: Been married thirteen years this coming July.

Q: Have any children?

A: No, sir.

Q: Is your wife in Chicago at the present time?

A: Yes, sir.

Q: Where is your Chicago address?

A: Trenier Hotel, 40th and Grand Blvd.

Q: You were playing professional ball with the White Sox in the season of 1919, were you?

A: Yes, sir.

Q: You played in the World Series between the Chicago Americans Baseball Club and the Cincinnati Baseball club, did you?

A: I did.

Q: What position did you play?

A: Left field.

Q: Were you present at a meeting at the Ansonia Hotel in New York about two or three weeks before–a conference there with a number of ball players?

A: I was not, no, sir.

Q: Did anybody pay you any money to help throw that series in favor of Cincinnati?

A: They did.

Q: How much did they pay?

A: They promised me $20,000 and paid me five.

Q: Who promised you the twenty thousand?
A: "Chick" Gandil.
Q: Who is Chick Gandil?
A: He was their first baseman on the White Sox club.
Q: Who paid you the $5,000?
A: Lefty Williams brought it in my room and threw it down.
Q: Who is Lefty Williams?
A: The pitcher on the White Sox club.
Q: Where did he bring it, where is your room?
A: At the time I was staying at the Lexington Hotel, I believe it is.
Q: On 21st and Michigan?
A: 22nd and Michigan, yes.
Q: Who was in the room at the time?
A: Lefty and myself, I was there, and he came in.
Q: Where was Mrs. Jackson?
A: Mrs. Jackson–let me see–I think she was in the bathroom. It was suite; yes, she was in the bathroom, I am pretty sure.
Q: Does she know that you got $5,000 for helping throw these games?
A: She did that night, yes.
Q: You said you told Mrs. Jackson that evening?
A: Did, yes.
Q: What did she say about it?
A: She said she thought it was an awful thing to do.
Q: When was it that this money was brought to your room and that you talked to Mrs. Jackson?
A: It was the second trip to Cincinnati. That night we were leaving.
Q: That was after the fourth game?
A: I believe it was, yes.
Q: Refreshing your recollection, the first two games that you remember were played in Cincinnati?
A: Yes, sir.
Q: And the second two were played here?
A: Yes.
Q: This was after four games?
A: Yes, sir.
Q: You were going back to Cincinnati?
A: Yes, sir.
Q: What time of day was that he came to your rooms?
A: It was between, I would say, 7 and 8 o'clock in the evening, right after the game.
Q: After the fourth game? Do you remember who won that game?
A: Dick Kerr, I believe.

Q: Cincinnati won that game. Cicotte pitched and Cincinnati won; do you remember now? Cincinnati beat you 2 to nothing?

A: Yes, sir.

Q: Were you at a conference of these men, these players on the Sox team, at the Warner Hotel sometime previous to then?

A: No, sir, I was not present, but I knew they had the meeting, so I was told.

Q: Who told you?

A: Williams.

Q: Who else talked to you about this besides Claude Williams?

A: Claude didn't talk to me direct about it, he just told me things that had been said.

Q: What did he tell you?

A: He told me about this meeting in particular, he said the gang was there, and this fellow Attel, Abe Attel, I believe, and Bill Burns is the man that give him the double crossing, so Gandil told me.

Q: You say Abe Attel and Bill Burns are the two people that Claude William told you gave you the double cross?

A: Chick Gandil told me that.

Q: Then you talked to Chick Gandil and Claude Williams both about this?

A: Talked to Claude Williams about it, yes, and Gandil more so, because he is the man that promised me this stuff.

Q: How much did he promise you?

A: $20,000 if I would take part.

Q: And you said you would?

A: Yes, sir.

Q: When did he promise you the $20,000?

A: It was to be paid after each game.

Q: How much?

A: Split it up some way, I don't know just how much it amounts to, but during the series it would amount to $20,000. Finally Williams brought me this $5,000, threw it down.

Q: What did you say to Williams when he threw down the $5,000?

A: I asked him what the hell had come off here.

Q: What did he say?

A: He said Gandil said we all got a screw through Abe Attel. Gandill said that we got double-crossed through Abe Attel, he got the money and refused to turn it over to him. I don't think Gandil was crossed as much as he crossed us.

Q: You think Gandil may have gotten the money and held it from you, is that right?

A: That's what I think, I think he kept the majority of it.

Q: What did you do then?

A: I went to him and asked him what was the matter. He said Abe Attel game him the jazzing. He said, "Take that or let it alone." As quick as the series was over I left town, I went right on out.

Q: Did you ever meet Abe Attel?

A: Not to my knowledge, no sir. I wouldn't know him if I would see him.

Q: Did you ever meet Bill Burns?

A: Yes, sir.

Q: Where did you first meet Bill Burns?

A: When I first came to the American League to play ball I first met him.

Q: Where was he then?

A: He was at Detroit when I met him.

Q: Do you know whether or not he was in on this deal?

A: Well, I know what Gandil told me, that he and Attel was man that…

Q: Bill Burns and Abe Attel?

A: Yes.

Q: Were the men that what?

A: And some other gentlemen, I can't recall their names. There was three of them.

Q: A Jewish name, if you know, would you know it if you were to hear it?

A: No, sir, I would not.

Q: Do you know whether or not Gideon of St. Louis was in on this in any way?

A: No, sir, I only know he was with Risburg and McMullin all the time.

Q: Whom, Gideon?

A: That's all I know. I seen him around with them.

Q: What is his first name?

A: Joe.

Q: Joe Gideon? Do you know whether or not Rawlins of the Philadelphia National League Club was in on this in any way?

A: No, sir, I do not.

Q: You know Rawlins?

A: I only know him by name.

Q: You know Gideon?

A: Yes.

Q: Where did you see McMullin and Risburg together?

A: In Cincinnati one night in the smoking room of a Pullman car.

Q: Where else?

A: And I saw them on the street together in Cincinnati. I didn't see them in Chicago here, because I didn't live in that neighborhood, though I would see Joe at the ball grounds.

Q: You saw Gideon?

A: Yes.

Q: At the ball park during the World's Series?

A: Yes, I saw him here one day, I saw him in here.

Q: And you were to be paid $5,000 after each game, is that right?

A: Well, Attel was supposed to give the $100,000. It was to be split up, paid to him, I believe, and $15,000 a day or something like that, after each game.

Q: That is to Gandil?

A: Yes.

Q: At the end of the first game you didn't get any money, did you?

A: No, I did not, no, sir.

Q: Then you went ahead and throw the second game, thinking you would get it then, is that right?

A: We went ahead and threw the second game, we went after him again. I said to him, "What are you going to do?" "Everything is all right," he says, "What the hell is the matter?"

Q: After the third game what did you say to him?

A: After the third game I says, "Somebody is getting a nice little jazz, everybody is crossed." He said, "Well, Abe Attel and Bill Burns had crossed him," that is what he said to me.

Q: He said Abe Attel and Bill Burns had crossed him?

A: Yes, sir.

Q: After throwing the fourth game, did you talk to him then before Williams brought you the money?

A: No, sir; I didn't talk to him then, no, sir. Williams and I talked.

Q: Who was your best chum on the team, who did you go with in the club?

A: Williams and Lind. I hardly ever pal with any of them there except those two.

Q: Who did Gandil pal with mostly on the team?

A: Risburg.

Q: Who did McMullin pal with mostly on the team?

A: I cannot recall who McMullin roomed with.

Q: Who did he go with?

A: You would see him and Charlie together, and Chick, quite a bit.

Q: Chick Gandil and Charlie Risburg?

A: All times, not only on this occasion.

Q: Do you know who was the first man that the gamblers approached, that Burnes and Attel approached on your team?

A: Why, Gandil

Q: What makes you think Gandil?

A: Well, he was the whole works of it, the instigator of it, the fellow that mentioned it to me. He told me that I could take it or let it go, they were going through with it.

Q: Didn't you think it was the right thing for you to go and tell Cominkey about it?

A: I did tell them once, "I am not going to be in it." I will just get out of that altogether.

Q: Who did you tell that to

A: Chick Gandil

Q: What did he say?

A: He said I was into it already and I might as well stay in. I said, "I can got o [sic] the boss and have every damn one of you pulled out of the limelight." He said, "It wouldn't be well for me if I did that."

Q: Gandil said to you?

A: Yes, sir.

Q: What did you say?

A: Well, I told him any time they wanted to have me knocked off, to have me knocked off.

Q: What did he say?

A: Just laughed.

Q: When did that conversation take place, that you said anytime they wanted to have you knocked off, to have you knocked off.

A: That was the fourth game, the fifth night going back to Cincinnati. I met Chick Gandil and his wife going to the 12th Street Station. They got out the cab there. I was standing on the corner.

Q: Do you recall the fourth game that Cicotte pitched?

A: Yes, sir.

Q: Did you see any fake plays made by yourself or anybody on that game, that would help throw the game?

A: Only the wildness of Cicotte.

Q: What was that?

A: Hitting a batter, that is the only thing that told me they were going through with it.

Q: Did you make any intentional errors yourself that day?

A: No, sir, not during the whole Series.

Q: Did you Play to win?

A: Yes.

Q: And run the bases to win?

A: Yes, sir.

Q: And fielded the balls at the outfield to win?

A: I did.

Q: Did you ever hear anyone accusing Cicotte of crossing the signals that were given to him by Schalk?

A: No, sir, I did not.

Q: Do you know whether or not any of those signals were crossed by Cicotte?

A: No, sir, I couldn't say.

Q: After the fourth game you went to Cincinnati and you had the $5,000, is that right?

A: Yes, sir.

Q: Where did you put the $5,000, did you put it in the bank or keep it on your person?

A: I put it in my pocket.

Q: What denominations, in silver or bills?

A: In bills.

Q: How big were the bills?

A: Some hundreds, mostly fifties.

Q: What did Mrs. Jackson say about it after she found it out again?

A: She felt awful bad about it, cried about it a while.

Q: Did it ever occur to you to tell about this before this?

A: Yes, where I offered to come here last fall in the investigation, I would have told it last fall if they would have brought me in.

Q: And you are telling me this now, of course, of your own free will, you want to tell the truth, is that the idea, of all you know?

A: Yes, sir.

Q: In the second game, did you see any plays made by any of those fellows that would lead you to believe that they were trying to throw the game, that is the game that Claude Williams pitched with Cincinnati?

A: There was wildness, too, that cost that game. Two walks, I think, and a triple by this fellow, two or three men out.

Q: Was there any other move that would lead you to believe they were throwing the game?

A: No, sir, I didn't see any plays that I thought was throwing the game.

Q: In the third game Kerr pitched three, 1 to nothing. Did you see anything there that would lead you to believe anyone was trying to throw the game?

A: No, sir. I think if you would look that record up, I drove in two and hit one.

Q: You made a home run, didn't you?

A: That was in the last game here.

Q: The fourth game Cicotte pitched again? It was played out here in Chicago and Chicago lost it 2 to nothing? Do you remember that?

A: Yes, sir.

Q: Did you see anything wrong about that game that would lead you to believe there was an intentional fixing?

A: The only thing that I was sore about that game, the throw I made to the plate, Cicotte tried to intercept it.

Q: It would have gone to the first base if he had not intercepted it?

A: Yes.

Q: Did you do anything to throw those games?

A: No, sir.

Q: Any game in the Series?

A: Not a one. I didn't have an error or make no misplay.

Q: Supposing the White Sox would have won this Series, the World's Series, what would have done then with the $5,000?

A: I guess I would have kept it, that was all I could do. I tried to win all the time.

Q: To keep on with these games, the fifth game, did you see anything wrong with that or any of the games, did you see any plays that you would say might have been made to throw that particular game?

A: Well, I only saw one play in the whole Series, I don't remember what game it was in, either, it was in Cincinnati.

Q: Who made it?

A: Charles Risburg.

Q: What was that?

A: It looked like a perfect double play. And he only gets one, gets the ball and runs over to the bag with it in place of throwing it in front of the bag.

Q: After the Series were all over, did you have any talk with any of these men?

A: No, sir, I left the next night.

Q: Where did you go?

A: Savannah, Georgia.

Q: Weren't you very much peeved that you only got $5,000 and you expected to get twenty?

A: No, I was ashamed of myself.

Q: Have you ever talked with Chick Gandil since that time?

A: No, I never saw him since.

Q: When was the last time you saw him and talked to him?

A: It was on the following morning after the Series were over, that day in Comiskey's office, waiting in there.

Q: What did you say to him at that time?

A: I told him there was a hell of a lot of scandal going around for what had happened. He said, "To hell with it." He was about half drunk. I went on out and left that night.

Q: Did you drink much Mr. Jackson?

A: Now and then, I don't make no regular practice of it.

Q: Do you get drunk?

A: No, sir.

Q: Have you been drunk since you have been with the Chicago White Sox team?

A: Yes, sir.

Q: Where?

A: Atlantic City.

Q: You were not playing . . .

A: Off days.

Q: Did Mr. Comiskey or Mr. Gleason know you were drunk at that time?

A: I don't judge they did, no, sir

Q: Who was with you when you got drunk?

A: Claude Williams, John Fownier and myself.

Q: That is some years ago, he played with the Chicago team, is that right?

A: I think it was '18

Q: You haven't been drunk since you played with the Chicago team.

A: Not what you would call drunk, no.

Q: Did you ever talk to Happy Felsch since that time, about those games?

A: I believe I mentioned it to Happy the other day, too; yes, I know I did.

Q: What did you say to him?

A: I told him they would have him down before the Grand Jury before long, the way things looked.

Q: What did he say?

A: He said, "All right."

Q: What day was that, Mr. Jackson?

A: I don't remember what day it was, but one day last week.

Q: Were you playing ball?

A: We were walking across the field, yes, sir. Just before practice, I believe, and we were taking our position for practice that day.

Q: Do you know whether or not Happy Felsch received some of this money?

A: I don't know that he received any more than what the boys said.

Q: What did the boys say about him?

A: They said each fellow got some money.

Q: Did they say how much?

A: $5,000, I understand, Felsch.

Q: You wouldn't say that any one got more than $5,000; in other words, if I was to tell you one man got $10,000, you wouldn't doubt it, would you; you don't know?

A: Yes, I know the man you would refer to.

Q: Do you know how much he got?

A: I know what he said.

Q: Do you know how much he said he got?

A: $10,000.

Q: Who do you think I mean, then?

A: Eddie Cicotte.

Q: When did Eddie Cicotte tell you he got $10,000.

A: The next morning after the meeting we had in his room.

Q: Did you tell him how much you got?

A: I did.

Q: What did you tell him?

A: I told him I got five thousand.

Q: What did he say?

A: He said I was a God damn fool for not getting it in my hand like he did.

Q: What did he mean by that?

A: I don't know, that he wouldn't trust anybody, I guess.

Q: What did he mean, that's what he meant by it?

A: Why, he meant he would not trust them, they had to pay him before he did anything.

Q: He meant then you ought to have got your money before you played, is that it?

A: Yes, that's it.

Q: Did you have a talk with any of the other players about how much they got?

A: I understand McMullen got five and Risburg five thousand, that's the way I understand.

Q: How do you understand that?

A: Just by talking to different fellows.

Q: To whom?

A: Different fellows.

Q: Did you talk to McMullen himself?

A: Very little I never talked to Mac any more than just hello and go on.

Q: Did you ever ask him how much he got?

A: Yes

Q: What did he say?

A: Never made me any answer, walked right out.

Q: Did you ever ask Charlie how much he got?

A: Yes.

Q: What did he say?

A: Asked me how much I got.

Q: What did you tell him?

A: Told him.

Q: What did you tell him?

A: I told him I got $5,000.

Q: What did he say?

A: He said, "I guess that's all I got."

Q: Did you believe him at the time?

A: No, sir, I think he was telling a damn lie.

Q: What?

A: I think he was lying.
Q: Did you tell him at the time he said it he was lying?
A: Yes.
Q: You thought he was lying even at that time, did you?
A: Yes, sir.
Q: When was that time?
A: That was this spring. We were talking in Memphis, he and I were taking walk.
Q: On your training trip?
A: Yes, sir.
Q: Did you ever talk to anybody else how much they got?
A: No sir, I didn't.
Q: You never asked Williams how much he got?
A: Williams, I have, yes.
Q: What did he say?
A: He said he got $5,000 at that time.
Q: You think he gave you the truth?
A: No, sir, I do not.
Q: What do you say?
A: No, I did not.
Q: What do you think?
A: I think that those fellers cut it up to suit themselves, what little they did have.
Q: Who is that?
A: The gang.
Q: What gang?
A: Charlie.
Q: Charlie Risburg?
A: Yes.
Q: Who else?
A: McMullen and Williams.
Q: Who else?
A: Cicotte, they were gambling.
Q: Weren't you in on the inner circle?
A: No, I never was with them, no, sir. It was mentioned to me in Boston. As I told you before, they asked me what would I consider, $10,000? And I said no, then they offered me twenty.
Q: Who mentioned it first to you?
A: Gandil.
Q: Who was with you?
A: We were all alone.
Q: What did he say?

A: He asked me would I consider $10,000 to frame up something and I asked him frame what? And he told me and I said no.

Q: What did he say?

A: Just walked away from me, and when I returned here to Chicago he told me that he would give me twenty and I said no again, and on the bridge where you go into the club house he told me I could either take it or let it alone, they were going through.

Q: What did they say?

A: They said, "You might as well say yes or say no and play ball or anything you want." I told them I would take their word.

Q: What else did you say?

A: Nothing.

Q: Did you talk to anyone else about it?

A: That's all I talked to.

Q: Did you ever talk to Buck Weaver about it?

A: No, sir, I never talked to Buck Weaver, never talked very much.

Q: Did you know the time Buck was in on the deal?

A: They told me he was; he never told me himself.

Q: Who told you?

A: Chick told me.

Q: Did Mrs. Jackson ever talk to Mrs. Weaver about it that you know of?

A: No, sir, not that I know of; no, sir.

Q: Is Mrs. Jackson a friend of Mrs. Weaver's, and did they chum together frequently–or did they?

A: They are all chummy there on the ball ground, sit together there on the stand, most all the ball players' wives sit together.

Q: Who did Mrs. Jackson sit with most?

A: Mrs. Williams and her sit together.

Q: Did Mrs. Jackson talk to Mrs. Williams about it?

A: Not that I know of.

Q: Did Mrs. Williams ever talk to Mrs. Jackson about it?

A: I don't know, they never talked when I was around, I don't know what they did when I wasn't around.

Q: Go back to Attel and Burns, just what do you know about them?

A: All I know is what Gandil told me over there, I talked to Bill myself later.

Q: What did you talk to Burns later?

A: It was the day the World's Series started.

Q: What did you say to him and what did he say to you?

A: I met him in the lobby of the hotel, we sat there; I can't remember the name of the hotel.

Q: Sinton Hotel?

A: Sinton Hotel, yes.

Q: That is in Cincinnati?
A: Yes. I said, "How is everything?"
Q: What did he say?
A: He said, "Everything is fine."
Q: Then what happened?
A: He told me about this stuff and I didn't know so much, I hadn't been aound and I didn't know so much. He said, "Where is Chick?" I said, "I don't know." He walked away from me. I didn't know enough to talk to him about what they were going to plan or what they had planned, I wouldn't know it if I had seen him, I only knew what I had been told, that's all I knew.
Q: Who was the third party in with Burns and Attel?
A: I don't know their names, I know there was three names.

The Foreman:

Q: What made you think that Gandil was double-crossing you, rather than Attel and Burns?
A: What made me think it was, Gandil going out on the coast, so I was told, I was surmising what I heard, they came back and told me he had a summer home, big automobile, doesn't do a lick of work; I know I can't do that way.

Mr. Replogle:

Q: In other words, if he double crossed you fellows he couldn't come back and face them, and he had plenty of money to stay out there. It wasn't at the time that you thought Gandil was double crossing you, you thought Gandil was telling the truth, is that right?
A: No, I told Williams after the first day it was a crooked deal all the way through, Gandil was not on the square with us.
Q: Had you ever played crooked baseball before this?
A: No, sir, I never had.
Q: Did anybody ever approach you to throw a game before this?
A: No, sir, never did.
Q: Did anybody approach you to throw a game since that time, to throw the World's Series?
A: No, sir.
Q: Do you have any suspicion about the White Sox, any of the players throw any of the games this summer?
A: Well, there have been some funny looking games, runs, I could have just my own belief about it, I wouldn't accuse the men.

Q: Where at?

A: A couple in New York, this last Eastern trip, looked bad, but I couldn't come out and open and bold and accuse anybody of throwing those games.

Q: Who pitched?

A: Williams got one awful beating up there, 25 to something there.

Q: Who else?

A: I don't remember whether Cicotte started the game there or not.

Q: Do you remember the last series you played in Boston? Last three straight games, did any of those games look suspicious to you?

A: There was a lot of funny pitching, lot of walking.

Q: Who was pitching those games?

A: Kerr and Williams and Cicotte.

Q: Was Kerr in on this in any way, do you think?

A: I don't think so.

Q: Were any of the other six players in it except the ones we have mentioned?

A: Not to my knowledge.

Q: Do you remember the Washington series here the last time Washington played here, that you lost three straight games?

A: No, sir.

Q: Did any of those games look suspicious to you?

A: I didn't pay any attention to them, looking for errors, and that, I was out trying to beat them.

Q: Was anything whispered around the club that you know of, that you should beat New York and then drop these games for those other teams so that Cleveland would win?

A: No, sir, I never heard that.

Q: Did you hear anything in your ball team to the effect that if the White Sox would take second place and would get part of the World's Series money because you won second place in the pennant race and then get the City Series money, that you would make more money than if you won the pennant and won the World's Series?

A: No, sir.

Q: Did any of the players ever tell you that?

A: No, sir, never told me that.

Q: Did that ever occur to you, yourself?

A: No sir. I wanted to win, this year, above all times.

Q: Why?

A: Because–I wanted to get in there and try and beat some National League club to death, that's what I wanted to do.

Q: You didn't want to do that so bad last year, did you?

A: Well, down in my heart I did, yes.

Q: Did you hear any of the players that mentioned that proposition to you that I have just mentioned?

A: No, not to me, no, sir; they have not.

Q: Did you write and ask him for the other $15,000?

A: No, sir.

Q: Why didn't you?

A: I didn't think it would do any good, I didn't pay any attention to that.

Q: Did you ever talk to Claude Williams about it since the Series?

A: We have talked about it once or twice, yes.

Q: When?

A: Sometime this summer, I don't remember when it was.

Q: In what city, if you can recall?

A: I think it was here, in Chicago.

Q: Where in Chicago, at the ballpark?

A: No, we were out riding in his car.

Q: What did you say to him and what did he say to you?

A: We were just talking about how funny it looked that Gandil didn't come back, and he must have made an awful lot out of it, crossed up the boys. We both decided he crossed them up.

Q: You think now Williams may have crossed you, too?

A: Well, dealing with crooks, you know, you get crooked every way. This is my first experience and last.

Q: Where else did you talk to Williams, outside of the time you were out riding in his car?

A: Somewhere we were at, I believe in Washington.

Q: When was that?

A: That was this summer, I think.

Q: How long ago?

A: I think it was the second Eastern trip.

Q: What did you say to him at that time, and what did he say to you?

A: We just brought up the World's Series, I told him what a damned fool I thought I was, and he was of the same opinion, so we just let it go at that.

Q: Does your contract with the Sox Baseball team call for $6,000?

A: $8,000.

Q: What party of the money did you get when you were sold by Cleveland to Comiskey?

A: I think they gave me $1,000 out of the sale.

Q: That's all you got out of it, just $1,000?

A: Yes.

Q: Do you know how much Mr. Comiskey paid the Cleveland Club for you?

A: I do not, no, sir.

Q: You knew it was a big sum of money, did you?

A: So they said.

Q: You were satisfied with $8,000 a year, were you?

A: That's all I could get out of them.

Q: Did you get $8,000 in 1919?

A: No, sir.

Q: What did you get in that year, that was last year?

A: I believe they gave me $6,000, last year.

Q: That is for the season, not for the year?

A: Yes, just the playing season, yes, sir.

Q: That also includes all your expenses on the trips, doesn't it?

A: Yes, sir.

Q: Railroad fare, board, room and so forth?

A: Railroad, fare, room and board.

Q: You were pretty well satisfied with that, weren't you?

A: They wouldn't give you any more, that's all you could get. I was pretty lucky to get a contract like that with him when I came over here.

Q: What were you getting with Cleveland?

A: I was getting six the last year, and I had been in that automobile wreck, and it looked like I was through as a ball player.

Q: That automobile wreck in Cleveland?

A: Yes; I had my leg all tore up, my knee cap came out, it looked like I would be through as a ball player.

Q: $6,000 is the most you ever got until this year, is that right?

A: (NO ANSWER)

Q: Did you ever talk to any of the other men about this, now, that I have not asked you about?

A: No, sir.

Q: Do you know anything more about it than I have asked you?

A: No, sir, I don't believe I do.

Q: Can you think of anything else of importance that I have not asked you?

A: This other fellow, if I could think of his name, I can't think of his name.

Q: Did Cicotte ever tell you who paid him the money?

A: He told me about somebody paying him money, yes; but I don't know their names, never did know any of their names, except Bill Burns and Abe Attell, that's the only two names that I know. I did not attend the meetings.

Q: You say Williams gave you your money; what ball player paid Cicotte his money?

A: These gamblers paid him, I think, all along, from what I learn.

Q: Did Williams ever tell you who paid him?

A: Never did.

Q: Did you ever ask Williams where he got this $5,000?
A: Yes.
Q: What did he say?
A: Up at Gandil's apartment, he said.
Q: Have you ever talked to Burns since the World's Series?
A: No, sir.
Q: Do you know where he lives, where he is?
A: No, sir.
Q: You talked to Gideon this summer?
A: Yes; "Hello, how are you?" and something like that.
Q: Do you now whether or not Gideon is in on the deal?
A: No, sir, I do not.
Q: Do you think he was?
A: (NO ANSWER)
Q: Does Williams know where you are now?
A: I don't think so.

Mr. Replocle:

It is an off day, no game today (Whereupon the Grand Jury adjourned to Wednesday, September 29, 1920, at 9:30 o'clock A.M.

Appendix C

PRACTICE STATEMENT

My FBI supervisor came into my office with a letter in his hand. He handed it to me and said, "What do we do about this?" He told me that a prominent citizen received the letter through the mail and brought it to the police department. The police department forwarded it to the FBI. The letter contained an extortion demand. My supervisor asked me to analyze the letter. He said that if I determined the letter to be a viable threat, he would deploy the necessary resources to catch the extortionist. These resources included the SWAT team, the surveillance team, surveillance aircraft, and a legion of Special Agents to support the effort.

I faced a volatile conundrum. This would be the first letter I analyzed outside the training environment. The pressure was on. If I determined the letter presented a viable threat and it turned out to be a hoax, a lot of resources would be needlessly expended. If I determined the letter to be a hoax, and the writer presented a real threat, innocent people might get hurt. My reputation as a behavioral analyst was riding on my analysis of this letter. I could have taken the easy way out and determined that to be on the safe side the resources should be deployed. This solution would have satisfied the near-term problem; however, in the long-term, this strategy would not suffice. The FBI receives countless letters each year from disgruntled citizens that contain threats or veiled threats. The FBI would rapidly deplete its resources if it responded to each letter.

I want you to pretend that you are in my position. Your job is to conduct a PNA of the letter and then decide if the writer is serious about his extortion threat. How dangerous is the writer? What are the writer's physical characteristics? The bonus question is, "What color hair does the writer have?"

My PNA of the extortion letter and the outcome of the case can be found in Appendix D. Conduct your own PNA of the letter before reviewing my analysis. Remember to develop Competing Hypotheses to avoid the Primacy Effect.

The letter read as follows:

We require you to make an involuntary contribution to our organization in the amount of $500,000 cash USD. Failure to pay will risk the health and well being of any one of your family of 4 children ages 12 to 2, brothers, sisters and both your parents (George & Denise). Your refusal to comply with this demand will result in serious retaliation of a *permanent* nature. ANY INVOLVEMENT OF THE LAW WILL RESULT IN RETALIATION! Keep in mind that although your contribution will hurt financially, it won't ruin you. Preserving your family intact is much more important. This is the time for clear thinking. After this successful operation, our goal will be met and we leave you in peace. Obviously, do not contact the authorities or anyone else – if any of our team is apprehended the remaining members will carry out the retaliation. You are under visual and electronic surveillance so be smart and don't do anything risky.

The choice is simple – pay us or wonder when . . .

INSTRUCTIONS:

Place $500,000 USD (nothing greater than unmarked $100 bills) in a cloth pillowcase and seal with duct tape. Place the cloth pillowcase inside at least 4 black heavy-duty plastic trash bags and seal securely with duct tape. Do not place anything other than the money in the cloth sack or inside the plastic bags. We will immediately scan for metal objects, electronic devices, chemical agents, etc. If we find anything, we will abandon the bag and consider the operation forfeit with the consequences to be paid by you. On October 23 1998, between 10 pm and 11pm travel in your Ford truck in a circular pattern starting on Victoria to Olivas Park Dr (turn left) to Harbor (turn left) to Gonzales Road (turn left) back to Victoria (turn left). Continue in this counterclockwise circle at a maximum speed of 45 miles per hour. At some time during the hour you will see a sign on your right side with the letter H appearing on the roadside. Making sure of no other traffic, on or near the sign, slow but do not stop the truck and throw the package out the passenger window a distance of no less than 15 feet. If you do not throw the package correctly, you forfeit. After throwing the package, leave the area immediately and return home. You will continue to be under surveillance until we have successfully retrieved the package and verified its contents. If you do not see the sign, wait until October 24, 1998 10 pm to 11 pm and try again. There will be no third chance. If there are any problems, the fault is yours! No discussion and no second chance! Make no mistake; we are a deadly and serious team of professionals!

Appendix D

PNA OF PRACTICE STATEMENT

1) **We require you to make an involuntary contribution to our organization in the amount of $500,000 cash USD.**
   a) The Personal Identifier "We" and the Word Clue "organization" suggests more than one person may be involved.
   b) The writer did not identify which organization he represented. If the writer considered the organization the most important focus, then he would have mentioned it by name. One Hypothesis posits that the writer may be out for himself and just using the term organization as subterfuge. A Competing Hypothesis posits that the writer may want to secure money for his organization without drawing law enforcement attention, thus allowing the group to continue its work.
   c) The Word Clue "involuntary contribution" suggests the writer may be uncomfortable with making an actual extortion demand. This may suggest that the writer does not engage in criminal activity on a regular basis.
   d) The Word Clue "USD" is unusual in that USC is more commonly used. This may be a typographical error; although, the writer uses USD twice in the letter. This suggests that writer is educated, possibly in the business field. Traditional criminals simply want cash; they do not know what USC is much less USD.
2) **Failure to pay will risk the health and well being of anyone of your family of 4 children ages 9 to 1, brothers, sisters and both your parents (George & Denise).**
   a) The writer probably knows the identity of his target(s), which suggests that he collected background information prior to sending the letter. This reference also suggests that the writer put some thought into the crime. The writer should be considered as a serious threat for this reason.
   b) The Word Clue "Failure to pay will risk the health and well being of anyone of your family" suggests that the writer was afraid to use more

harsh terms. The writer is probably not a career criminal in that traditional criminals are not afraid to use foul language and words such as kill, beat, etc. This may also be an attempt by the writer to appeal to the reader's emotions.

3) **Your refusal to comply with this demand will result in serious retaliation of a *permanent* nature.**
   a) The writer italicized the word permanent to emphasize the seriousness of the retaliation.
   b) The Word Clue "permanent nature" suggests that the he has not yet made a serious commitment to killing his victims.
   c) The Word Qualifier "serious" indicates that he wanted to send the message that the retaliation would be severe.

4) **ANY INVOLVEMENT OF THE LAW WILL RESULT IN RETALIATION!**
   a) The use of all Capitalization suggests that the writer wanted to emphasize the message contained in this sentence.
   b) In this sentence, the writer did not use the Word Qualifier "serious" to describe the word "retaliation" as compared to Sentence 3. This Word Qualifier also serves as a Change in Language. The writer changed "serious retaliation" in Sentence 3 to RETALIATION in this sentence, which suggests that the writer is not firm in his commitment to retaliation.

5) **Keep in mind that although your contribution will hurt financially it won't ruin you.**
   a) The Word Clue "your contribution will hurt financially it won't ruin you" indicates that the writer is trying to justify his crime by reminding the victim that he will still have some money left over after making the payment. The writer may be trying to justify his crime by thinking along the lines that it is all right to steal from big corporations and insurance companies because they can afford it. The writer drew a line by stealing a certain quantity of money from the victim not to cause him to go broke.
   b) The Word Clue "contribution" suggests that the writer may have a socialist philosophy because he avoided more harsh words to describe his demands.

6) **Preserving your family intact is much more important.**
   a) The Word Clue "Preserving your family intact" may be an attempt by the writer to appeal to the reader's emotions by setting up a contrast between a few dollars that "won't ruin you" compared to the well-being of his family.

7) **This is the time for clear thinking.**
   a) Word Clue "This is the time for clear thinking" suggests that the writer has given some thought as to how the victim would initially react to the

extortion letter. The writer demonstrated some ability to empathize with the victim, which indicates that the writer is probably not a psychopath.

8) **After this successful operation as our goal will be met and we leave you in peace.**

   a) The writer emphasizes that all he wants is to get the money and the group will leave in peace. Career criminals do not use the term we will leave you in peace. The writer seems to be telling the victim, "No hard feelings, rich person, we are only taking the fair share you should be giving."

   b) The Push-Pull Word "this" suggests the writer may have conducted similar operations in the past.

   c) The use of the Personal Identifier *we* suggests the writer is not acting alone.

9) **Obviously, do not contact the authorities or anyone else–if any of our team is apprehended the remaining members will carry out the retaliation.**

   a) The Word Clues "our" and "remaining members" suggests that the writer is not acting alone.

   b) The Word Clue "carry out the retaliation" is less active than "will retaliate," which suggests that the writer is not entirely committed to violence.

10) **You are under visual and electronic surveillance so be smart and don't do anything risky.**

   a) The Word Clues "under visual and electronic surveillance" suggest a possible attempt by the writer to portray himself or his organization as being more powerful than they may actually be.

11) **The choice is simple–pay us or wonder when . . .**

   a) The Word Clue "wonder when…" suggests that the writer cannot commit to violence.

INSTRUCTIONS:

12) **Place $500,000 cash USD (nothing greater than unmarked $100 bills) in a cloth pillowcase and seal with duct tape**

   a) The Word Clue "USD" supports the hypothesis that the writer intended to use "USD" instead of "USC."

   b) The Word Clue "greater than unmarked $100 bills" indicates that the writer may not be professionally employed because the United States does not generally circulate any bills larger than $100 bills.

   c) The Word Clue "unmarked" suggests that the writer is aware of techniques used by the police to track money.

13) **Place the cloth pillowcase inside at least 4 black heavy-duty plastic trash bags and seal securely with duct tape.**

a) The writer instructs the victim to "Place the cloth pillowcase inside at least 4 black heavy-duty plastic trash bags and securely with duct tape." There is a specific reason for these instructions and that reason could be to prevent the package from breaking open when the victim throws the bag out of the window of a moving car. The writer probably made several practice runs and learned that the package breaks open if the money is placed in less than four heavy-duty plastic trash bags. Three bags would probably be sufficient. To be safe, the writer calls for four.

14) **Do not place anything other than the money in the cloth sack or inside the plastic bags.**

a) This sentence suggests that the writer is aware of devices used by law enforcement to track packages.

15) **We will immediately scan for metal objects, electronic devices, chemical agents, etc.**

a) The sentence supports the hypothesis that the writer is aware of law enforcement techniques to track packages.

16) **If we find *anything*, we will abandon the bag and consider the operation forfeit with the consequences to be paid by you.**

a) The writer again distances himself from the crime by writing "If we find anything we will abandon the bag and consider the operation forfeit with the consequences to be paid by you." The writer is trying to justify his crime by placing the blame on the victim. The writer does not want to face the fact that he is, in fact, to blame, for it was his actions that started the chain of events

17) **On October 23, 1998, between 10pm and 11pm travel in your Ford truck in a circular pattern starting on Victoria to Olivas Park Dr (turn left) to Harbor (turn left) to Gonzales Road (turn left) back to Victoria (turn left) continue in this counter clockwise circle at a Maximum speed of 45 miles per hour.**

a) These instructions are very specific which suggests that the writer has given a great deal of thought and practice as to how the money is to be delivered.

b) By driving in a circular motion, the writer has probably predetermined that he can detect any law enforcement presence or the drone of a surveillance plane overhead.

c) The writer is obviously familiar with the route and is comfortable and secure in that area. The writer may live in the surrounding area or spends a lot of time in the neighborhood.

d) This area is probably an open area where the writer and others can easily see what is happening and, more importantly, conduct countersurveillance. If the writer is an environmentalist, he will be comfortable spending several hours outside moving about to keep an eye on the surroundings as opposed to seeking a comfortable place indoors and conduct static countersurveillance.

18) **At some time during the hour you will see a sign on your right side with the letter H appear on the roadside.**

a) This sentence demonstrates that the writer made some practice runs in preparation for the crime.

19) **Making sure of no other traffic, on or near the sign, slow but do not stop the truck and throw the package out the passenger window a distance of no less than 15 feet.**

a) This sentence demonstrates that the writer made some practice runs in preparation for the crime.

20) **If you do not throw the package correctly, you forfeit.**

a) The Change of Language from "serious retaliation" to "RETALATION" to "wonder when . . ." to "forfeit" supports the hypothesis that the writer is probably not committed to violence.

21) **After throwing the package leave the area immediately and return home.**

a) No comment

22) **You will continue to be under surveillance until we have successfully retrieved the package and verified its contents.**

a) The Word Clue "continue" indicates that the writer will conduct surveillance.

b) The Personal Identifier "we" suggests that there is more than one person involved.

23) **If you do not see the sign, wait until October 24, 1998 10pm to 11pm and try again.**

a) The writer may want to see if there are any flaws in his scheme and give himself time to fix the problems. The writer may also want to determine if there is a law enforcement presence. However, if this were the case, a traditional criminal would probably give the victim a second chance but by using a route the criminal feels in is more under his control. The overall impression of this sentence is a casual one. "On your way home, stop by my office. If I'm not there, no big deal, come back the next day." Theoretically, this should be the most important thing the writer is doing that day and would make time.

24) **Make no mistake; we are a deadly and serious team of professionals!**

a) Only amateurs have to tell others they are professionals.

Description of the Writer
Sex: Male
Race: White

Age: 30+
Hair Color: Red
Residence: The writer lives or works in the greater Oxnard area.
Marital status: Single, possibly married but no children
Occupation: If the writer is employed, he is underemployed and works a minimum wage type job probably with animals or out-of-doors. The writer has some experience with business. Writer could have possibly worked for the victim as a ranch hand.
Education: The writer is educated, or has, at least, attended college. This is evinced by correct spelling and the proper use of grammar. The writer is probably a college graduate. This assumption is based on grammar structure and articulation. On the Flesch Reading Ease scale the letter rated 60.1. The Flesch Reading Ease scale rates text on a 100-point scale; the higher the score, the easier it is to understand the document. For most standard documents, an optimum score is approximately 60 to 70. On the Flesch-Kincaid Grade Level scale the letter scored 8.7. The Flesch-Kincaid Grade Level scale rates text on a U.S. grade-level. For most standard documents, an optimum score is 7.0 to 8.0.
Relationship to Victim: The writer is probably not from the victim's inner circle of friends because he does not know intimate information regarding the victim; however, the writer does know enough information about the victim to have some had some relationship with the victim albeit from a distance. All the information the writer provided can be gathered by surveillance or working as a ranch hand for the victim.
Personality Traits
- The writer is not a career criminal. This is probably his first or second attempt at a scheme of this magnitude.
- The writer is a mature person in that he can wait for the post office to deliver the mail, wait several days for the drop, and then provide an alternate date for the drop. The writer has a lot of faith in the USPS. A telephone call would have been more efficient and serve as immediate gratification.
- The writer has a conscience, a sense of right and wrong in that he uses the term "involuntary contribution." The writer justifies his crime by thinking that the involuntary contribution is some kind of tax-deductible contribution on the part of the victim. Traditional criminals seldom make such elaborate justifications–they want it, they steal it.
- The writer has dedicated himself to his organization's cause or his personal cause to the point where he is willing to risk going to jail. The writer sees the cause as something greater than himself.
- The possibility exists that the writer has set up an elaborate prank to embarrass the victim. The writer would do this to establish control over

the victim by making him drive around in circles for an hour. However, the overall tone of the letter does not suggest that this is the case because the writer expended a great deal of time researching the victim, his family, and the drop off procedure.

Propensity for Violence

- The writer should be considered dangerous in that he has dedicated a significant amount of his time to research the victim and his family, the victim's financial condition, and the type of vehicles the victim drives. Additionally, the writer has obviously made some practice runs in preparation for the money drop.
- Ninety-seven percent of the letter was written with active verbs, which suggests that the writer is action orientated. This action is probably directed toward the cause his organization espouses and not toward traditional criminal activities.
- The soft verbiage and nonspecific threats suggests that the writer is philosophically dedicated to the cause but is far less willing to translate that philosophical fervor into physical violence. At the time the writer wrote the letter, he had not yet committed himself to harming the victim or his family. Traditional criminals are not afraid to use foul language or words such as: kill, beat, tear to bits to emphasize their point.

Conclusion

The writer's extortion threat should be taken seriously. However, based on the contents of the letter, if the scheme does not work, the writer would probably shrug his shoulders and move on to another scheme to make money.

Outcome

Based on the PNA of the letter, I recommended to my supervisor that the writer was a threat, his propensity to violence was low, and that he would show up to pick up the package. My supervisor deployed the full resources of the FBI. The SWAT team put on their camouflage suits and deployed in the mid-afternoon to prepare for the 11 p.m. drop. They laid motionless in the open fields surrounding the drop site, no doubt enduring the bites of a variety of insects. The airplane and surveillance teams formed a perimeter. My supervisor even ordered out the Mobile Command Center (MCC). The Special Agent in Charge (SAC) of the Los Angeles Office was notified of the extortion attempt and decided to personally direct the operation from the MCC. When the SAC made this decision, the Assistant Special Agents in Charge (ASACs) felt obligated to join the SAC in the MCC. The ASACs had to appear as though they were contributing to the operation (showing off to the SAC) and gave orders to countless Special Agents streaming in and out of the MCC. My supervisor pulled me aside and said, "This guy better show up or we're both in trouble." I just stood there bobbing my head up and down. Later the case agent approached and asked me how sure I was that the guy would show up. I told him that I was quite sure and made the prediction that the writer had red hair.

At 9:08 p.m. a man cautiously walked up to the drop site and placed a construction type sign near the curb. The sign had a large, handwritten letter H written. When this information was transmitted to the MCC, I gave a large sigh of relief, on the inside of course. The tension in the MCC increased steadily the closer we got to 11:00 p.m.

At 10:30 p.m., an FBI agent pretending to be the victim, got into the victim's Ford truck and drove to the drop site. He followed the instructions in the letter faithfully and threw the package supposedly containing the money from the front passenger window. The waiting game began.

At 11:14 p.m. a shadowy figure emerged from the tree line, walked several feet, and stopped. His head swiveled slowly surveying the area. A few moments later, the dark figure moved forward several more feet and stopped. Unbeknownst to the extortionist, he stepped on the sole of the shoe worn by a SWAT agent, who was laid prone surveying the drop site. The SWAT agent held his breath until the extortionist move forward. The extortionist worked his way to the drop site and picked up the package supposedly containing the money. A half-dozen SWAT agents sprang from their concealments and ran toward the extortionist. He ran several blocks to where he parked his truck, got in, and tried to make his getaway. Meanwhile, Special Agents positioned two blocks away blocked the road with their cars cutting off any escape. The truck stopped abruptly and the driver was taken into custody. The case agent pulled the sky mask off the driver's head to reveal a full head of red hair.

The truth is I had no objective reason to believe that the writer had red hair. It was just a feeling I got when I analyzed the letter. Sometimes I use this extortion in classroom exercises and ask the students what color hair they think the writer had and more times than not they say, "Red hair." I wonder if this is a coincidence or is there something the writer wrote in his letter that unconsciously leads readers to form the impression that the writer had red hair. Needless to say, my stock rose significantly in the Los Angeles FBI officer and gave me the confidence to continue my work as a behavioral analyst.

INDEX

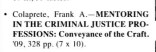